French

Grammar

R. Adamson & B. A. Edelston

TEACH YOURSELF BOOKS

For UK orders: please contact Bookpoint Ltd, 39 Milton Park, Abingdon, Oxon OX14 4TD. Telephone: (44) 01235 400414, Fax: (44) 01235 400454. Lines are open from 9.00–6.00, Monday to Saturday, with a 24 hour message answering service. Email address: orders@bookpoint.co.uk

For U.S.A. & Canada orders: please contact NTC/Contemporary Publishing, 4255 West Touhy Avenue, Lincolnwood, Illinois 60646 – 1975, U.S.A. Telephone: (847) 679 5500, Fax: (847) 679 2494.

Long renowned as the authoritative source for self-guided learning – with more than 30 million copies sold worldwide – the *Teach Yourself* series includes over 200 titles in the fields of languages, craft, hobbies, sports, and other leisure activities.

British Library Cataloguing in Publication Data
A catalogue record for this title is available from The British Library

Library of Congress Catalog Card Number: On File

First published in UK 1998 by Hodder Headline Plc, 338 Euston Road, London NW1 3BH.

First published in US 1998 by NTC/Contemporary Publishing, 4255 West Touhy Avenue, Lincolnwood (Chicago), Illinois 60646–1975 U.S.A.

The 'Teach Yourself' name and logo are registered trade marks of Hodder & Stoughton Ltd.

Copyright © 1998 Robin Adamson and Brigitte Edelston

Consultant editor: Sarah Butler

Typeset by Transet Limited, Coventry, England
Printed in Great Britain for Hodder & Stoughton Educational, a division of Hodder Headline Plc, 338 Euston Road, London NW1 3BH by Cox & Wyman Ltd, Reading, Berkshire.

Impression number   10 9 8 7 6 5 4

Year   2004 2003 2002 2001 2000

CONTENTS

Introduction: How to use this book, the storyline. __ v

1 | *Greetings and introductions*: **Les présentations** – introducing people, counting to 100, greetings, talking about yourself / someone else, asking for and giving personal information. _____ 1

2 | *People, hobbies, likes and dislikes*: **Les loisirs** – days and dates. _____ 16

3 | *Describing people, places and things*: **Les gens, les endroits, les choses** – descriptions, daily activities, telling the time. _____ 29

4 | *What is available?*: **Les courses** – saying what you would like, finding out prices, where to get things, talking about quantities and sizes. _____ 48

5 | *Saying what you prefer*: **Les achats, les choix** – talking about preferences, comparing things, places and people. _____ 60

6 | *Where you are and what you are going to do*: **Les voyages** – locating/asking questions about people, places and things. _____ 74

7 | *Who owns what?*: **Les biens, le logement** – personal ownership and belonging. _____ 91

8 | *What can you do? What do you want to do? What do you have to do?*: **Mark et Stéphanie en France** – permission, instructions. _____ 101

9 | *Telling people what to do!*: **Les directions, les projets des Dickson** – advising and telling people what to do and what not to do. _____ 113

10 | *Processes and procedures*: **Projets de vacances** – describing a series of events; relating events to one another, saying why something happened. _____ 124

11 | *Future plans and events*: **Les projets des Lemaire, l'emploi** – talking and writing about hopes and plans. _____ 135

12 | *Getting things done*: **La banque et l'argent** – giving orders and instructions. _____ 147

13 | *Talking about past events*: **Le voyage des Dickson** – saying what took place over a period of time, presenting things that happened in the recent past._____ 158

14 | *Past habits and activities*: **Souvenirs, souvenirs d'enfance** – discussing situations and isolated events in the past, saying how often you did things. _____ 169

15 | *Going back in the past*: **L'informatique, le voyage** – saying that something happened before or after something else, writing an account of past activities, saying that something was done by someone to someone else._____ 178

16 | *Wishing and wanting; probability and possibility*: **Le tourisme** – saying what you want and what you wish for, envisaging probability and possibility, longer and more complex sentences. _____ 187

17 | *Saying how you feel about something*: **L'avenir: vos désirs, vos anxiétés et vos projets** – saying what you intend to do and why, putting restrictions on your own and other people's actions, expressing doubt, hopes, fears._____ 198

18 | *Imagining what could happen*: **Les fiançailles et le mariage** – saying what would have to take place before something else could happen, imagining how you would react in certain circumstances, saying what you thought would happen. _____ 211

En contexte – Transcriptions _____ 221

Pour vérifier – Key_____ 227

Verb tables _____ 232

Index _____ 245

Abbreviations

masc./m.	masculine
fem./f.	feminine
sing.	singular
plu./pl.	plural
infinit.	infinitive
past part./pp	past participle
pt.p	present participle
Q	question
A	answer

INTRODUCTION

How to use this book

This book is based on a grammatical progression and is intended for a variety of learners from beginners to those wanting to brush up their grammar skills. However, each Unit can stand alone and you can work through the Units in any order you like to suit your own requirements. If you want to use French for a particular language function, the **Index** and the **Contents** will help you find the most useful Unit to look up.

If you want to check specific grammar points use the **Index** on page 245. For more information on irregular verbs see the **Verb Tables** page 232.

Each Unit is structured in the same way. There is a **Summary** of the Unit followed by six sections:

> **Avant de commencer** Before starting – Introduction, reference to previous points
> **Comment dit-on?** Examples covering the different functions covered in this Unit
> **Résumé grammatical** The Grammatical summary
> **En Contexte** Examples in context
> **Pour vérifier** To check what you have learnt
> **Pour aller plus loin** To go further

In **Avant de commencer** examples are given in both French and English to encourage you to look closely at structures and to analyse them from a comparative point of view. The best way to learn is to build on what you can already do. Useful cross-references to previous Units are also given.

The **Comment dit-on?** section is a collection of examples and dialogues, phrases that take you through the Lemaire – Dickson family story illustrating the grammatical functions of the unit. It is a good idea to read these all out loud to get the sound of the constructions.

The specific grammar points are explained in the **Résumé grammatical** and more examples are given to make understanding easier. If you want to go on to more advanced grammar, you can do this in **Pour aller plus loin**. This is not compulsory and real beginners are advised to cover it later – once Units 1 to 9 have been understood and assimilated.

The language functions and grammatical points are used again in **En contexte**. Here you will find practical dialogues bringing everything together in a natural and communicative way. Translations of **En contexte** are included from Unit 1 to 8 to make the section easier to understand and to encourage and help you to learn by yourself. For Units 9 to 18 transcriptions in English are available for reference at the end of the book on pages 221–6. The corrections to the exercises in **Pour vérifier** are also given at the end of the book on pages 227–31. **Pour vérifier** will give you useful feedback on your understanding and progress and will tell you if you need to go back to specific points.

The storyline

The storyline, with its characters, runs through the whole book. In each Unit you will meet the same people and follow some of their activities. There are two families, a French family, *les Lemaire*, living in Saint-Amand-les-Eaux in the north of France and a Scottish family, *the Dicksons*, living in Dundee in Scotland.

The Lemaire family have two children, Stéphanie, aged 20 and Nicolas, aged 17. Stéphanie is on work experience with an oil company. She met Mark Dickson at the beginning of her stay in Aberdeen. They are planning to become engaged at the end of the summer. Stéphanie and Mark go to St Amand at the beginning of May and the Dicksons are planning to spend a few days with Stéphanie's parents in July. They have enrolled to learn French at evening classes in preparation for the big event.

How are Alison Dickson, a history and geography teacher, and Patrick, a supermarket manager, going to communicate with the Lemaires? Georges Lemaire, a skilled plumber, and Isabelle, a capable housewife involved in voluntary work with the catholic church, do not speak English at all. Will the engagement date be decided during their stay? …

We hope you enjoy discovering French grammar while getting to know the Lemaire and the Dickson families.

1 GREETINGS AND INTRODUCTIONS

Thème   Les présentations

Georges introduces his family
Stéphanie introduces Mark to the Lemaires

In this Unit you will learn to:

1 Introduce yourself / someone else
2 Count to 100
3 Greet people
4 Talk about yourself / someone else
5 Ask questions about someone (age, address, nationality, occupation, family circumstances)

Structures grammaticales

1 Subject pronouns: **je** (*I*), **tu** (*you*), **il** (*he*), **elle** (*she*), **on** (*one/we/they*), **nous** (*we*), **vous** (*you*), **ils/elles** (*they*)
2 Verbs: present tense of **avoir** (*to have*), **être** (*to be*)
3 -**er** verbs: regular **habiter** (*to live*); irregular **aller** (*to go*)
4 A reflexive verb: **s'appeler** (*to be called*)
5 Using **tu** or **vous**?
6 Asking questions
7 The negative form: **ne...pas / n'...pas** (*not*)
8 Stressed pronouns: **moi, toi, lui/elle, nous, vous, eux/elles**
9 Gender

Pour aller plus loin

1 Expressions with **avoir** and **être**
2 Changes in spelling of -**er** verbs
3 Questions: inversion of verb and subject pronoun
4 Gender rules and exceptions

Avant de commencer

So that you can say a little about yourself in French, it is important to learn some key verbs, such as **avoir** *to have*, **être** *to be*, **habiter** *to live*, **s'appeler** *to be called* and the subject pronouns (i.e. **je** *I*, **tu** *you*, **il** *he* etc.). With a few numbers and a little vocabulary you are well on your way.

Comment dit-on?

1 Introducing yourself / someone else

Bonjour, **je m'appelle**	*Hello, my name is*
Georges Lemaire.	*Georges Lemaire.*
J'ai 46 ans.	*I'm 46 years old.*
J'habite St Amand-les-Eaux.	*I live in St Amand-les-Eaux.*
Je suis Georges.	*I'm Georges.*
Je vous **présente** ma famille.	*This is my family.*

2 Numbers to 100

Here is a list of numbers to 100. Learn them at your own pace and refer to the list frequently.

■ Note that after 60, the French count in 20's. *70* is **soixante-dix**, *80* is **quatre-vingts** and *90* is **quatre-vingt-dix**.

0	zéro	10	dix	20	vingt
1	un	11	onze	21	vingt et un
2	deux	12	douze	22	vingt-deux
3	trois	13	treize	23	vingt-trois
4	quatre	14	quatorze	24	vingt-quatre
5	cinq	15	quinze	25	vingt-cinq
6	six	16	seize	26	vingt-six
7	sept	17	dix-sept	27	vingt-sept
8	huit	18	dix-huit	28	vingt-huit
9	neuf	19	dix-neuf	29	vingt-neuf

30 trente	40 quarante	50 cinquante	60 soixante
31 trente et un	41 quarante et un	51 cinquante et un	61 soixante et un
32 trente-deux	42 quarante-deux	52 cinquante-deux	62 soixante-deux

70 soixante-dix	80 quatre-vingts	90 quatre-vingt-dix
71 soixante et onze	81 quatre-vingt-un	91 quatre-vingt-onze
72 soixante-douze	82 quatre-vingt-deux	92 quatre-vingt-douze
73 soixante-treize	83 quatre-vingt-trois	93 quatre-vingt-treize
74 soixante-quatorze		100 cent
75 soixante-quinze		
76 soixante-seize		
77 soixante-dix-sept		
78 soixante-dix-huit		
79 soixante-dix-neuf		

3 Greeting people

Stéphanie présente son petit ami Mark à la famille Lemaire. (*Stéphanie introduces her boyfriend Mark to the Lemaire family.*)

Stéphanie	Mark, **je** te **présente** mon père et ma mère.	*Mark, this is my father and my mother.*
Mark	Enchanté.	*Pleased to meet you.*
Stéphanie	**Je** vous **présente** Mark, mon copain.	*This is my friend Mark.*
Isabelle ⎫ **Georges** ⎭	Ravis de faire votre connaissance.	*Delighted to make your acquaintance.*
Georges	Comment **allez-vous**?	*How do you do?*
Mark	Bien, merci.	*I'm well, thank you.*
Stéphanie	Voici mon frère, Nicolas.	*This is my brother Nicolas.*
Mark	Salut, ça **va**?	*Hi, how are you?*
Nicolas	Ça **va** bien, merci. Et toi? Comment **tu vas**?	*Fine, thank you. What about you? How's it going?*

4 Talking about yourself / someone else

Voici ma femme Isabelle:	*This is my wife Isabelle:*
Elle a 43 (quarante-trois) ans.	*She's 43.*
Moi, **j'ai** 46 (quarante-six) ans.	*(Myself) As for me, I'm 46 years old.*
Nous avons deux enfants.	*We have two children.*
Ils s'appellent Stéphanie et et Nicolas.	*They're called Stéphanie and Nicolas.*
Stéphanie **a** 20 (vingt) ans et Nicolas **a** 17 (dix-sept) ans.	*Stéphanie is 20 and Nicolas is 17.*

5 Asking questions about someone else

Georges	**Vous habitez** Aberdeen aussi?	*Do you live in Aberdeen too?*
Mark	Oui, **je suis** ingénieur dans une compagnie pétrolière.	*Yes, I'm an engineer in an oil company.*
Isabelle	Est-ce que vos parents **habitent** Aberdeen?	*Do your parents live in Aberdeen?*
Mark	Non, **ils** n'**habitent** pas Aberdeen. **Ils habitent** Dundee.	*No, they don't live in Aberdeen. They live in Dundee.*
Isabelle	**Êtes-vous** né en Ecosse?	*Were you born in Scotland?*
Mark	Oui, à Dundee.	*Yes, in Dundee.*
Georges	**Vous aimez** Aberdeen?	*Do you like Aberdeen?*
Mark	Oui, beaucoup.	*Yes, very much.*

Résumé grammatical

1 Subject pronouns

The subject pronouns and accompanying verbs are shown in bold type in **Comment dit-on?** above. Here they are in full:

1st person singular	**je** (**j'** in front of vowel /vowel sound)	*I*
2nd	**tu**	*you*
3rd	**il/elle/on**	*he/she/one*
1st person plural	**nous**	*we*
2nd	**vous**	*you*
3rd	**ils/elles**	*they*

2 *Verbs* avoir *and* être

Look for the different forms of **être** and **avoir** and the accompanying nouns or subject pronouns in the examples in **Comment dit-on?** *1* and *4*.

avoir *to have*
j'**ai**
tu **as**
il/elle/on **a**
nous **avons**
vous **avez**
ils/elles **ont**

être *to be*
je **suis**
tu **es**
il/elle/on **est**
nous **sommes**
vous **êtes**
ils/elles **sont**

M. Lemaire (il) **est** plombier.	*Mr Lemaire (he) is a plumber.*
Mme Lemaire (elle) **est** femme au foyer.	*Mrs Lemaire (she) is a housewife.*
Elle **a** 43 ans.	*She is 43.*
Ils **ont** deux enfants.	*They have two children.*

Remember that in French you use the verb **avoir** to say your age.

Nicolas **a** dix-sept ans.	*Nicolas is 17.*
J'**ai** 46 ans.	*I am 46.*

3 *Verbs in* -er

a) *Regular verbs such as* **habiter** *to live*

80% of French verbs are in -er and most of them are regular.

Pronoun	Stem	Ending
j'	habit-	**E**
tu	habit-	**ES**
il/elle/on	habit-	**E**
nous	habit-	**ONS**
vous	habit-	**EZ**
ils/elles	habit-	**ENT**

List of regular -er verbs	
aider	to help
aimer	to like
chercher	to look for
commander	to order
danser	to dance
déjeuner	to have breakfast
demander	to ask
désirer	to wish
détester	to hate
discuter	to discuss
écouter	to listen to
emprunter	to borrow
expliquer	to explain
fermer	to close
fumer	to smoke
gagner	to win
jouer	to play
laisser	to leave
louer	to rent/hire
marcher	to walk
monter	to go up
oublier	to forget
parler	to talk
porter	to carry
raconter	to tell
remercier	to thank

To conjugate -er verbs you just: take the -er off the infinitive, this gives you the *stem*; then add the endings.

For example:
habiter: take the -er off the infinitive to get the stem (**habit-**); then add the endings given below, matching them to the subjects. (Notice that because the **h** at the beginning of **habiter** is not pronounced, the first sound is **a** and so the **e** on **je** is dropped.)

habiter
j'habit**E** Londres
   I live in London
tu habit**ES** Paris
   you live in Paris
il/elle habit**E** Marseille
   he/she lives in Marseilles
nous habit**ONS** Édimbourg
   we live in Edinburgh
vous habit**EZ** Cardiff
   you live in Cardiff
ils/elles habit**ENT** Lille
   they live in Lille

Les Lemaire habit**ent**
St Amand-les-Eaux
dans le nord de la France.

The Lemaires live in
St Amand-les-Eaux
in the north of France.

Useful verbs such as **aimer** *to like*, **détester** *to hate*, **donner** *to give*, **quitter** *to leave*, follow the same pattern.

■ You should start compiling your own list now in your notebook and keep adding to it as you learn.

The stems of some -**er** verbs change their spelling with some subjects:

appeler   *to call*
préférer *to prefer*

These verbs are given in full on page 244.

b) *A key irregular verb*

Aller, *to go* does not follow the pattern given above for **habiter**. It is used in expressions such as:

Ça **va**?	*How is it going?*
Comment **allez**-vous?	*How do you do?*

aller

je **vais** très bien	*I'm very well*
tu **vas** à Dundee	*you are going to Dundee*
il/elle/on **va** au travail	*he/she/one (we go) goes to work*
nous **allons** à l'arrêt de bus	*we're going to the bus stop*
vous **allez** à St Amand	*you're going to St Amand*
ils/elles **vont** en France	*they're going to France*

4 A reflexive verb

s'appeler	je **m'**appelle Stéphanie	*I'm called Stéphanie*
	tu **t'**appelles Mark?	*you're called Mark?*
	il/elle/on **s'**appelle Dickson	*he/she/we are called Dickson*
	nous **nous** appelons Lemaire	*we're called Lemaire*
	vous **vous** appelez Alison?	*you're called Alison?*
	ils/elles **s'**appellent Dupont	*they're called Dupont*

In French you say *I call myself, we call ourselves, …* This type of verb is called **reflexive**. You will find out more about reflexive verbs in Unit 3 **Résumé grammatical 2, 3**.

Stéphanie a un frère.	*Stéphanie has a brother.*
Il **s'appelle** Nicolas.	*He is called Nicolas.*
Ils **s'appellent** Lemaire.	*They're called Lemaire.*

5 Using **tu** *or* **vous**

Did you notice, in **Comment dit-on?** *3*, that Nicolas said:

Comment tu vas? when talking to Mark. He uses **tu**, the informal, friendly form, as opposed to: **Comment allez-vous?** which is a formal way of speaking to *one* person. Georges said: **Comment allez-vous?** He addresses Mark more formally because they do not know one another.

Here are some guidelines on when to use the formal **vous** and the informal **tu**:

TU for	VOUS for
■ friends	■ adults meeting someone for the first time
■ family	■ someone you don't know well
■ children	■ someone with whom you do not have a
■ students	friendly / personal relationship; i.e. unless
■ teenagers	your doctor or a shop assistant was a
■ animals	personal friend of yours you would always
	say **vous**.
	■ people you want to show respect to:
	a superior / somebody in authority,
	an employee, in-laws, etc.

6 Asking questions

As you can see from the above examples, there are three ways of asking questions:

a) use a statement structure and raise your voice

Ça va? (↑)
Vous habitez Aberdeen? (↑)

b) add the question structure est-ce-que *at the beginning of the sentence*

Est-ce que vos parents habitent Aberdeen?

c) change the order of the verb and the subject pronoun

Êtes-vous né en Écosse?

This is called inversion. When an -**er** verb and the pronoun **il/elle/on** are inverted, if the verb ends in a vowel, you add a -**t**- preceded and followed by a hyphen:

Aime-**t**-il Dundee?   *Does he like Dundee?*
Joue-**t**-elle au football?   *Does she play football?*

These three ways of asking questions can also be used with question words, *when? how?* etc. See Unit 2 **Résumé grammatical** *8.*

7 The negative forms: ne ... pas / n'... pas

Compare these two sentences:

J'habite Aberdeen.   *I live in Aberdeen.*
Je **n'**habite **pas** Dundee.   *I do not live in Dundee.*

To say that you 'do *not* do something/are *not*' you use the structure **ne ... pas**. **Ne** comes after the subject. **Pas** comes after the verb.

Les Lemaire **ne** sont **pas** écossais.   *The Lemaires are not Scottish.*

Ne, like **je**, drops the **e** and becomes **n'** in front of a vowel or vowel sound:

Stéphanie **n'**habite **pas** Lille.   *Stéphanie does not live in Lille.*
Mark **n'**aime **pas** Londres.   *Mark doesn't like London.*

8 Stressed pronouns: moi, toi, lui/elle

Stressed pronouns are useful if you want to find out something about someone.

a) speaking to one person, you say:

et *toi*? (informal register), or **et *vous*?** (formal register)

J'aime ma famille. **Et toi?**   *I love my family. What about you?*
Je n'aime pas le football. **Et vous?**   *I don't like football. Do you?*

b) speaking to several people you say:

et vous?

Nous aimons beaucoup   *We like England very much.*
l'Angleterre. **Et vous?**   *Do you?*

c) referring to other (third) persons you say:

et elle? (feminine singular); **et lui?** (masculine singular)
et elles? (feminine plural); **et eux?** (masculine plural)

Sandy va bien maintenant. **Et lui?**   *Sandy is fine now.*
                                            What about him?
Tous les garçons sont ici. **Et elle?**   *All the boys are here. What about her?*

allons en France. **Et eux?**   *We're going to France.*
                                  How about them?

These pronouns are called **stressed pronouns**, because the speaker puts the emphasis on the pronoun. Here is a complete list of stressed pronouns and the subject pronouns they correspond to.

moi	*me*	corresponds to	**je**
toi	*you*	→	**tu**
lui	*him*	→	**il**
elle	*her*	→	**elle**
soi	*oneself*	→	**on**
nous	*us*	→	**nous**
vous	*you*	→	**vous**
eux	*them*	→	**ils**
elles	*them*	→	**elles**

Stressed pronouns can also be used to add emphasis to the subject pronoun:

Moi, je m'appelle Georges.   *(Myself), I'm called Georges.*

They can be used after **et** (*and*) and after prepositions such as **après** (*after*), **avant** (*before*) etc. See Unit 6, **Résumé grammatical 3**.

Moi, je vais bien. **Et toi?**   *I am well. What about you?*
Après **vous**. Après **toi**.   *After you.*

9 Gender

Just as in English, there are feminine and masculine **subject** pronouns in French:

■ for *she* in French you use **elle**
■ for several girls or women (*they*), you use **elles**
■ for *he* you use **il**
■ for more than one man or a mixed group (*they*) you use **ils**

There are also feminine and masculine **stressed** pronouns:

■ for *and her* you use **elle**: et *elle*
■ for *and them* (feminine group) you use **elles**: et *elles*
■ for *and him* you use **lui**: et *lui*
■ for *and them* (masculine or mixed group) you use **eux**: et *eux*

However, not only people have gender in French. All nouns, objects, fruit and vegetables – everything has gender. For example **une table** (*a table*) is feminine → **elle**. **Une voiture** (*a car*) is also feminine. As you progress through the book you will discover that gender is extremely important in French because it affects verb and adjective endings, pronouns etc.

■ In your notebook, keep separate lists of masculine and feminine nouns, and add to them as you learn more nouns.

Here is a grid to help you separate French nouns into these two groups:

Masculine	Feminine
■ days of the week	■ most words ending in -e
■ male members of the family	■ female members of the family
■ vegetables and countries not ending in -e	■ vegetables and countries ending in -e
■ nouns ending in -**isme**, -**asme**, -**age**, -**ège**, -**ème**, -**ède**	■ words ending with a double consonant + -**e** (**une allumette** *a match*)
	■ nouns ending in -**tion**/-**sion**

En contexte

In this passage look for **verbs**, **subject pronouns** and **verb endings**.

Nicolas	Moi, j'ai 17 ans. Et toi? Quel âge as-tu?	*(Me/myself) I'm 17. And you? How old are you?*
Mark	J'ai 24 ans. Tu es lycéen?	*I'm 24. Are you a student?*
Nicolas	Oui, je suis en première, section S. Et toi, tu travailles?	*Yes, I'm in (6th year) science stream. And how about you, do you work?*
Mark	Oui, je suis ingénieur dans une compagnie pétrolière à Aberdeen. Est-ce que tu aimes l'école?	*Yes, I'm an engineer with an oil company in Aberdeen. Do you like school?*
Nicolas	Non, pas du tout. Je n'aime pas les profs, surtout mon prof d'anglais … Toi et moi, nous partageons la même chambre. On monte?	*No, not at all. I don't like the teachers, especially my English teacher … You and I are sharing the same room. Shall we go up? I'll help*

	Je t'aide à porter tes valises.	*you carry your suitcases.*
	D'accord?	*All right?*
Mark	Oui, merci.	*Yes, thank you.*
Nicolas	Comment s'appellent	*What are your parents*
	tes parents?	*called?*
Mark	Ils s'appellent Patrick	*They're called Patrick*
	et Alison.	*and Alison.*
Nicolas	Tu as des frères et des soeurs?	*Do you have brothers and sisters?*
Mark	Oui, j'ai un frère et une soeur.	*Yes, I have a brother and a sister.*
	Mon frère s'appelle Andrew	*My brother's called Andrew*
	et ma soeur s'appelle Sandy.	*and my sister's called Sandy.*
Nicolas	Est-ce que tes parents	*Do your parents work?*
	travaillent?	
Mark	Ma mère est professeur	*My mother is a history and*
	d'histoire-géographie. Mon	*geography teacher. My*
	père est directeur de	*father is the manager of a*
	supermarché.	*supermarket.*

Pour vérifier

Voici la famille Dickson

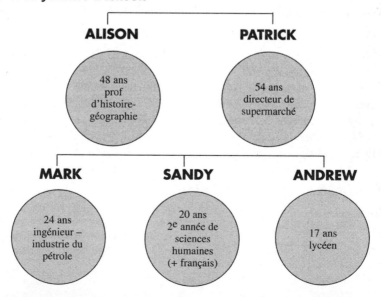

ALISON — 48 ans prof d'histoire-géographie

PATRICK — 54 ans directeur de supermarché

MARK — 24 ans ingénieur – industrie du pétrole

SANDY — 20 ans 2e année de sciences humaines (+ français)

ANDREW — 17 ans lycéen

1 Introduce the Dickson family in French by filling in the gaps:

    a)   Je vous _____ Alison. Elle _____ 48 ans.

    b)   Elle _____ professeur d'histoire-géographie.

    c)   Voici Patrick. _____. _____ 54 ans.

    d)   Il _____ _____.

    e)   Ils _____ trois enfants: Mark, Sandy, Andrew.

    f)   Andrew _____ travaille ___. Il _____ à l'école.

2 Complete the following questions:

    a)   Comment _____ les parents de Mark?

    b)   Quel âge _____ Sandy?

    c)   _____ Sandy travaille?

    d)   Les Dickson _____ -ils (à) Aberdeen?

    e)   Et Stéphanie? _____ – ___ – ___ (à) Dundee?

3 Answer in French the questions you have just completed in **2** above.

Pour aller plus loin

1 Expressions with avoir *and* être

Avoir is sometimes used in French where **être** (*to be*) is used in English:

J'**ai** 20 ans.	*I am 20 years old.*
J'**ai** faim.	*I am hungry.*
J'**ai** froid.	*I am cold.*
J'**ai** chaud.	*I am hot.*

Avoir and **être** are also used as auxiliary verbs in some past tenses: the perfect (see Unit 13, **Résumé grammatical 2, 3**), the pluperfect (see Unit 15, **Résumé grammatical 1**) and the perfect subjunctive (see Unit 17, **Résumé grammatical 5**).

2 Changes in spelling -er *verbs*

Some **-er** verbs have a change in spelling in some tenses. See Verb Tables page 232.

a) Verbs ending in -yer

envoyer *to send*	
j'**envoie**	nous **envoyons**
tu **envoies**	vous **envoyez**
il/elle/on **envoie**	ils/elles **envoient**

b) Verbs ending in -ger

Verbs such as **manger** *to eat*, **nager** *to swim*, **plonger** *to dive* add an **-e** in the first person plural (**nous** form) to retain the same pronunciation (a soft **g**) as in the infinitive:

nous mangeons, nous nageons, nous plongeons, ...

c) Verbs ending in -cer

Verbs such as **commencer** (*to begin*) have a cedilla on the **c** in the first person plural (**nous** form) to retain the soft **c** sound of the infinitive:

nous commençons

d) Verbs ending in -ter/-ler

Verbs such as **jeter** or **appeler** double the **t** or **l** except for the **nous** and **vous** forms:

jeter *to throw*	
je **jette**	nous **jetons**
tu **jettes**	vous **jetez**
il/elle/on **jette**	ils/elles **jettent**

épeler *to spell*	
j'**épelle**	nous **épelons**
tu **épelles**	vous **épelez**
il/elle/on **épelle**	ils/elles **épellent**

or add a grave accent:

acheter *to buy*	
j'**achète**	nous **achetons**
tu **achètes**	vous **achetez**
il/elle/on **achète**	ils/elles **achètent**

3 Questions: Inversion of verb and subject pronoun

As-tu faim?   *Are you hungry?*
Ont-ils des frères et des soeurs?   *Do they have brothers and sisters?*

It is only possible to invert a verb and a pronoun. If a noun such as **Mark** or **la soeur de Mark** is used, you use a matching pronoun after the verb while retaining the noun:

Mark, a-**t**-il faim?   *Is Mark hungry?*
La soeur de Mark (Sandy)   *Does Mark's sister (Sandy)*
aime-**t**-elle Dundee?   *like Dundee?*
Alison, joue-**t**-elle au tennis?   *Does Alison play tennis?*

4 Gender rules and exceptions

The guidelines given in the **Résumé grammatical 9** are useful suggestions which you should bear in mind, but do not be surprised if you encounter words which break the rules:

■ Most words ending in **-age**, for example, are masculine except: **la cage** (*the cage*), **la nage** (*swimming*), **l'image** (*image, picture*), **la page** (*page*), **la plage** (*the beach*), **la rage** (*rabies*).

■ Most words ending in **-tion** are feminine, but there are exceptions such as **le bastion** (*stronghold*).

■ Although most animals, like humans, have both a masculine and a feminine form, there are some animals which are always feminine in gender: **la girafe** (*giraffe*), **l'autruche** (*ostrich*), **la perruche** (*budgie*).

■ Some professions remain masculine and do not have a feminine form:

le professeur (*teacher*)   Il est professeur. Elle est professeur.
l'auteur (*author*)   Il est auteur. Elle est auteur.
le juge (*judge*)   Il est juge. Elle est juge.
le chauffeur (*driver*)   Il est chauffeur. Elle est chauffeur.

■ Some words have a different meaning depending on whether they are masculine or feminine:

le livre (*book*)   **la livre** (*pound*)
le mort (*dead man*)   **la mort** (*death*)
le physique (*physique*)   **la physique** (*physics*)
le poste (*post/job*)   **la poste** (*post office*)

2 PEOPLE, HOBBIES, LIKES AND DISLIKES

Thème   Les loisirs

The Lemaires' and Dicksons' hobbies

In this Unit you will learn to:

1   Discuss hobbies, likes and dislikes
2   Ask about hobbies, likes and dislikes, places
3   Days and dates

Structures grammaticales

1   Definite articles **le, la, l', les** (*the*) and
    indefinite articles **un, une, des** (*a, an*)
2   Articles with nouns in the plural
3   Contracted articles: definite articles after *at/with/to*: **au, aux** and after
    of/from: **du, des**
4   Partitive articles: **du, de la, de l', des** (*some/any*)
5   Demonstrative adjectives: **ce/cet, cette, ces** (*this, that, these, those*)
6   Possessive adjectives: **mon/ma/mes** (*my*)
7   The verb **faire** (*to do*) in the present tense
8   Question words: **comment?, qui?, quand?** (*how?, who?, when?*)

Pour aller plus loin

1   Partitive articles after negatives
2   Irregular plurals
3   More about demonstratives
4   More about possessive adjectives
5   When to use **faire** and **jouer**

Avant de commencer

As you saw in Unit 1, **Résumé grammatical 2**, the article in French is omitted after **être** before a profession. You say:

Il est professeur.   *He is a teacher.*

This is an exception to the ground rule, as articles are usually used in French.

Mark aime **le** football.   *Mark likes football.*
Nicolas a **des** amis sur l'internet.   *Nicolas has friends on the Internet.*

1 In this Unit you will learn when to use the definite articles **le, la, les** and when to use the indefinite articles **un, une, des**:

Georges regarde **un** match de   *Georges is watching a football*
football à **la** télévision.   *match on the television.*
Il adore **le** football.   *He loves football.*

2 You will find out more about the plural of nouns and the use of definite and indefinite articles in French with plural nouns. In some cases you will see they are used in French when they would not be used in English:

Nicolas aime **les** ordinateurs.   *Nicolas likes computers.*
Nicolas rencontre **des** amis ce soir.   *Nicolas is meeting friends this evening.*

3 You will learn to say *any / some* in French:

Avez-vous **des** passe-temps?   *Do you have any hobbies?*
J'ai **des** amis français.   *I have some French friends.*

4 You will also learn how definite articles contract with the prepositions **à** (*at/with/to*) and **de** (*of/from*):

Nicolas va **au** cinéma.   *Nicolas goes to the cinema.*
Nicolas joue **du** piano.   *Nicolas plays the piano.*

5 An article can be replaced by a demonstrative adjective (**ce/cet, cette, ces**) if you want to refer specifically to one or more things. In the following examples the demonstrative adjective singles out a particular video, a specific picture or specific ideas:

Nicolas préfère **cette** vidéo.   *Nicolas prefers this video.*
Stéphanie adore **ce** tableau de Monet.   *Stéphanie likes this painting by*
                                                 Monet very much.
Aimez-vous **ces** idées d'avant-garde?   *Do you like these avant-garde ideas?*

6 A noun can also be preceded by a possessive adjective (**mon/ma/mes**, …) which indicates possession or refers to family members etc:

Leur père, Georges, a des trophées de chasse.	*Their father, Georges, has hunting trophies.*
Stéphanie admire **sa** mère car elle fait du travail bénévole.	*Stéphanie admires her mother because she does voluntary work.*

7 The verb **faire** is a very useful verb when you are talking about your hobbies/ activities. In this Unit you will learn to use it in the present tense:

Mark **fait** du football et du rugby.	*Mark plays football and rugby.*

8 You have already met (Unit 1 **En Contexte**) the question words **quel?** (*what*) in **Quel âge as-tu?** (*How old are you?*) and **comment?** (*how*) in **Comment allez-vous?** (*How are you?*). In this Unit you will meet more question words **où?** (*where?*), **quand?** (*when?*) etc:

Quand est-ce que Mark joue au rugby?	*When does Mark play rugby?*
Où joue-t-il au rugby?	*Where does he play rugby?*

Look carefully at all the structures in the following examples before moving on to the **Résumé grammatical**.

Comment dit-on?

1 Discussing hobbies, likes and dislikes

Georges adore **le** football. Moi, je préfère **la** broderie et **le** canevas.	*Georges adores football. Myself, I prefer embroidery and cross-stitch.*
Nicolas déteste **le** sport. Il préfère **les** ordinateurs.	*Nicolas hates sport. He prefers computers.*
Mark joue **au** squash. Il fait **du** ski et **de la** plongée sous-marine.	*Mark plays squash. He skis and dives.*
Nicolas adore **la** cuisine d'Isabelle, surtout **sa** purée Parmentier.	*Nicolas loves Isabelle's cooking especially her Parmentier purée.*

2 Asking about hobbies, likes and dislikes, places

Qu'est-ce que tu fais comme loisirs?	*What do you do in your spare time?*
Qu'est-ce que tu aimes?	*What do you like?*
Quel plat préfères-tu?	*What is your favourite dish?*
Que détestes-tu?	*What do you hate?*
Quand jouez-vous au squash?	*When do you play squash?*
Qui joue avec vous?	*Who plays with you?*
Où se trouve Aberdeen?	*Where is Aberdeen?*
Comment allez-vous au travail?	*How do you go to work?*

3 Days and dates

Mark joue au squash **le lundi** et **le mardi**.	*Mark plays squash on Mondays and Tuesdays.*
Il joue au rugby **le samedi** ou **le dimanche après-midi**.	*He plays rugby on Saturday or Sunday afternoons.*
Est-ce que tu joues au rugby **samedi**?	*Are you playing rugby this Saturday?*
Georges est né **le 26 novembre** 1931.	*Georges was born on November 26th, 1931.*
Stéphanie est née **le 1er janvier**.	*Stéphanie was born on January 1st.*
Mark est né **le 3 septembre**.	*Mark was born on September 3rd.*

Résumé grammatical

1 Definite and indefinite articles

These vary in French according to the **gender** of the noun (Unit 1 **Résumé grammatical 9**) and to the **number** of the noun (singular or plural).

	definite article: *the*	indefinite article: *a, an, -*
masc. sing.	**le, l'** (in front of a vowel)	**un**
fem. sing.	**la, l'** (in front of a vowel)	**une**
masc. fem. plural	**les**	**des**

a) Definite article

The definite article is used in French even when you are talking about something in general terms. In English you talk and write about *football/swimming* etc., but in French you use the definite article **le / la** in front of the noun (depending on its gender): **le football** (*football*), **la natation** (*swimming*) etc. See **Comment dit-on?** *1*.

Aimez-vous **le** football?	*Do you like football?*
Stéphanie aime **le** chant.	*Stéphanie likes singing.*
Georges regarde **le** football sur *Canal +*.	*Georges watches football on Canal plus.*
Georges regarde **le** match Paris-Nice.	*Georges is watching the Paris-Nice match.* (a specific match)

b) Indefinite article

The indefinite article also varies according to the gender of the noun. You use **un** in front of a masculine noun and **une** in front of a feminine noun.

Mark habite **un** appartement à Aberdeen.	*Mark lives in a flat in Aberdeen.*
Nicolas va à la vidéothèque et emprunte **une** vidéo.	*Nicolas goes to the video library and borrows a video.*
Georges regarde **un** match de football à la télévision.	*Georges is watching a football match on the television.* (not specific)

2 Articles with nouns in the plural

French normally adds an -s to nouns to show that they are plural. Plural articles also have the ending -s. The plural of **le / la** (*the*) is **les**, and the plural of **un / une** (*a / an*) is **des**. Note that, in English, plural nouns are most often used *without* an article, while in French an article *is* used.

Il y a souvent **des** matches de football sur *Canal +*.	*There are often football games on Canal +.*
Nicolas adore **les** plats comme **les** frites et **les** pizzas.	*Nicolas adores dishes such as chips and pizzas.*

3 Contracted articles

The definite articles **le, les** contract with **de** (*of / from*) and **à** (*at / with / to*) to become **du / des** and **au / aux**.

Here is a pattern to help you. You will need to keep referring to this section. Contracted articles are used often and can be surprising as there are no equivalents in English.

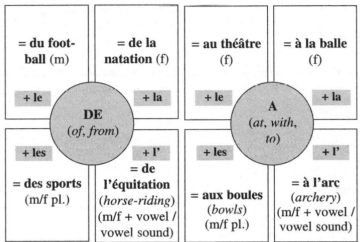

Mark joue **au** squash.	*Mark plays squash.*
Georges fait **du** ball-trap.	*Georges does clay pigeon shooting.*
Nicolas va souvent **au** cinéma.	*Nicolas often goes to the cinema.*
Il aime jouer **aux** échecs.	*He likes to play chess.*
Isabelle reste **à la** maison ou va **au** centre d'accueil du presbytère.	*Isabelle stays at home or goes to the drop-in centre at the presbytery.*
Alison joue **du** piano.	*Alison plays the piano.*

■ Note that **aimer** can be followed directly by an infinitive (e.g. **jouer**).

4 Partitive articles: some, any

If you want to talk about a quantity or use *some* or *any* you use **de** with the definite article. This is called the **partitive article**. As you saw in *3* above, there is a contraction with **le** and **les** and you say:

> J'ai **du** temps libre. (**de** combines with **le** to become **du**)
> J'ai **des** problèmes. (**de** combines with **les** to become **des**)

More about these in Unit 4 **Résumé grammatical 2**.

5 Demonstrative adjectives: this, that, these, those

These also vary according to the gender and number of nouns. Look at the
following grid and examples and refer to it when demonstratives occur in
other situations.

masc. sing.	fem. sing.	masc. fem. plural
ce	cette	ces
cet + vowel/		
vowel sound		
this / that	*this / that*	*these / those*

Ce match est formidable.   *This match is wonderful.*
Cet ordinateur est bien.   *This computer is good.*
Cette émission est intéressante.   *This TV programme is interesting.*
J'aime bien ces tableaux.   *I really like these paintings.*

6 Possessive adjectives: mon, ma, mes

In French it is important to remember that possessive adjectives agree in
number and gender with what is possessed and not with the person who
owns it (More about this in Unit 7 **Résumé grammatical 1**). The gender
of the person who owns something is totally irrelevant in French and does
not affect the choice of possessive adjective.

Nicolas taquine **sa** soeur (fem.) et   *Nicolas teases his sister and*
Stéphanie n'aime pas toujours   *Stéphanie doesn't always like*
son frère (masc.)   *her brother.*

Here is a complete grid for immediate use and further reference:

masc. sing.	fem. sing.	masc. fem. plural	
mon	**ma**	**mes**	*my*
	mon + vowel		
ton	**ta**	**tes**	*your*
	ton + vowel		
son	**sa**	**ses**	*his/her/its*
	son + vowel		
notre	**notre**	**nos**	*our*
votre	**votre**	**vos**	*your*
leur	**leur**	**leurs**	*their*

See **Avant de commencer 6**.

7 The verb faire

Faire is a very useful verb to talk about your leisure activities. See **Comment dit-on?** *1* and **Résumé grammatical** *3*. It is an irregular verb and is conjugated as follows:

faire		
	je **fais** le ménage	*I do the housework*
	tu **fais** du sport	*you play sport*
	il/elle/on **fait** du football	*he/she plays football*
	nous **faisons** des promenades	*we go for a walk*
	vous **faites** du travail bénévole	*you do voluntary work*
	ils/elles **font** du ski	*they go skiing*
	Mark **fait** du football, du ski et de la plongée sous-marine.	*Mark plays football and goes skiing and diving.*

The present tense in French is also used where in English you would use the form *is* + ing: Mark **fait** du football. (*Mark is playing football.*) The present tense can also be used in speech to talk about future actions, which are indicated by time expressions in the context e.g. **demain** (*tomorrow*), **l'année prochaine** (*next year*). See the future tense in Unit 11 **Avant de commencer 1, 2** and **Résumé grammatical** *1, 2*.

Demain, il **fait** de la plongée.   *He is diving tomorrow.*

8 Question words

The three ways of asking questions that were given in Unit 1 **Résumé grammatical 6**, can also be used with question words.

Quel âge tu as?	*How old are you?*
Quel âge est-ce que tu as?	*How old are you?*
Quel âge as-tu?	*What age are you?*
J'ai 24 ans.	*I'm 24.*

Quel? is an adjective and it varies according to the gender and number of the noun it accompanies:

Quels sports (masc. plural) tu fais?	*What sports do you play?*
Quelle est votre date (fem. sing.) de naissance?	*What is your date of birth?*
Quelles activités (fem. plural) est-ce que tu fais?	*Which activities do you do?*

Other interrogative words:

Comment?	Comment s'appellent-ils?	*(How) What are they called?*
Qui?	Qui joue avec moi?	*Who is playing with me?*
Que?, qu'?	Qu'est-ce que tu fais?	*What are you doing?*
Où?	Où habitez-vous?	*Where do you live?*
Pourquoi?	Pourquoi dites-vous ça?	*Why do you say that?*
Quand?	Quand faites-vous du sport?	*When do you play sport?*
	Quand allez-vous en vacances?	*When do you go on holiday?*
Combien / combien de?	Combien de temps est-ce que Mark reste en France?	*How long is Mark staying in France?*

Note that in spoken French the interrogative word can be placed at the end of the sentence:

Vous faites du sport **quand**?
Vous habitez **où**?

■ Here are the names of other days and months so that you can say what the date is and answer some of the questions above:

Aujourd'hui, c'est **le lundi**   *Today is Monday,*
2 (deux) février.   *February 2nd.*

le ...

lundi (*Monday*)	1er janvier (*January*)	5 mai	9 septembre
mardi (*Tuesday*)	2 février (*February*)	6 juin	10 octobre
mercredi (*Wednesday*)	3 mars (*March*)	7 juillet	11 novembre
jeudi (*Thursday*)	4 avril (*April*) etc.	8 août	12 décembre
vendredi (*Friday*)			
samedi (*Saturday*)			
dimanche (*Sunday*)			

In French, days and months are always written in lower case.

You only use an ordinal number – **le premier** (*the first*) – for the first of the month. After that, say **le deux**, **le trois**, **le quatre** etc. when you say the date.

Note the difference between:

Qu'est-ce que tu fais **lundi**?	*What are you doing on Monday?*
Qu'est-ce que tu fais **ce lundi**?	*What are you doing this Monday?*

and

Qu'est-ce que tu fais **le lundi**?	*What do you do on Mondays?* *(every Monday).*

You also use **le** when talking about a specific day followed by a date.

Qu'est-ce que tu fais **le** **lundi 20 mars**?	*What will you be doing* *on Monday, March 20th?*

En contexte

Look for the different **articles** and **question forms** in the dialogue below.

Stéphanie	Mark, Nicolas! Le dîner est prêt.	*Mark, Nicolas! Dinner is ready.*
Nicolas	Nous arrivons.	*We're coming.*
Isabelle	Georges, on mange. Qu'est-ce que tu fais?	*Georges we are eating. What are you doing?*
Georges	Je regarde un match de foot.	*I'm watching a football match.*
Isabelle to Mark		
Isabelle	Georges adore le football. Moi, je préfère la cuisine et la couture. Est-ce que vous jouez au football?	*Georges adores football. Myself, I prefer cooking and sewing. Do you play football?*
Mark	Oui, je joue au football et aussi au rugby.	*Yes I play football and also rugby.*
Stéphanie	Il joue aussi au squash, au golf et il fait de la plongée sous-marine.	*He plays squash, golf and goes diving.*
Nicolas	Maman, qu'est-ce qu'on mange?	*Mum, what are we having?*
Isabelle	Nicolas n'aime pas le sport. Il préfère son ordinateur et son estomac. N'est-ce pas, Nicolas?	*Nicolas doesn't like sport. He prefers his computer and his stomach. Isn't that right, Nicolas?*
Stéphanie	Qu'est-ce que tu fais ce soir?	*What are you doing this evening?*

| Nicolas | Je vais au cinéma puis à la pizzéria. | *I am going to the cinéma and then to the pizza parlour.* |
| Isabelle | Quand rentres-tu? Pas trop tard, j'espère. | *When are you coming home? Not too late, I hope.* |

Pour vérifier

Mark montre des photos de sa famille. Georges et Isabelle posent des questions.

Mark is showing pictures of his family. Georges and Isabelle are asking questions. As they don't know one another well, they are using **vous**.

1   Complete the following questions and answers, using question words, articles and possessive adjectives. (One word per gap)

   a)   _____'est-ce que _____ maman fait comme passe-temps?

   b)   Elle aime ___ randonnées en montagne, ___ photographie et faire ___ ski.

   c)   Et _____ père? _____ sports fait-il?

   d)   Il joue ___ golf.

   e)   ___ est-ce qu'il joue au golf? (where)

   f)   ___ est sur ___ photo?

   g)   C'est ___ frère Andrew et ici c'est ___ soeur Sandy.

   h)   ___ 'est-ce qu'elle fait dans ___ vie?

   i)   Elle est étudiante. Elle fait ___ études de sciences humaines et de français.

2   One way of asking questions with interrogative words is suggested in the following sentences. Find the other two ways.

   Comment est-ce que tu t'appelles?
   Où habites-tu?
   Tu joues au rugby quand?

3   Give your date of birth and the date today.

Pour aller plus loin

1 Partitive articles after negatives

After negatives or after expressions of quantity (Unit 4, **Résumé grammatical** *3*) the Partitive Article – **du, de la, de l'**, **des** – becomes simply **de** or **d'**:

Nicolas n'a **pas d'**argent.	*Nicolas doesn't have any money.*
	Nicolas has no money.
Il a **beaucoup de** temps libre.	*He's got a lot of free time.*

2 Irregular plurals

Most plurals are indicated by -s. However, there are nouns which have irregular plurals. Here are some that form the plural with -x:

a) Most nouns in -**eau/-eu**:

le bateau	les bateaux	*boats*
le gâteau	les gâteaux	*cakes*
le cheveu	les cheveux	*hair*
le jeu	les jeux	*games*

b) Some nouns in -**al**:

le cheval	les chevaux	*horses*
le journal	les journaux	*newspapers*

c) Nouns in -**ou** add an -s except: **hibou** (*owl*), **joujou** (*toy*), **caillou** (*stone*), **chou** (*cabbage*), **genou** (*knee*), **pou** (*louse*) which add -x:

le hibou	les hiboux
le pou	les poux

3 More about demonstratives

To be more specific in pinpointing something, you can use a demonstrative adjective and add -**ci** or -**là** (*here* or *there*) after the noun. A hyphen is used between the noun and -**ci** and -**là**:

Cette raquette-**ci**.	*This particular racket.*
Ce ballon-**là**.	*That ball there.*

4 *More about possessive adjectives*

The possessive adjectives **mon, ton, son** are used before a vowel, even if
the noun is feminine. This can seem surprising, but it is to make the
pronunciation easier:

Mon/ton/son amie   *My/your/his/her girl friend.*
Mon/ton/son ordinateur   *My/your/his/her/its computer.*

5 *When to use* **faire** *and* **jouer**

(See **Comment dit-on?** *1*, **Résumé grammatical** *3*). With **jouer** (*to play*)
you use **à** for sports et **de** with musical instruments:

Il **joue au** rugby.   *He plays rugby.*
Vous **jouez du** piano.   *You play the piano.*

Jouer à can be replaced by **faire de**:

Il **fait du** rugby.   *He plays rugby.*

Faire can also be used for activities other than sports:

Nicolas **fait du** dessin assisté   *Nicolas does computer-aided*
par ordinateur.   *design.*
Isabelle **fait de la** couture.   *Isabelle sews.*
J'aime **faire des** promenades.   *I like to go for walks.*

3 | DESCRIBING PEOPLE, PLACES AND THINGS

Thèmes   Les gens, les endroits, les choses

What the Lemaires and the Dicksons look like
More about their daily activities

In this Unit you will learn to:

1   Describe people: talk about their age, their size and their appearance
2   Describe their clothes
3   Talk about daily activities
4   Describe things and places
5   Telling the time

Structures grammaticales

1   Adjectives
2   Reflexive verbs
3   Questions with reflexive verbs
4   More numbers (from 100 onwards, saying *1st*, *2nd*, *3rd* ..., saying
    you are in your *twenties* etc. ...)

Pour aller plus loin

1   More about adjectives – position of adjectives
2   Adjectives with adverbs
3   Present participles: the *-ing* form of verbs

Avant de commencer

As you saw in Unit 2 **Résumé grammatical** *1 – 6*, the gender and number of nouns affect other words in the sentence, such as articles, interrogative adjectives **quel?**, **quels?**, **quelle?**, **quelles?** and demonstrative adjectives **ce/cet**, **cette**, **ces**.

1 In this Unit you will see that adjectives also agree in gender and number with the nouns they relate to. This means that their endings change, unlike in English where they remain the same:

Mark est **grand**.   *Mark is tall.*
Sandy est **grande**.   *Sandy is tall.*

In English most adjectives come before the noun. In French, they usually come after the noun:

Mark a les cheveux **noirs**.   *Mark has black hair.*

– except for a few short adjectives, which you will also meet in this Unit:

Andrew et son copain ont de   *Andrew and his mate have great*
belles bicyclettes.   *bicycles.*

You will see that some adjectives can have different meanings according to whether they come before or after the noun:

Patrick aime avoir une voiture   *Patrick likes to have a **clean***
propre et bien entretenue.   *and well maintained car.*
Andrew voudrait sa **propre** voiture.   *Andrew would like his **own** car.*

2 You have already met the reflexive verb **s'appeler** in Unit 1 **Résumé grammatical** *4*. Reflexive verbs use the extra pronoun **se** which changes according to the subject (**je**, **tu**, **il** ...):

Quand **vous** réveillez-vous?   *When do you wake up?*
À quelle heure **te** couches-tu?   *(At) what time do you go to bed?*

The extra pronoun (reflexive pronoun) can mean *myself, yourself, yourselves* etc:

Je **me** lave.   *I wash (myself).*

– but it can also mean *one another, each other*:

Nous **nous** parlons souvent.   *We often talk to each other.*
Stéphanie et Nicolas **se**   *Stéphanie and Nicolas often argue*
disputent souvent.   *(with one another).*

3 In this Unit you will also meet numbers from 100 onwards and learn to say the approximate age of someone (e.g. *in his late twenties / thirties*).

Comment dit-on?

Read the following examples, identify all the **adjectives** and look carefully at their **position** and their **agreement** with the nouns they refer to.

1 Describing people

Mark est un **beau** garçon **bronzé**.	*Mark is a good-looking boy with a tan.*
Il mesure 1,82m.	*He is 1.82m tall.*
Il a les yeux **bleus** et les	*He has blue eyes and*
cheveux **noirs**.	*black hair.*
Il est **musclé** car il est très **sportif**.	*He has good muscles because he is very keen on sport.*
Son père a les cheveux **gris** et les	*His father has grey hair and*
yeux **bleus**.	*blue eyes.*
Sa mère Alison a les cheveux	*His mum Alison has light*
brun clair et elle a les	*brown hair and greyish*
yeux **gris-vert**.	*green eyes.*
Elle mesure 1,57m. Elle est **mince**	*She is 1.57m tall. She is slim and*
et très **élégante**. Elle a la	*very smart. She is in her forties.*
quarantaine.	
Sandy est **brune**. Elle est très **jolie**.	*Sandy is dark. She is very pretty.*
Elle travaille comme modèle pour	*She works as a model for a*
un magazine de mode.	*fashion magazine.*
Andrew a les cheveux **noirs bouclés**.	*Andrew has curly black hair.*
Il a l'air très **coquin**.	*He looks very cheeky.*
Il mesure 1,70m et il est **bronzé**.	*He is 1.70m tall and is suntanned.*

2 Describing people's clothing

Alison porte une **jolie** jupe **bleue**,	*Alison is wearing a pretty blue*
un **beau** chemisier **blanc** et des	*skirt, a nice white blouse and*
chaussures **assorties**.	*matching shoes.*
C'est une jupe **longue, classique**,	*It is a long skirt, in a classical style,*
taille 40.	*size 12.*
Patrick porte un **vieux** survêtement,	*Patrick is wearing an old tracksuit,*
car il fait du jardinage.	*because he is gardening.*

3 Talking about daily activities

Andrew est souvent à l'extérieur.	*Andrew is often outdoors.*
Il **se lève** très tôt pour distribuer les journaux en vélo.	*He gets up very early to deliver newspapers on his bike.*
Il **se douche** en vitesse.	*He has a quick shower.*
Il **s'habille** rapidement et il déjeune.	*He gets dressed quickly and has breakfast.*
Il **se dépêche** de distribuer les journaux car il **se rend** à l'école à 8h30.	*He delivers the papers quickly because he goes to school at 8.30.*
Le soir, il **s'amuse** avec ses amis.	*In the evenings he enjoys himself with his friends.*

4 Describing things/places

Il **se déplace** en vélo.	*He goes around on his bike.*
Son vélo est un V.T.T. **bleu** et **blanc** avec 22 vitesses.	*His bike is a blue and white mountain bike with 22 gears.*
Il travaille pour un **petit** magasin **populaire**, qui vend des journaux près de chez lui.	*He works for a small popular shop selling newspapers near his house.*
Il n'a pas le temps de ranger sa chambre. Elle est mal **rangée**.	*He doesn't have time to tidy up his bedroom. It is untidy.*
Alison porte de **jolies** boucles d'oreille **rondes**.	*Alison is wearing pretty round earrings.*
Ce sont des boucles d'oreille en or, très **chic**.	*They are very smart gold earrings.*

5 Telling the time

Je me réveille **à 7 heures** du matin et je me couche **à 11 heures** du soir.	*I get up at 7 in the morning and go to bed at eleven in the evening.*
Andrew se lève **à 6 heures et demie** pour distribuer les journaux.	*Andrew gets up at half past 6 to deliver papers.*
Ses cours commencent **à 8h45** et finissent **à 15h55**.	*His lessons start at a quarter to nine and finish at five to four.*
Il sort avec des amis et rentre **à 23h15**.	*He goes out with friends and comes home at a quarter past eleven.*

Résumé grammatical

1 Adjectives

a) être + adjective

To describe a person or an object, the verb **être** can be used to link the noun and the adjective that relates to it:

Mark est très **sportif**.	*Mark is very keen on sport.*
La chambre d'Andrew est mal **rangée**.	*Andrew's bedroom is untidy.*

If there is more than one adjective after **être**, they are separated by **et** (*and*), **ou** (*or*), **mais** (*but*) or by a comma:

Patrick est **grand** et **fort**.	*Patrick is big and strong.*
Le vélo est **bleu**, **blanc** et **rouge**.	*The bike is blue, white and red.*

Most adjectives end: in any letter if they are masculine singular
in -s if they are masculine plural
in -e if they are feminine singular
in -es if they are feminine plural

Mark est intelligent.	*Mark is intelligent.*
Patrick, Mark et Andrew sont sportifs.	*Patrick, Mark and Andrew are keen on sport.*
Alison est élégante et bien habillée.	*Alison is elegant and well dressed.*
Sa bicyclette est bleue et blanche.	*His bike is blue and white.*
Ses chaussures sont assorties à sa robe.	*Her shoes match her dress.*

As you can see from the above examples and **Comment dit-on? *1***, after the verb **être** adjectives agree in gender and number with the subject.

b) Noun + adjective

Most adjectives follow the noun:

Mark a les yeux **bleus**.	*Mark has blue eyes.*
Il a les cheveux **noirs**.	*He has black hair.*

These adjectives also agree in number and gender with the noun they qualify:

Patrick porte un survêtement **usagé** (masc. sing.).	*Patrick wears a worn tracksuit.*
Alison porte une jupe **bleue** (fem. sing.), une veste **bleue** (fem. sing.) et des chaussures **assorties** (fem. pl.).	*Alison is wearing a blue skirt, a blue jacket and matching shoes.*
Andrew a les cheveux **bouclés** (masc. pl.).	*Andrew has curly hair.*

c) Change of spelling

Some adjectives change their endings when they qualify a feminine noun.

■ Adjectives ending in -**eau**

masc. sing.	fem. sing.	masc. plural	fem. plural	
beau	**belle**	**beaux**	**belles**	*beautiful*
un **beau** garçon	une **belle** fille	de **beaux** garçons	de **belles** filles	
nouveau	**nouvelle**	**nouveaux**	**nouvelles**	*new / recent*
un **nouveau** film	une **nouvelle** amie	de **nouveaux** amis	de **nouvelles** amies	

See **Résumé grammatical 1d** for the position of **beau** and **nouveau**.

■ Adjectives ending in -**euf**

masc. sing.	fem. sing.	masc. plural	fem. plural	
neuf	**neuve**	**neufs**	**neuves**	*new, not old*
un vélo **neuf**	une robe **neuve**	des vêtements **neufs**	des robes **neuves**	
veuf	**veuve**	**veufs**	**veuves**	*widowed*
un homme **veuf**	un femme **veuve**	des hommes **veufs**	des femmes **veuves**	

■ Adjectives ending in **-eur** become **-euse**

masc. sing.	fem. sing.	masc. plural	fem. plural	
menteur	**menteuse**	**menteurs**	**menteuses**	*lying*
il est	elle est	ils sont	elles sont	
menteur	**menteuse**	**menteurs**	**menteuses**	
rieur	**rieuse**	**rieurs**	**rieuses**	*cheerful*
il est	elle est	ils sont	elles sont	
rieur	**rieuse**	**rieurs**	**rieuses**	

Many adjectives ending in **-teur** have **-trice** in the feminine:

masc. sing.	fem. sing.	masc. plural	fem. plural	
innovateur	**innovatrice**	**innovateurs**	**innovatrices**	*innovative*
un projet	une idée	ils sont	elles sont	
innovateur	**innovatrice**	**innovateurs**	**innovatrices**	

■ Adjectives ending in **-l, -n, -s** double the consonant and add **-e**:

masc. sing.	fem. sing.	masc. plural	fem. plural	
bas	**basse**	**bas**	**basses**	*low*
cruel	**cruelle**	**cruels**	**cruelles**	*cruel*
gentil	**gentille**	**gentils**	**gentilles**	*nice, kind*
gros	**grosse**	**gros**	**grosses**	*fat*
mignon	**mignonne**	**mignons**	**mignonnes**	*cute*
pareil	**pareille**	**pareils**	**pareilles**	*same*

Nicolas a une **grosse** chatte.　　　*Nicolas has a big (female) cat.*
Elle est **gentille,** plutôt **mignonne,**　　*She is nice, rather cute, but cruel*
mais **cruelle** avec les oiseaux.　　*with birds.*
Ces deux jupes sont **pareilles**.　　*These two skirts are alike.*

■ Adjectives ending in **-t** either double the **-t**:

masc. sing.	fem. sing.	masc. plural	fem. plural	
coquet	**coquette**	**coquets**	**coquettes**	*smart*

Alison est très **coquette**.　　*Alison is very particular about*
　　her appearance.

or add a grave accent **è** and an **e** (→ **ète**):

masc. sing.	fem. sing.	masc. plural	fem. plural	
complet	complète	complets	complètes	*complete / full*

Cette auberge de jeunesse est **complète**.

This youth hostel is full.

■ Adjectives ending in **-er** also add a grave accent and an **-e** in the feminine:

masc. sing.	fem. sing.	masc. plural	fem. plural	
cher	chère	chers	chères	*dear, expensive*
dernier	dernière	derniers	dernières	*last*

Chères amies ...
L'année **dernière** je ...

Dear (female) friends ...
Last year I ...

■ Adjectives ending in **-ic** become **-ique**:

masc. sing.	fem. sing.	masc. plural	fem. plural	
public	publique	publics	publiques	*public*

■ Some adjectives are highly irregular:

masc. sing.	fem. sing.	masc. plural	fem. plural	
blanc	blanche	blancs	blanches	*white*
favori	favorite	favoris	favorites	*favourite*
frais	fraîche	frais	fraîches	*fresh*
franc	franche	francs	franches	*frank, straight*
vieil + vowel				
vieux	vieille	vieux	vieilles	*old*

Nicolas regarde son émission **favorite**.

Nicolas is watching his favourite programme.

d) Adjective + noun

■ Some adjectives come before the noun. See **Comment dit-on? 2**.

These are usually short common adjectives, such as **beau, bon, grand** etc.

Here is a list of other adjectives that usually come *before the noun*:

autre	*other*
*beau (bel)	*handsome*
bon	*good*
chaque	*each*
grand	*tall*
gros	*big / fat*
haut	*high*
jeune	*young*
joli	*pretty*
long	*long*
mauvais	*bad*
*nouveau (nouvel)	*new*
grand	*big*
petit	*small*
tel	*such*
vaste	*vast*
*vieux (vieil)	*old*
vilain	*naughty*

Most of them are one-syllable adjectives except **mauvais** and **vilain**.

These adjectives also agree in number and gender with the noun they relate to.

Patrick porte aussi de **vieilles** baskets.
Patrick is also wearing old trainers.

Patrick porte un **vieux** survêtement.
Patrick is wearing an old tracksuit.

Andrew a la grippe.
Andrew's got the flu.

Il a **mauvaise** mine.
He looks poorly.

*when the masculine adjectives **beau, nouveau, vieux** come before a singular noun beginning with a vowel or a vowel sound, they change their endings to become **bel, nouvel** and **vieil**.

Patrick est un très **bel** homme.   *Patrick is a very handsome man.*
Andrew va acheter un **nouvel** album. *Andrew's going to buy a new album.*
Ce n'est pas un **vieil** homme.   *He is not an old man.*

■ Colour adjectives, although short, come after the noun.

Alison porte une jupe **bleue**.   *Alison is wearing a blue skirt.*
Patrick porte un survêtement **gris**. *Patrick is wearing a grey tracksuit.*

...o the rules on agreement of adjectives

...ves remain unchanged:

...tives derived from fruit and nuts:

Nouns	Adjectives	Examples
un marron / des marrons (*wild chestnut*)	marron	des yeux marron
une noisette / des noisettes (*hazelnut*)	noisette	des yeux noisette
une orange / des oranges (*orange*)	orange	des boules orange

■ chic – des boucles d'oreille très **chic**

■ hyphenated adjectives with two colours do not change their spelling:

Elle a les yeux **gris-vert**.   *She has greyish green eyes.*

When there are two adjectives, a colour and an adjective that refers to it, neither of them agrees:

Il a les yeux **bleu clair**.   *He has light blue eyes.*
Les nuages sont **gris foncé**.   *The clouds are dark grey.*

Note the difference between the spelling of the adjectives in the following examples:

Elle a les cheveux **bruns** et **foncés**.   *She has dark brown hair.*
Elle a les yeux **brun foncé**.   *She has dark brown eyes.*

2 Reflexive verbs

Reflexive verbs (where the subject and the object are the same person) are easily noticeable in French as they have an extra pronoun: **se** in front of the infinitive, which changes form according to the subject of the verb (See Unit 1 **Résumé grammatical 4**).

They mean that:

a) the subject is doing something to himself / herself (*myself, yourself, himself / herself / oneself* etc.):

Andrew **se lève** tôt, il **se douche**, il **s'habille** et **se dépêche**.	*Andrew gets up early, has a shower (showers), gets dressed and hurries up.*

As you can see from the above examples and **Comment dit-on?** *3*, the object of a reflexive verb is not always expressed in English. The formula *to get dressed* is more usual in English than *to dress oneself*.

In French the subject performs the action on him/herself, i.e. *Andrew gets himself up, showers himself* etc.

b) the subject and another person or other persons (also subject of the verb) are doing something to one another:

Stéphanie et Nicolas **se disputent** souvent, mais ils **s'aiment** quand même.	*Stéphanie and Nicolas often quarrel, but they like each other all the same.*

The idea of interaction (each other/one another) is not always explicit in English:

Mark et Stéphanie **se rencontrent** toujours après le travail.	*Mark and Stéphanie always meet after work.*

3 Questions with reflexive verbs

When asking questions with reflexive verbs using inversion, remember that the reflexive (object) pronoun does not move. It always remains before the verb.

Comment **t'**appelles-tu? / Comment est-ce que tu **t'**appelles? / Comment **vous** appelez-vous?	*What are you called? / What's your name?*
Vous promenez-vous à la campagne?	*Do you walk in the country?*
Vous entendez-vous bien?	*Do you get on well?*

4 More numbers

a) For asking / telling the time:

Quelle heure est-il?	*What time is it?*

■   For the 12-hour clock system you simply add the expression in bold below to indicate *a quarter past, half past, a quarter to* …:

Il est une heure.	*It's one o'clock.*

Il est une heure **et quart**.	*It's a quarter past one.*
Il est une heure **et demie**.	*It's half past one.*
Il est deux heures **moins le quart**.	*It's a quarter to two.*
Il est midi.	*It's noon.*
Il est minuit.	*It's midnight.*

This 12-hour system does not indicate whether it is in the morning or in the afternoon. If it is not obvious from the context, it is necessary, just as in English, to add the time of day:

Il est une heure **du matin**.	*It's one o'clock in the morning.*
Il est une heure **de l'après-midi**.	*It's one o'clock in the afternoon.*
Il est onze heures **du soir**.	*It's eleven o'clock at night / in the evening.*

■ The 24-hour system is used more formally in business timetables, schedules etc. In this system, you do not use **et quart, et demie, moins le quart**, but simply the number of minutes: **quinze, trente, quarante-cinq**:

Il est 23h00 (vingt-trois heures).	*It's 23.00.*
Il est 23h15 (vingt-trois heures quinze).	*It's 23.15.*
Il est 23h30 (vingt-trois heures trente).	*It's 23.30.*
Il est 23h45 (vingt-trois heures quarante-cinq).	*It's 23.45.*

The word **heures** cannot be omitted.

b) Ordinal numbers

To speak about *first, the first,* you say:

le premier / la première, les premiers, les premières.

These numbers agree with the person or noun referred to:

Mark se lève le premier.   *Mark gets up first.*
Stéphanie quitte le travail **la première**.
    Stéphanie leaves work first.

To say *second, third, 4th ...,* again put the definite article **le/la/les** first, and then add **-ième/s** to the number:

Nicolas est le **deuxième** de sa classe en maths.
Nicolas is second in his class in maths.

Georges regarde souvent **la cinquième**.
Georges often watches the fifth channel.

le deuxième
le troisième
le quatrième
le cinquième
le sixième
le septième
le huitième
le neuvième
le dixième
le vingtième
le vingt et unième
le vingt-deuxième
le vingt-troisième ...

■ **le second / la seconde** can replace **le deuxième / la deuxième** when talking about ranks / classes:

C'est **la seconde** fois qu'il gagne.	*It's the second time that he has won.*
Il voyage en **seconde** classe.	*He travels second class.*
En **second** lieu …	*Secondly …*

c) ***To say that someone is in their twenties, thirties etc.***

You remove the -e from the number and add **-aine**. These numbers are always feminine:

Isabelle a **la quarantaine**.	*Isabelle is in her forties.*
Alison a aussi **la quarantaine**, mais Patrick a une petite **cinquantaine**.	*Alison is also in her forties, but Patrick is in his early fifties.*

d) ***To count after 100***

100	cent, cent un, cent deux, cent trois …
200	deux cents , deux cent un, deux cent deux, deux cent trois …
300	trois cents, trois cent un, trois cent deux …
370	trois cent soixante-dix, trois cent soixante et onze …
1 000	mille, mille un, mille deux …
2 000	deux mille, deux mille un, deux mille deux …
10 000	dix mille …
10 280	dix mille deux cent quatre-vingts …
10 372	dix mille trois cent soixante-douze …
1 000 000	un million …
2 000 000	deux millions, deux millions un …
2 120 000	deux millions cent vingt mille …
1 000 000 000	un milliard …
1000 000 115	un milliard cent quinze …

Note that **vingt** and **cent** are spelt with an **-s** when they are not followed by other numbers:

quatre-vingts but **quatre-vingt-deux**
deux cents but **deux cent deux**
mille never adds an **-s**

With numbers after 1000, a full stop or a space is used in French, whereas a comma is used in English:

1.000	mille	1,000	*a thousand*
2.331	deux mille trois cent trente et un	2,331	*two thousand three hundred and thirty-one*

The words **million** and **milliard** take **de** when they are followed by a noun:

Il y a plus de 56.000.000 **de** gens en France.
(cinquante-six millions)

There are over 56,000,000 people in France.

En contexte

When reading this dialogue look for **expressions of time, reflexive verbs** and **adjectives**.

Mark et Stéphanie parlent d'Aberdeen et de leur appartement.
Mark and Stéphanie are talking about Aberdeen and their flat.

Mark	Je me lève vers 7 heures. Je me douche et je m'habille. Stéphanie se réveille un peu plus tard. Nous quittons l'appartement vers 8 heures.	*I get up about 7 o'clock. I have a shower and get dressed. Stéphanie wakes up a little later. We leave the flat about 8 o'clock.*
Stéphanie	Nous partageons l'appartement mais Mark est souvent absent. Il se rend sur la plate-forme pétrolière pour plusieurs semaines. Je m'occupe donc de l'appartement.	*We share the flat but Mark is away. He goes to the oil platform for several weeks. So I look after the flat.*
Isabelle	Il est joli?	*Is it pretty?*
Stéphanie	Oui, c'est un petit appartement situé dans le centre-ville. Il est bien décoré, clair, bien chauffé et très confortable. Les voisins sont très sympathiques.	*Yes it is a small flat situated in the town centre. It is well decorated, well lit, well heated and very comfortable. The neighbours are very friendly.*
Mark	Stéphanie et moi, nous nous rencontrons souvent pour le déjeuner. Nous rentrons ensemble le soir.	*We often meet for lunch, Stéphanie and I. We go home together in the evening.*

Pour vérifier

La famille Lemaire

1   a)   Complete the sentences given below, using the information
        provided on Georges and Isabelle and the adjectives in brackets.

Georges (blond) (grand) (long) **visage** **yeux** (bleu) **cheveux** (bouclé) **1.92m** **46 ans**	**Isabelle** **cheveux** (brun), (mi-long) (mince), (joli) **yeux** (marron) **43 ans**	**Stéphanie** (joli) **yeux** (bleu) (blond) **cheveux** (blond) (bouclé) (mince)

George est un homme _____.

Il mesure _____.

Il est _____. Il ___ les cheveux

_____ et les yeux _____.

Isabelle a les _____ _____,

_____.

Elle est _____ et _____.

Elle a les _____ _____.

Ils ont la _____ (*in their forties*).

> **Nicolas**
> **cheveux** (blond)
> **yeux** (noisette)
> (grand)
> (mince)
> **1.90m**

b)   Write a few sentences to describe Stéphanie and Nicolas.

2   Say and write the following figures / times in French (in words).

231 456

245 985

3 500 765

6.15, 3.45, 3.05 (using the 12-hour system)

13.55, 22.35, 23.45 (using the 24-hour system)

Pour aller plus loin

1 More about adjectives

a) Adjectives following a verb.

As seen previously in **Résumé grammatical *1***, adjectives can follow the verb **être**, and they agree with the subject:

Il est **fatigué**.   *He is tired.*

They can also follow other verbs and qualify the subject.

■ verbs of state, such as **sembler** (*to look*), **paraître/apparaître** (*to appear*):

Il semble **épuisé**.   He seems exhausted.
Elle paraît **épuisée**.   She looks exhausted.

■ verbs of action, such as **rentrer** (*to come back*), **sortir** (*to go out*):

Ils rentrent **fatigués** le soir.   *They get home tired in the evening.*

When a noun is qualified by two adjectives, they can be placed after the noun and are linked by **et** (*and*), **mais** (*but*) or **ou** (*or*).

Cette voiture paraît ancienne   *This car looks old but/and*
mais / et bien entretenue.   *well kept.*

b) Position of adjectives

■ Some adjectives can have a different meaning according to their position *before* or *after* the noun:

Georges est un homme **grand**.   *George is a tall man.*
Le Général de Gaulle est un **grand** *General de Gaulle is a great man in*
homme de l'histoire française.   *French history.*

Ce n'est pas la **même** idée.   *It is not the same idea.*
L'idée **même** m'amuse.   *The very idea amuses me.*

Isabelle rencontre souvent des   *Isabelle often meets poor people.*
gens **pauvres**.
L'entreprise caritative fait   *The charity does a lot for these*
beaucoup pour ces **pauvres** gens. *unfortunate people.*

Here is a list of adjectives which have a different meaning depending on their position:

ancien + noun = former	une **ancienne** élève	*a former pupil* (female)
noun + **ancien** = old	un village **ancien**	*an old village*
certain + noun = certain	un **certain** 'je ne sais quoi'	*a certain 'je ne sais quoi'*
noun + **certain** = sure	un fait **certain**	*a sure fact*
cher + noun = dear	**chers** amis	*dear friends*
noun + **cher** = expensive	une voiture **chère**	*an expensive car*
même + noun = same	C'est la **même** chose.	*It's the same thing.*
noun + **même** = itself	C'est cette personne **même**.	*It's the very same person.*
propre + noun = own	Son **propre** ordinateur.	*His own computer.*
noun + **propre** = clean	Il a un appartement **propre**.	*He has a clean flat.*

■ If several adjectives which usually go before the noun are used, such as **joli**, **nouveau** (**Résumé grammatical 1d**), only one adjective goes before the noun and the other adjectives go after the noun:

Alison porte une **jolie** jupe nouvelle.   *Alison is wearing a pretty new skirt.*

Other adjectives may follow the second adjective, provided a comma or a link word such as **et** (*and*), **mais** (*but*), **ou** (*or*) is used.

Andrew a un **beau** VTT **neuf et**
propre.

*Andrew has a nice new clean
mountain bike.*

Patrick porte un **vieux** survêtement
foncé, légèrement **usé**.

*Patrick is wearing an old dark
tracksuit, slightly worn.*

■ A few adjectives can be joined to other adjectives: **demi-/mi-/semi-** (*half*) (+ hyphen) do not agree when they are joined to another adjective.

The main adjective agrees with the noun it relates to:

Isabelle a les cheveux **mi**-longs.   *Isabelle has longish hair.*
Elle aime le lait **demi**-écrémé.   *She likes semi-skimmed milk.*
C'est une région **semi**-autonome.   *It's a semi-autonomous region.*

■ Some noun + adjective combinations are so common that they act as a single noun. In this case, the adjective agrees with the noun:

Les **grands**-parents   *Grand-parents*

| Il faut faire attention aux **ronds**-points. | *One must be careful at roundabouts.* |

c) **Tel/telle/tels/telles** (*such*) can be used with or without an indefinite article. In each case, the meaning is slightly different:

| Une **telle** personne. | *Such a person.* |
| **Telle** personne. | *A certain person.* |

d) **Adjectives ending in -*ic* in English** often end in -**ique** (fem. / masc.) in French:

Noun	**Adjective**
l'ecclésiastique	ecclésiastique(s)
l'économie	économique(s)
l'élastique	élastique(s)

■ **public** is an exception:

| le public | public / publique / publics / publiques |

2 Adjectives with adverbs

a) Adjectives can be preceded by adverbs (Unit 6 **Résumé grammatical 4 c**), such as **très** (*very*), **trop** (*too much*), **complètement** (*completely*) etc. if they come after the verb **être** or another verb:

| Ils sont **trop fatigués**. | *They are too tired.* |
| Ils rentrent **complètement épuisés**. | *They come back completely exhausted.* |

b) Adjectives which go before the noun can also be preceded by **trop** (*too*), **très** (*very*):

| Isabelle est une **très petite** femme. | *Isabelle is a very small woman.* |

If an adjective which usually goes before the noun is modified by an adverb – except **très** (*very*) and occasionally, **trop** (*too*), it comes after the noun:

| Isabelle est une femme **vraiment petite**. | *Isabelle is a really small woman.* |

3 Present participles: the -ing form

For most verbs you just take off the -**ons** from the second person plural (**nous** form) of the present tense and add -**ant**, for example:

descendre *to go down*	nous descendons	descend-	+ ant	descendant
partir *to leave*	nous partons	part-	+ ant	partant
précéder *to precede*	nous précédons	précéd-	+ ant	précédant

There are three exceptions to this ground rule:

avoir	nous avons	ayant
être	nous sommes	étant
savoir	nous savons	sachant

Present participles are **verbs**, always ending in -**ant**. They do not agree in number or gender with the subject:

Andrew et Mark **étant** jeunes, beaux et forts, ils sont très populaires avec les filles.
Being young, handsome and strong Andrew and Mark are very popular with girls.

L'horloge s'**étant** arrêtée, je ne connais pas l'heure exacte.
The clock having stopped, I do not know the exact time.

Many **adjectives** in French also end in -**ant** but they agree in gender and number with the noun they relate to:

Cette émission est intéress**ante**.
This programme is interesting.

Les acteurs sont très amus**ants**.
The actors are very funny.

If you are using a French word ending in -**ant**, it is important to check to see if it is an adjective or a verb.

4 | WHAT IS AVAILABLE?

Thème   Les courses

Mark and Stéphanie go shopping
Mark buys presents for his family

In this Unit you will learn to:

1 Say what you want or need
2 Ask what / which one someone would like
3 Find out where to get things and prices
4 Talk about quantities and sizes

Structures grammaticales

1 Verbs and expressions to say what you want or need: **je voudrais** (*I'd like*), **avoir besoin de** (*to need*)
2 Partitive articles **du, de la, de l', des** (*some, any*)
3 Expressions of quantity and size
4 Question adjectives and pronouns: *what/which, which one*(s)
5 More negatives: **ne...plus** (*no longer/no more*), **ne...jamais** (*never*)

Pour aller plus loin

1 More about articles
2 More expressions of quantity
3 More about using articles after negatives
4 **ne...personne, personne ne,** (*nobody*), **rien ne, ne...rien** (*nothing*)
5 **Avoir besoin de** (*to need*) in the negative
6 **La plupart de** (*most of*)

Avant de commencer

Look back at Unit 1 **Résumé grammatical 3, 8** for verbs which can express what you want / desire, such as **aimer, désirer** + noun or + infinitive:

Nous **aimons** la France.   *We like France.*
Nicolas **désire** sortir.   *Nicolas wants to go out.*

1 In this Unit, you will meet other verbs and expressions to express needs, likes and dislikes:

Nicolas **voudrait** acheter un cédérom. *Nicolas would like to buy a CD rom.*
Nicolas **a besoin de** nouvelles   *Nicolas needs some new*
disquettes.   *disks.*

2 You will also learn to use more partitive articles **du, de la, de l'**, **des** (*some, any*). See Unit 2 **Résumé grammatical 4**.

Mark voudrait acheter **des** cadeaux   *Mark would like to buy some*
pour sa famille.   *presents for his family.*

3 You will meet expressions of quantity:

Mark voudrait acheter **deux boîtes**   *Mark would like to buy two*
de chocolats pour des amis et   *boxes of chocolates for some*
une bouteille de bon vin   *friends and a bottle of good wine*
pour son père.   *for his father.*

4 To ask what sorts of thing someone does, you can use interrogative adjectives **quel(s)**, **quelle(s)** (*which/what*), which agree with the noun they accompany. See Unit 2 **Résumé grammatical 8**. Also look back at Unit 1 **Résumé grammatical 6**, if you have problems with asking questions.

Quelle sorte voulez-vous?   *What type do you want?*
Qu'est-ce que vous désirez?   *What do you want?*
                                         (What would you like?)

In this Unit you will meet interrogative pronouns **lequel?**, **laquelle?** (*which one(s)?* which replace the noun they refer to and help you to ask more specific questions:

Lequel (masc. sing.) voulez-vous?   *Which one do you want?*
Lequel préférez-vous?   *Which one do you prefer?*

5 You have already used the negative **ne … pas** (*not*). See Unit 1 **Résumé grammatical 7**. In this Unit you will meet other useful negatives such as **ne … plus** (*no longer, no more*):

| Mark **n'**aime **pas** faire les courses. | *Mark does not like shopping.* |
| Mark **n'a plus** beaucoup de temps pour faire ses achats. | *Mark doesn't have a lot of time to do his shopping any more.* |

Comment dit-on?

1 Saying what you need or want

Stéphanie, je **voudrais** acheter des cadeaux pour mon père, ma mère, Andrew et Sandy.

Stéphanie, I would like to buy presents for my father, my mother Andrew and Sandy.

Je **voudrais** une bonne bouteille pour mon père.

I'd like a good bottle of wine for my father.

Je **désire** acheter un St Émilion ou un Bourgogne.

I want to buy a St Émilion or a wine from Burgundy.

Je **voudrais** acheter un CD ou un T-shirt pour Andrew.

I'd like to buy a CD or a T-shirt for Andrew.

Pour maman, j'**aimerais** acheter du parfum à l'aéroport.

For mum I'd like to buy some perfume at the airport.

J'**ai** aussi **besoin de** lames à rasoir pour moi.

I also need some razor blades for myself.

2 Asking what/which one someone would like

Quel parfum voudrais-tu acheter? — *Which perfume would you like to buy?*
Lequel préfères-tu? — *Which one do you prefer?*
Une **eau de toilette** est aussi très bien. — *An eau de toilette is also quite good.*
Laquelle préfères-tu? — *Which one do you prefer?*
Il y a de jolis T-shirts. — *There are some nice T-shirts.*
Lesquels préfères-tu? — *Which ones do you prefer?*

3 Finding out where to get things and prices

Qu'est-ce que vous avez **comme** vins? — *What wines do you have?*
Où est-ce qu'il y a un marchand de vins? — *Where is there a wine store?*
Combien coûte ce vin? — *How much does this wine cost?*
Ça fait combien en tout? — *How much is it all together?*
C'est combien? — *How much is it?*

4 Quantities and sizes

Je désire **une bouteille de** vin.	*I want a bottle of wine.*
Je voudrais **deux boîtes de** chocolats.	*I'd like two boxes of chocolates.*
Pour sa mère, Stéphanie a **une liste de** courses. Elle voudrait:	*Stéphanie has a shopping list for her mother. She would like:*
1 kilo de pommes de terre, **une demi-livre de** beurre, **500 g de** pâté, **deux litres de** vin rouge, **deux briques de** lait, **un paquet de** sucre.	*1 kg of potatoes, half a pound of butter, 500 g of pâté, two litres of red wine, two cartons of milk, a packet of sugar.*
Je voudrais un T-shirt **demi-patron** ou **patron**.	*I'd like a medium size or large size T-shirt.*
Je ne veux **plus rien**, merci.	*I don't need anything else, thank you.*

Résumé grammatical

1 Verbs and expressions to say what you want or need

■ désirer

The verb **désirer** can be followed by a noun:

Je **désire du jambon** fumé.	*I want/I'd like some smoked ham.*

It can also be followed by an infinitive:

Je **désire faire** des achats.	*I want/I'd like to do some shopping.*

The verb **désirer** is used in French to say *what you want* and to ask *what someone also wants*: **Que désirez-vous?** However, it is not the most commonly used expression to say *what you would like*. The most polite way is to use the conditional of **vouloir** (*to want*). See Unit 8 **Résumé grammatical *1c*** and Unit 18 **Résumé grammatical *3***.

■ **vouloir**   The conditional of **vouloir**:   je **voudrais**   tu **voudrais**   il/elle/on **voudrait**   nous **voudrions**   vous **voudriez**   ils/elles **voudraient**

Using **vouloir** in the **present** tense to say what you want: Je **veux** un café au lait (*I want a white coffee.*) could be too abrupt. See Unit 8 **Résumé grammatical *1c***.

Je **voudrais** un café et deux croissants.	*I'd like a coffee and two croissants.*
Mark **voudrait** acheter un St. Émilion pour son père.	*Mark would like to buy a St. Émilion for his father.*
Nous **voudrions** regarder les T-shirts.	*We'd like to look at the T-shirts.*

■ **avoir besoin de** (*to need*)

Mark **a besoin de** beaucoup d'argent pour acheter ses cadeaux.	*Mark needs a lot of money to buy his presents.*

2 Partitive articles: some, any

See grid, Unit 2 **Résumé grammatical** *3*.

Partitive articles follow the same contraction rule as **de** + definite article:

    le combines with **de** to make **du**
    les combines with **de** to make **des**

Here is a complete list of partitive articles:

masc. sing.	fem. sing.	masc. plural	fem. plural
du	**de la**	**des**	**des**
de l' + vowel	**de l'** + vowel		
du fromage	**de la margarine**	**des croissants**	**des baguettes**
(*some cheese*)	(*some margarine*)	(*some croissants*)	(*some baguettes*)
de l'ail	**de l'aspirine**		
(*some garlic*)	(*some aspirin*)		

Mark voudrait **du** vin rouge.	*Mark would like some red wine.*
Il voudrait aussi acheter **des** fleurs pour Isabelle.	*He would also like to buy some flowers for Isabelle.*
Stéphanie achète **du** beurre, **du** pâté, **de** l'ail, **de la** limonade, **de** l'huile, des pommes de terre ... pour sa mère.	*Stéphanie buys some butter, paté, garlic, lemonade, oil, potatoes ... for her mother.*

As you can see from the above examples, articles in a list are repeated in French, even if they have the same gender and number.

3 Expressions of quantity and size

The partitive article becomes **de**, not only after a negative (Unit 2 **Pour aller plus loin 1**), but also after expressions of quantity.

Je voudrais **un peu de** fromage.	*I would like a little cheese.*
Nous voudrions **un morceau de** brie, **un paquet de** café moulu et **une boîte de** choucroute garnie.	*We would like a piece of brie, a packet of ground coffee and a tin of sauerkraut with meat.*

Non-specific quantities and sizes		Precise quantities
assez de	*enough of*	**un litre de** (100cl)
beaucoup de	*a lot of*	*a litre of*
moins de	*less*	**une bouteille de**
plus de	*more*	(75cl) *a bottle of*
une boîte de	*a box/tin of*	**100 grammes de**
un bouquet de	*a bunch of*	*100 g of*
une brique de	*a carton of* (milk, juice)	**1 kg de**
une carafe de	*a carafe of*	*one kilo of*
une cuillerée de	*a spoonful of*	**une livre de**
un morceau de	*a piece of*	*one pound of*
un pack de ...	*several cartons/bottles of ...*	**une demi-livre de**
un paquet de	*a packet of*	*half a pound of*
une plaque de	*a bar of*	
une plaquette de	*a bar of*	
un pichet de	*a pichet* (jugful/carafe) *of*	
une pincée de	*a pinch of*	
une portion de	*a portion of/helping of*	
une tasse de	*a cup of*	
une tranche de	*a slice of*	
un verre de	*a glass of*	

Pour faire une mousse au chocolat, Isabelle a besoin de **500g,** **de** chocolat, de six oeufs et de **200 cl de** crème fraîche.	*To make a chocolate mousse Isabelle needs 500g of chocolate, six eggs and 200 cl of fresh cream.*

4 Question adjectives and pronouns

Interrogative **adjectives**, Unit 2 **Résumé grammatical 8**, are shown in the grid below. As you can see, they are followed by a noun, and they agree with it in number and gender.

Interrogative adjectives:

masc. sing.	fem. sing.	masc. plural	fem. plural
quel	quelle	quels	quelles
quel parfum?	quelle crème?	quels T-shirts?	quelles pommes?
(Which perfume?)	*(Which cream?)*	*(Which T-shirts?)*	*(Which apples?)*

Interrogative **pronouns** replace the noun. They are formed with the definite article **le/la/les** + **quel/le/s**. They agree with the noun they replace in gender and number: *le*quel, *la*quelle, etc.

Interrogative pronouns:

masc. sing.	fem. sing.	masc. plural	fem. plural
lequel	laquelle	lesquels	lesquelles
Lequel voulez-vous?	Laquelle désirez-vous?	Lesquels prenez-vous?	Lesquelles désirez-vous?
(Which one do you want?)	*(Which one do you want?)*	*(Which ones are you taking?)*	*(Which ones do you want?)*

More examples with interrogative pronouns:

Je voudrais un T-shirt. — *I'd like a T-shirt.*
Lequel désirez-vous? — *Which one would you like?*
Il y a deux sortes de crèmes hydratantes. — *There are two types of moisturising lotion.*
Laquelle préfères-tu? — *Which one do you prefer?*
Ta mère aime les parfums français? — *Does your mum like French perfumes?*
Lesquels préfère-t-elle? — *Which ones does she prefer?*
Ces fleurs sont toutes très jolies. — *These flowers are all very pretty.*
Lesquelles préférez-vous? — *Which ones do you prefer?*

5 More negatives

As you will remember, in the case of the negative **ne**...**pas**, the **ne** comes after the subject and the **pas** comes after the verb (See Unit 1 **Résumé grammatical** *7*). The same applies to other negatives.

List of useful negatives:	
ne...plus	*no longer, not any of*
ne...jamais	*no longer, never*
ne...guère	*hardly*
ne...point	*emphatic 'no'*
ne...rien	*nothing*
ne...que	*only*
ne...personne	*nobody*
ne...aucun(e)	*no, none*
ne...ni...ni	*neither...nor*

Je **n**'ai **rien** à faire.	*I have nothing to do.*
Je suis au régime. Je **ne** mange **ni** gâteaux **ni** bonbons.	*I am on a diet. I eat neither cakes nor sweets.*
Je **ne** veux **qu**'un verre d'eau.	*I only want a glass of water.*
Je **n**'ai **aucune** idée au sujet d'un cadeau pour Sandy.	*I have no ideas about a present for Sandy.*
Il **n**'y a **personne** à la caisse.	*There is nobody on the till.*
Des ennuis, je **n**'en veux **point**.	*I do not want **any** worries.*

When negatives are used as expressions of quantity meaning *not / never... any of*, they are followed by **de** without an article (See Unit 2 **Pour aller plus loin** *1* and above **Résumé grammatical** *3*).

Stéphanie ne boit **jamais de** whisky.	*Stéphanie never drinks whisky.*
Mark ne veut **plus de** fromage.	*Mark does not want any more cheese.*
Il n'achète **jamais de** roquefort.	*He never buys roquefort.*
Je n'ai **pas de** monnaie.	*I haven't got any change.*
Je ne bois **plus de** vin rouge.	*I don't drink red wine any more.*

En contexte

Make a list of the **interrogative adjectives** and **interrogative pronouns** used in the dialogue. Identify the **nouns** which the interrogative pronouns replace.

Au supermarché *At the supermarket*

Stéphanie	On va au rayon vêtements.	*Let's go to the clothes department.*
	Il y a beaucoup de vêtements en solde.	*There are lots of clothes in the sale.*
Mark	D'accord.	*All right.*
Stéphanie	Ces T-shirts sont jolis. Lequel préfères-tu?	*These T-shirts are pretty. Which one do you prefer?*
Mark	Je préfère le bleu avec la vue de la Tour Eiffel.	*I prefer the blue one with the picture of the Eiffel Tower.*
Stéphanie	De quelle taille as-tu besoin?	*What size do you need?*
Mark	Je ne sais pas quelle taille. 'Patron'? Qu'est-ce que ça veut dire?	*I do not know what size. 'Patron'? What does that mean?*
Stéphanie	Ça veut dire *large*. Grand patron c'est *extra large*.	*It means large. 'Grand patron' is extra large.*
Mark	Je voudrais taille patron. Mon frère est grand pour son âge.	*I'd like the large size. My brother is big for his age.*
Stéphanie	Qu'est-ce que tu achètes pour Sandy?	*What are you buying for for Sandy?*
Mark	Je n'ai aucune idée.	*I have no idea.*
Stéphanie	Peut-être des magazines français ou un roman?	*Perhaps French magazines or a novel?*
Mark	Lesquels à ton avis?	*Which ones, do you think?*
Stéphanie	*Marie-Claire, le Point, l'Express.*	Marie-Claire, le Point, l'Express.
Mark	Quel roman suggères-tu?	*Which novel do you suggest?*
Stéphanie	On va à la librairie. Ils ont plus de choix.	*We'll go to the bookshop. They have more choice.*
Mark	Laquelle? La librairie sur la place?	*Which one, the bookshop on the market-place?*
Stéphanie	Oui, mais d'abord il faut passer à la caisse.	*Yes, but first of all we'll have to go to the till.*

Pour vérifier

1 Rewrite the sentences below by putting the words in the right order.
Add capital letters and hyphens wherever necessary.

a) je un rouges kilo belles voudrais de pommes.

b) taille vous acheter quelle désirez ?

c) je plus ne de veux viande merci

d) nous ma acheter mère du voudrions parfum pour

e) vous laquelle ces voudriez de robes ?

2 a) Add the appropriate articles in the following sentence:

Isabelle voudrait ___ pâté, ___ beurre, ___ fromage, ___ pommes
de terre, ___ limonade, ___ croissants.

b) Add an appropriate expression of quantity to the phrases below:
Stéphanie would like to cook for her mother. She needs ...

Stéphanie a besoin de/d':

___ bouteille de bordeaux.

___ gros poulet.

un ___ oignons

500 _____ ___ champignons.

une _____ ___ beurre.

5 _____ ___ pommes de terre.

3 Your friend would like to buy the following items. Ask him/her which
one s/he prefers.

Je voudrais:

une chemise (*shirt*)	Laquelle préfères-tu?
un pantalon (*trousers*)	_____ préfères-tu?
des bonbons (*sweets*)	_____ préfères-tu?
des cerises (*cherries*)	_____ préfères-tu?
du whisky	_____ préfères-tu?

Pour aller plus loin

1 More about articles

All articles normally have to be repeated in a list in French. See Unit 2
Comment dit-on? *1, 3* and Unit 4 **Résumé grammatical 2**.

Voici les activités offertes: **les**
randonnées, **le** golf, **la** natation...

Here are the available activities:
walks in the forest, golf, swimming...

However, they are sometimes omitted in advertisements or in brochures:

Voici les nombreuses activités
offertes par St Amand:
randonnées en forêt, golf,
natation, ball-trap, canoë-kayac...

Here are the numerous activities
available at St Amand:
walks in the forest, golf, swimming,
clay-pigeon shooting, canoeing...

■ As gender is crucial in French, get into the good habit of always using the correct article with every noun. Don't forget to keep adding to the lists of masculine and feminine nouns in your notebook.

2 More expressions of quantity

The adjective **demi/e-**: (**une demi-livre** *half a pound*) can be used with many nouns to mean *half.*

un **demi**-fromage	*half a cheese*
un **demi**-camembert	*half a camembert*
une **demi**-heure	*half an hour*

When it comes **before** the noun, **demi-** is joined to it by a hyphen and it is invariable, whatever the gender of the noun. If **demi** follows the noun, it agrees with it in gender:

une heure et **demie**	*an hour and a half*
deux portions et **demie**	*two and a half portions*

3 Using articles after negatives

a) Articles are not used after the negatives: **ne...pas**, **ne...guère**, **ne...point**, **ne...jamais**, **ne...plus** when talking about quantities, or when *any/some* are used. See **Résumé grammatical 5**.

In these cases you say: **pas** *de*, **guère** *de*, **point** *de*, **jamais** *de*, **plus** *de*:

Elle **n'**a **pas d'**excuses.	*She doesn't have any excuses.*
Vous **n'**avez **guère de** patience.	*You have hardly any patience.*
Il **ne** mange **jamais de** poisson.	*He never eats fish (any fish).*
Je **n'**ai **plus d'**argent.	*I don't have any more money.*

b) However, if you want to refer to something specific, the definite article (example 1, below) or the contracted article (example 2, below) can be used and you can say:

Ils n'ont pas le chocolat, indiqué dans la recette, pour faire une bonne mousse au chocolat.	*They haven't got the chocolate mentioned in the recipe to make a good chocolate mousse.*
Je n'ai plus du vin que vous aimez tant.	*I haven't got any more of the wine you like so much.*

c) The indefinite article can also be used after a negative and you can say:

Il n'a plus un sou.	*He is penniless (doesn't have a penny).*
Il n'a pas une seule excuse.	*He doesn't have a single excuse.*

4 ne ... personne, personne ne (nobody); ne ... rien, rien ne (nothing)

Personne can be the subject of the sentence. In that case, it comes before the **ne / n'**:

Personne ne sait pourquoi.	*Nobody knows why.*

When **rien** is the subject of the sentence, it also comes before the **ne / n'**.

Rien ne l'intéresse.	*Nothing interests him/her.*

5 avoir besoin de ... (to need) in the negative

Note that the preposition **de** always follows **besoin** when it is used with a negative:

Je n'ai pas besoin de sel.	*I do not need any salt.*
Je n'ai besoin de rien.	*I don't need anything/need nothing.*
Il n'a besoin de personne.	*He doesn't need anybody.*

6 La plupart de (most of)

After most expressions of quantity followed by **de**, e.g. **beaucoup de, un peu de** (**Résumé grammatical 3**), the partitive article becomes **de**. After the expression **la plupart de** (*most of*), the partitive article is **du/de l'/de la/des**:

La plupart des gens.	*Most of the people.*
La plupart du temps.	*Most of the time.*

5 | SAYING WHAT YOU PREFER

Thèmes   Les achats, les choix

Stéphanie and Mark choose more presents

In this Unit you will learn to:

1 Ask and say what someone prefers
2 Compare things, places, people

Structures grammaticales

1 Verbs in -**ir**, such as **choisir** (*to choose*) and verbs in -**re**, such as **vendre** (*to sell*)
2 Demonstrative pronouns (*this/that/these/those*)
3 More personal pronouns: direct object pronouns **me** (*me*), **te** (*you*), **le/la/les** (*him/her/them*) and the pronoun **en** (*some of it/of that*)
4 Comparatives (*less / more*)

Pour aller plus loin

1 The irregular verb **prendre** (*to take*), and **re**- before verbs (meaning *again*)
2 **C'est** or **il est / elle est?**
3 **Plus de** (*more than*)
4 The difference between **bon** (*good*) and **bien** (*well*), **meilleur** and **mieux** (*better*)

Avant de commencer

1 You have already met regular and irregular verbs ending in -er.
See Unit 1 **Résumé grammatical** *3*. In this Unit you will meet regular
verbs ending in -ir such as **choisir** and in -re such as **vendre**:

Je **choisis** ce livre-ci.	*I choose this book.*
Le supermarché **vend** des vins de	*The supermarket sells all qualities*
toutes qualités.	*of wine.*

2 Demonstrative adjectives **ce**, **cet**, **cette** (*that, this*), **ces** (*these, those*)
were explained in Unit 2 **Résumé grammatical** *5*. To pinpoint
something without repeating the noun, you need to use demonstrative
pronouns:

Quel vin désirez-vous?	*Which wine would you like?*
Je voudrais **celui**-ci.	*I'd like this one.*
Celui-là coûte combien?	*How much does that one cost?*
Ceci est important.	*This is important.*

3 You already know how to say that you like or want something.

Je **voudrais** un nouveau logiciel.	*I'd like a new computer programme.*
Je voudrais un café. Je **le** prends	*I'd like a coffee. I take it black*
noir et sans sucre.	*and without sugar.*

To avoid repeating the noun, you use direct object pronouns, which,
just as in English, are different from subject pronouns: *I* (subject),
me (object), *he* (subject), *him* (object) etc.

Il **la** voit tous les jours.	*He sees her every day.*
Je vais **l'**acheter demain.	*I am going to buy it tomorrow.*
(le cadeau de mon père)	*(the present for my dad).*
Je **le** choisis car il est bien.	*I choose it because it's good.*
J'**en** voudrais un peu.	*I'd like a little (of it).*

4 In this Unit you will learn how to compare things and so to express an
opinion.

Je préfère un vin **plus** doux.	*I prefer a sweeter wine.*
Je préfère les fruits **moins** amers.	*I prefer less bitter fruit.*

Comment dit-on?

1 Which one do you prefer?

Quel tableau préfères-tu?	*Which painting do you prefer?*
Celui-ci ou **celui-là**?	*This one or that one?*
Quelle carte choisis-tu?	*Which postcard do you choose?*
Je choisis **celle-ci**.	*I choose this one.*
Vous voulez **ceux-ci** (ces chocolats)?	*Do you want these (these chocolates?)*
Oui, je **les** prends.	*Yes, I'll have them.*
Lesquels voulez-vous?	*Which ones do you want?*
Je prends **ceux-ci**.	*I'll take these/those.*

2 Comparing things, places and people

Je préfère les endroits **moins** fréquentés.	*I prefer places which are less crowded.*
Cet ordinateur est **plus** puissant **que celui-là**.	*This computer is more powerful that that one.*
Les livres sont **plus** chers à la librairie **qu**'au supermarché.	*Books are more expensive at the bookshop than at the supermarket.*
Mais, le choix est **plus** grand à la librairie.	*But there is a wider choice at the bookshop.*

Résumé grammatical

1 Verbs in -ir/-re

a) -ir verbs

For regular -**ir** verbs you follow the same principle as for -**er** verbs. Take the -**ir** off the infinitive and add the endings given below.

Pronoun	Stem	Ending
je	chois-	IS
tu	chois-	IS
il/elle/on	chois-	IT
nous	chois-	ISSONS
vous	chois-	ISSEZ
ils/elles	chois-	ISSENT

Other regular verbs ending in -**ir** which follow the same rules are listed below.

accomplir	*to accomplish*
atterrir	*to land*
	(of a plane)
choisir	*to choose*
envahir	*to invade*
finir	*to finish*
fournir	*to provide*
grandir	*to grow up*
mûrir	*to ripen*
punir	*to punish*
rafraîchir	*to refresh*
ralentir	*to slow down*
réfléchir	*to think of*
réussir	*to succeed*
rougir	*to redden*
salir	*to dirty*
vieillir	*to grow old*

choisir:

je choisis un livre	*I choose a book*
tu choisis un disque compact	*you choose a compact disc*
il/elle/on choisit un nouvel ordinateur	*he/she(we are) is choosing a new computer*
nous choisissons du bon vin	*we choose good wine*
vous choisissez vos amis?	*do you choose your friends?*
ils/elles choisissent de nouveaux vêtements	*they are choosing new clothes*

Mark **réfléchit** et **choisit** un joli vase pour les fleurs d'Isabelle.	*Mark thinks and chooses a pretty vase for Isabelle's flowers.*
Mark et Stéphanie **réussissent** à trouver la plupart des cadeaux.	*Mark and Stéphanie succeed in finding most of the presents.*
Mark adore manger des cerises, mais elles ne **murissent** et ne **rougissent** qu'en juin.	*Mark loves to eat cherries but they only ripen and turn red in June.*

b) -re verbs

For regular **-re** verbs, take the **-re** off the infinitive to get the stem and add the endings given below:

Pronoun	Stem	Ending
je	vend-	S
tu	vend-	S
il/elle/on	vend-	-
nous	vend-	ONS
vous	vend-	EZ
ils/elles	vend-	ENT

Other regular **-re** verbs which follow the same rules are listed below.

correspondre	*to correspond*
défendre	*to defend*
dépendre de	*to depend on*
descendre	*to go down*
entendre	*to hear*
perdre	*to lose*
pondre	*to lay* (eggs)
rendre	*to give back*
répondre	*to answer*
tondre	*to mow*

vendre:

je vend**s** mes vieux livres	
I sell my old books	
tu vend**s** les tiens?	
do you sell yours?	
il/elle/on vend beaucoup de choses	*he/she/we sell a lot of things*
nous vend**ons** des produits verts	*we sell 'green' products*
vous vend**ez** quelque chose?	*do you sell anything?*
ils/elles vend**ent** des vêtements	*they sell clothes*

St Amand est célèbre pour les carillonneurs. Tu **entends** les cloches de St Amand?	*St Amand is famous for its bellringers. Can you hear the bells of St Amand?*
Le vendredi beaucoup de St Amandinois **se rendent** au marché pour acheter leurs fruits et légumes.	*On Fridays many people in St Amand go to the market to buy their fruit and vegetables.*

| Les boulangeries **vendent** du bon pain. | *The bakers sell good bread.* |
| Stéphanie et Mark montent les 370 marches de l'Abbaye et **redescendent**. | *Stéphanie and Mark go up the 370 steps of the Abbey and come down again.* |

2 Demonstrative pronouns

a) ce + être + adjective

To say *it is*, *this is*, **ce** is used with **être** + adjective when you are referring to something you have already been speaking or writing about:

Ce n'est pas important.	*This is not important.*
(... un problème)	*(... a problem)*
C'est plutôt cher. (... le prix)	*It is rather expensive. (... the price)*

It can also be used with **être** and a following noun:

| C'est un magasin bien achalandé. | *It is a well stocked shop.* |

b) ci (here), là (there)

If you are referring to something specific you add **ci** (*here*) and **là** (*there*) to **ce**:

> **ceci** (*this*); **cela** (*that*)

| **Ceci** est à moi. | *This is mine.* |
| **Cela** est à lui. | *That's his.* |

c) ça – cela

ça (*this/that*) is an abbreviation of **cela**:

| Je ne comprends pas **ça**. | *I don't understand that.* |
| **Ça** n'a pas d'importance. | *That doesn't matter.* |

d) ceci / cela

Ceci and **cela** refer to one object, one situation or something general.

e) However, if you are choosing between different objects, ideas or situations, you use the following demonstrative pronouns.

They replace a noun and agree with it in gender and number:

masc. sing.	fem. sing.	masc. pl.	fem. pl.
celui-ci	**celle-ci**	**ceux-ci**	**celles-ci**
(this one)	*(this one)*	*(these (ones))*	*(these ones)*
celui-là	**celle-là**	**ceux-là**	**celles-là**
(that one)	*(that one)*	*(those ones)*	*(those ones)*

See **Comment dit-on?** *1*.

J'ai besoin de piles pour mon baladeur.
I need some batteries for my walkman.

Lesquelles choisissez-vous?
Which ones will you choose?

Celles-ci.
These (ones).

Celles-là ne sont pas de longue durée.
Those (ones) are not long life.

Ces fleurs-ci sont jolies mais je prends **celles-là**.
Those flowers are pretty but I'll take those.

f) Demonstrative pronouns with **de** *and* **que / qui**

The following demonstrative pronouns:

> **celui** (masc. sing.)/**celle** (fem. sing.) (*this, that*)
> **ceux** (masc. plural) **celles** (fem pl) (*these, those*)

are used with:

> **de** to indicate possession. See Unit 7 **Résumé grammatical** *3*.
> **que / qui** (*that*). See Unit 11 **Résumé grammatical** *5*.

Ce vélo, c'est **celui de** Nicolas.
That bike is Nicolas'.

Celui que je voudrais.
The one (that) I'd like.

3 More personal pronouns

Remember that, although these pronouns usually refer to people "personal", they can also refer to **things**: **il/le/la** (*it*); **ils/les** (*they*)

a) Direct object pronouns

Subject pronouns		Direct object pronouns	
je	*I*	me	*me*
tu	*you*	te	*you*
il/elle/on	*he/she/one*	le/la	*him/her/it*
nous	*we*	nous	*us*
vous	*you*	vous	*you*
ils/elles	*they*	les	*them*

Direct object pronouns come **before** the verb but **after** the subject in a statement.

Alors, tu **les** prends? (les fleurs)	*Well are you taking them?* *(the flowers)*
Mark adore Stéphanie. Il **la** regarde avec passion.	*Mark adores Stéphanie. He looks at her passionately.*
Mark donne une pâquerette à Stéphanie. Elle tire les pétales un à un et dit: 'Je **t**'aime un peu, beaucoup, passionnément, à la folie, pas du tout.'	*Mark gives a daisy to Stéphanie. She pulls the petals one by one and says: 'I love you a little, a lot, passionately, madly, not at all.'*
Et toi, est-ce que tu **m**'aimes?	*And you, do you love me?*
Stéphanie laisse tomber sa liste de courses. Mark **la** ramasse.	*Stéphanie drops her shopping list. Mark picks it up.*
Patrick aime sa voiture.	*Patrick likes his car.*
Il **la** lave tous les week-ends.	*He washes it every week-end.*
Patrick s'occupe du gazon.	*Patrick looks after the lawn.*
Il **le** tond tous les week-ends.	*He mows it every week-end.*

b) en (some of it, of that) as personal pronoun

When you want to replace a noun by a pronoun, it is not always possible to use the direct object **le**, **la** when referring to things. For example, if you are talking about **quantities** – **du** poisson (*some fish*), **de** l'argent (*some money*) – you will need to use the pronoun **en** which means *some* (*of it/ of that*).

Je **le** veux. (something specific, precise)	*I want it.*

but

J'**en** veux.	*I want some (of it).*

Combien **en** voulez-vous?	*How much (of it) / how many*
	(of them) would you like?
J'**en** voudrais deux, s'il vous plaît.	*I'd like two (of them) please.*

4 Comparatives

There are three ways of comparing things or objects.

■ To say that something or someone is *as...as* something else you use: **aussi...que**.

| Mark est **aussi** intéressé par le | *Mark is as interested in sport as* |
| sport **que** son frère. | *his brother.* |

■ To say that something or someone is *less...than* you use: **moins...que**.

Nicolas est beaucoup **moins**	*Nicolas is much less athletic*
athlétique **qu'**Andrew.	*than Andrew.*
Les parents de Stéphanie parlent	*Stéphanie's parents talk less quickly*
moins vite **que** les gens dans la rue.	*than people in the street.*
Le vin coûte **moins** cher en France	*Wine costs less in France than in*
qu'en Grande-Bretagne.	*Great Britain.*

■ To say that something or someone is *more...than* you use: **plus...que**.

| Le vin de qualité supérieure coûte | *Top quality wine costs more than* |
| **plus** cher **que** le vin de table. | *table wine.* |

Just as in English, the comparison doesn't have to be specific. You can just say **aussi**, **plus**, **moins**, without saying **que** (*than*) (something else):

| Il coûte **plus** cher. | *It costs more.* |
| C'est **aussi** intéressant. | *It is just as interesting.* |

Two useful comparative adjectives

There are two adjectives which change their form when they are used as comparatives:

bon → becomes **meilleur/e/s** (*better*)
mauvais → becomes **pire/s** (*worse*)

Est-ce que le boudin blanc est	*Is boudin blanc better than haggis?*
meilleur que le haggis?	
Stéphanie pense que c'est **meilleur,**	*Stéphanie thinks that it is nicer,*
mais que les andouillettes sont **pires**.	*but that chitterlings are worse.*

There is one adverb which changes its form when it is used as a comparative:

bien → becomes **mieux** (*better*)

Je vais **mieux**. *I feel better.*

En contexte

When reading this dialogue look particularly for **demonstrative pronouns, direct object pronouns** and **-ir** and **-re** verb endings.

Mark achète des cadeaux à la librairie.
Mark is buying presents at the bookshop.

Stéphanie	Voici le rayon des magazines. Lesquels choisis-tu?	*Here is the magazine section. Which ones are you choosing?*
Mark	Celui-ci a l'air intéressant.	*This one looks interesting.*
Stéphanie	Si tu préfères un magazine plus littéraire, il y a *l'Express, le Point, le Nouvel Observateur.*	*If you'd rather have a more literary magazine, there are l'Express, le Point, le Nouvel Observateur.*
Mark	Je prends *le Point.* Je voudrais aussi des journaux régionaux, mais j'attends la fin de la semaine.	*I'll take le Point. I'd also like some regional papers, but I'll wait till the end of the week.*
Stéphanie	Voici le rayon des livres de poche. Voici deux romans populaires. Celui-ci est plus passionnant que celui-là. C'est l'histoire d'un ménage à trois à Paris.	*Here is the paperback section Here are two popular novels. This one is more exciting than that one. It's the story of a love triangle in Paris.*
Mark	Ce genre d'histoire te passionne. Moi, je préfère les livres de science fiction. C'est plus stimulant que les histoires d'amour.	*This type of story really appeals to you. As for me, I prefer science fiction books. They are more stimulating than love stories.*
Stéphanie	Merci beaucoup Mark!	*Thanks a lot Mark!*
Mark	Sandy est aussi sentimentale que toi. Alors je prends celui-ci.	*Sandy is as sentimental as you. So I'll take this one.*

La vendeuse	Et avec ceci, Monsieur?	*Something else, sir?*
Mark	C'est tout, merci madame.	*That's all, thank you.*
Stéphanie	Il y a un marchand de cadeaux	*There is a gift shop just next*
	juste à côté. Ils vendent de	*door. They sell gorgeous*
	jolies assiettes en porcelaine.	*china plates.*
	Celle-ci montre la place	*This one shows the square*
	et la station thermale. Celle-là	*and the spa centre. That one*
	montre l'Abbaye.	*shows the Abbey.*
Mark	Je préfère celle-ci. Elle est	*I prefer this one. It's a lot*
	beaucoup plus fine que l'autre.	*finer than the other one.*
	Et elle coûte aussi moins cher.	*And it also costs less.*
	D'accord, je la prends pour	*OK I'll take it for my*
	ma voisine.	*neighbour.*
La vendeuse	Monsieur, vous désirez un	*Would you like it gift-*
	emballage-cadeau?	*wrapped, sir?*
Mark	Oui, merci, madame.	*Yes, thank you, madam.*
La vendeuse	Je l'emballe aussi dans du	*I'll also wrap it in some*
	polystyrène pour la protéger.	*polystyrene to proctect it.*
Mark	Je vous en remercie.	*Many thanks.*

Pour vérifier

1   Write six pairs of sentences using a pronoun from the left-hand column and the word opposite it in the right-hand column. Use the verb **choisir** and the structure given in the example.

(Je) choisis (une assiette en porcelaine). Je prends (celle-ci).

a) je   une fleur
b) tu   un pot de confiture
c) il/elle/on   un stylo-plume
d) nous   un livre
e) vous   des brochures
f) ils/elles   des biscuits

2   a)   Add the appropriate endings to the verbs used in the following sentences:

A St Amand nous entend_____ **les cloches de l'Abbaye** sonner tous les jours.

Ils entend_____ **leurs voisins** partir très tôt.

Quand Mark joue au rugby, il sal_____**son maillot.**

Mark réfléch_____ et chois_____ **l'assiette en porcelaine** pour sa voisine.

b) Replace the expressions in bold above with the corresponding **object pronoun.**

3 Using the outlines in the box below, write two sentences, each one using a comparative.

Example: Il fait chaud – l'Afrique – le Pôle Nord
Il fait **plus** chaud en Afrique **qu'**au Pôle Nord.
Il fait **moins** chaud au Pôle Nord **qu'**en Afrique.

Un hôtel quatre étoiles – luxueux – un hôtel deux étoiles
La Tour Eiffel – haut – la Tour de Blackpool.
Mark – âgé – Stéphanie.

Pour aller plus loin

1 An irregular verb in -re: prendre

a) **Je, tu, il/elle/on** are regular; but the stem changes in the plural.

For other irregular **-re** and **-ir** verbs see Unit 6 **Résumé grammatical 2.**

prendre *to take*
je **prends**
tu **prends**
il/elle/on **prend**
nous **prenons**
vous **prenez**
ils/elles **prennent**

b) **re-** in verbs like **reprendre** (*to take back, to retake*)

You can add **re-** before many French verbs to mean that you do the action again.

recommencer *to restart*
refaire *to do again*
repartir *to go again*
reprendre *to take again*
reconnaître *to recognise*

2 C'est *or* il est?

Sometimes you have to choose between **c'est** (see **Résumé grammatical** *2*) and **il est**.

a) Il est / elle est + *adjective*

■ **Il est/elle est** is used when you are referring to a specific person:

Il / elle est **riche**.	*He/she is wealthy.*
(ton père/ma femme)	(your father/my wife)

or to a specific thing:

Elle est très **importante**.	*It is very important.*
(cette tâche)	(this task)

■ **Il est / elle est** + noun (without an article) is used when you are saying what someone's job or profession is. (See Unit 1 **Résumé grammatical** *2*):

Il est commerçant.	*He is a shopkeeper.*
Elle est professeur.	*She is a teacher.*

b) Il est *meaning it is*

■ **Il est** + adjective

There are many impersonal expressions in French based on **il est** meaning *it is*:

Il est important, il est probable, il est possible ... See Unit 10 **Pour aller plus loin** *2a* and Unit 17 **Résumé grammatical** *3c*:

■ **Il est** + adjective + **de** + infinitive (*it is* + adjective + *to*) is used to refer **forward** to something:

Il est important d'acheter des cadeaux avant de partir.	*It is important to buy presents before leaving.*
Il est difficile de comprendre cette liste.	*It is difficult to understand this list.*

c) C'est (*it is*) + *adjective*

(See **Résumé grammatical** *2*) refers **back** to an idea or situation but not to a person.

C'est vraiment très intéressant.	*It is really very interesting.*
C'est vrai, tu sais.	*It is true, you know.*

The structure **c'est** + noun + adjective can be used to refer to a person:

C'est un homme intelligent.   *He is an intelligent man.*
C'est une femme intelligente.   *She is an intelligent woman.*

3 Plus de *(more than)*

The expression *more than* is not always expressed by **plus que** when you are using figures. **Plus de** is used instead of **plus que** when figures are used:

Il fait **plus de** 30 degrés.   *It is more than (over) 30 degrees.*
Il y a **plus de** 100 élèves.   *There are more than (over) 100 pupils.*

4 Bon / bien *(good / well)*, meilleur / mieux *(better)*

The adverb **bien** *(well)* is sometimes used in French where in English you would use the adjective *good*:

Ce travail est **bien**.   *This is good work.*

Because there is sometimes a problem for English speakers in choosing between **bon** and **bien**, it might also be difficult to know when to use the comparatives **meilleur** and **mieux**. The **adjective meilleur/e/s** *(better)* is the comparative of **bon / bonne/s** *(good)*. It agrees with the appropriate noun in gender and number and goes before the noun it relates to.

Cette confiture est **meilleure**   *This jam is better than that.*
(lit. *more good*) que celle-là.
Mark a **meilleur** caractère   *Mark has a better temper*
qu'Andrew.   *than Andrew.*

The **adverb mieux** *(better)* is the comparative of **bien** *(well / fine)* and remains invariable (does not agree):

Ces nouvelles baskets sont **mieux**.*These new trainers are better.*

Mieux, being an adverb, follows the verb:

Ça va **mieux**.   *I am better. / Things are going better.*
Ça va **mieux**?   *Are you better? Are things any better?*

6 | WHERE YOU ARE AND WHAT YOU ARE GOING TO DO

Thème   Les voyages

Mark and Stéphanie visit St Amand
More about what they are going to do

In this Unit you will learn to:

1   Talk about where you are and where you are going
2   Talk about what you are going to do
3   Ask about people, places and things
4   Locate people, places and things

Structures grammaticales

1   The immediate future: **aller** + infinitive (*going to* + infinitive)
2   Irregular -**ir** and -**re** verbs
3   Prepositions *in*, *at*, *to*, *with*
4   Adverbs
5   Superlatives *the least / the most*

Pour aller plus loin

1   -**ir** / -**re** reflexive verbs
2   Verbs followed by prepositions
3   More about adverbs in set expressions

Avant de commencer

1 To say where you are going and what you are going to do, you can use the present tense in conversational French.

Je **vais** à Paris la semaine prochaine.   *I am going to Paris next week.*
J'**ai** une réunion dans deux semaines.   *I have a meeting in two weeks.*

The future action is indicated by the time expression: *next week / next year* ... In writing, or to emphasise the fact that the action will take place in the future, you will need to use the future tense (see Unit 11). However, just as in English, there is a way of saying that an action will take place in the immediate future (*going to* + infinitive): *I'm going to go abroad soon.*

In French you use the verb **aller** + the infinitive of the verb indicating the action:

Je **vais aller** à Paris la semaine   *I am going to go to Paris next*
prochaine.   *week.*

You have already learned how to conjugate **aller**, which is an irregular verb. If you are unsure refer back to Unit 1 **Résumé grammatical** *3*.

2 In this Unit you will also meet more irregular verbs ending in **-ir** and **-re** such as **prendre** (*to take*), **partir** (*to leave*).

Les français **prennent** souvent   *French people often take a month*
un mois de vacances en juillet   *off in July or August.*
ou en août.

Ils **partent** à la mer ou à   *They go to the seaside or to*
la montagne.   *the mountains.*

3 To say where you are going to, or to locate people, things or places, you need to use a preposition, for example: *to, in, with,* ...

St Amand-les-Eaux se trouve   *St Amand-les-Eaux is situated*
dans le nord **près de** la   *in the north near the*
frontière belge.   *Belgian border.*

4 To say **when, where, how, how often** you do something you use adverbs. In this Unit you will find out about common adverbs such as **souvent** (*often*). You will also find out how most other adverbs in French are formed, for example: **rarement** (*rarely*).

Isabelle va **souvent** à Paris.   *Isabelle often goes to Paris.*

Elle va à Paris **principalement** pour *She goes to Paris mainly for*
les expositions dans les musées.   *exhibitions in museums.*

5 You have used adjectives for comparisons in Unit 5 **Résumé
grammatical *4*** and **Comment dit-on?** *2*. In this Unit you will learn how
to use the superlative form, how to say *the most, the least* and so on.

Paris est **la plus** belle capitale   *Paris is the most beautiful capital*
du monde.   *in the world.*

Comment dit-on?

Look more closely at **verb structures**, **prepositions** and **adverbs** in the
following examples.

1 *Where you are and where you are going*

Mark **est** en vacances **à** St Amand-   *Mark is on holiday in St Amand-*
les-Eaux. St Amand offre de   *les-Eaux. St Amand has many*
nombreuses attractions touristiques.   *tourist attractions.*
Mark visite la station thermale.   *Mark visits the spa centre. It is*
Elle **se trouve près de** la source   *situated near the spring called*
du clos **de** l'Abbaye.   *the* clos de l'Abbaye.
Mark et Stéphanie se promènent   *Mark and Stéphanie are walking*
dans la forêt de St Amand.   *in the forest of St Amand.*
La forêt de St Amand **est au centre**   *St Amand forest is in the centre*
du Parc naturel régional.   *of the regional country park.*
Mark et Stéphanie **vont visiter**   *Mark and Stéphanie are going to*
l'Abbaye et **écouter** le carillon   *visit the Abbey and listen to the*
de 48 cloches.   *peal of 48 bells.*
Ils **vont** aussi **faire** des courses et *They are also going to go shopping*
prendre un verre **à** la terrasse   *and have a drink at a*
d'un café.   *pavement café.*

2 *What you are going to do*

Demain je **vais aller à** la pharmacie *Tomorrow I am going to go to the*
pour acheter des aspirines.   *chemist to buy some aspirins.*
Les parents **de** Mark **vont venir en** *Mark's parents are going to come*
France **afin de** rencontrer les   *to France to meet Stéphanie's*
parents **de** Stéphanie.   *parents.*

Les Dickson **vont suivre** des cours **du** soir en français.	*The Dicksons are going to take evening classes in French.*
Ils **vont venir en** France **en** juillet.	*They are going to come to France in August.*
Sandy **va** bientôt **passer** ses examens en français.	*Sandy is going to take her French exams soon.*
Elle **va** beaucoup **réviser** pendant plusieurs semaines.	*She is going to revise a lot for a few weeks.*

3 Asking about people, places and things

Qu'est-ce qu'il y a à voir dans la région?	*What is there to see in the area?*
Pourquoi la ville porte-t-elle ce nom?	*Why does the town have this name?*
Où est-elle située?	*Where is it situated?*
Pourquoi est-elle célèbre?	*Why is it famous?*
Quelles sont les spécialités de St Amand?	*What are the specialities of St Amand?*
Qui est le maire de St Amand?	*Who is the mayor of St Amand?*
Comment est-ce que ça s'appelle?	*What's that called?*

4 Locating people, places and things

Stéphanie et Mark **sont** au café **près de** la gare.	*Stéphanie and Mark are at the café near the station.*
La ville **est située dans** le nord de la France, **à** 30 km de Lille.	*The town is situated in the north of France, 30 kms from Lille.*
Le musée **se trouve sur** la place du marché.	*The museum is situated in the market place.*

Résumé grammatical

1 The immediate future

■ **aller** (*to go*) + infinitive

The immediate future tells you what is going to happen in the not too distant future and replaces the future tense in conversational French, when no specific point about the future is being made. See **Comment dit-on? 2.**

Les Dickson **vont mettre** leur français en pratique durant leurs vacances.	*The Dicksons are going to put their French to use during their holidays.*
Ils **vont faire** la connaissance de la famille de Stéphanie.	*They are going to meet Stéphanie's family.*
Où **allez**-vous **passer** vos vacances?	*Where are you going to spend your holidays?*
Nous n'**allons** pas **passer** les vacances en Italie.	*We aren't going to spend the holidays in Italy.*
Allez-vous **visiter** Marseille?	*Are you going to visit Marseilles?*

2 Irregular -ir and -re verbs

a) Verbs in -re

The stem of irregular -**re** verbs changes in the present tense with plural subjects.

For **prendre** the stem becomes **pren-** so that the plural forms of the present tense are:

nous prenons, vous prenez, ils prennent

The endings of the present tense of the other irregular -**re** verbs are: -**s**, -**s**, -**t**, -**ons**, -**ez**, -**ent**.

Here is a more complete list of irregular verbs in -**re**.

Note the way the stem changes in the plural:

boire *to drink*	bois, bois, boit,	buvons, buvez, boivent
croire *to believe*	crois, crois, croit,	croyons, croyez, croient
conduire *to drive*	conduis, conduis, conduit,	conduisons, conduisez, conduisent
connaître *to know*	connais, connais, connaît,	connaissons, connaissez, connaissent
dire *to say*	dis, dis, dit,	disons, dites, disent
écrire *to write*	écris, écris, écrit	écrivons, écrivez, écrivent
lire *to read*	lis, lis, lit,	lisons, lisez, lisent
prendre *to take*	prends, prends, prend,	prenons, prenez, prennent
suivre *to follow*	suis, suis, suit,	suivons, suivez, suivent
vivre *to live*	vis, vis, vit	vivons, vivez, vivent

For more information on irregular verbs, see the Verb Tables, page 232.

Cette année Mark et Stéphanie **prennent** une semaine de vacances en mai.	*This year Mark and Stéphanie are taking a week off in May.*
Les Dickson ne **connaissent** pas encore les Lemaire.	*The Dicksons do not know the Lemaires yet.*
Mark **écrit** quelques cartes. Stéphanie les **lit** et ajoute un petit mot.	*Mark writes some postcards. Stéphanie reads them and adds a few words.*

b) Irregular verbs in -ir

■ A small group of irregular verbs ending in -**ir** add the following endings to the stem:

-**e**, -**es**, -**e**, -**ons**, -**ez**, -**ent**.

The stem of these verbs does not change in the plural:

cueillir *to pick*	cueille, cueilles, cueille,	cueillons, cueillez, cucillent
offrir *to offer*	offre, offres, offre,	offrons, offrez, offrent
ouvrir *to open*	ouvre, ouvres, ouvre,	ouvrons, ouvrez, ouvrent
souffrir *to suffer*	souffre, souffres, souffre,	souffrons, souffrez, souffrent

Mark **cueille** un brin de muguet pour Stéphanie.	*Mark picks a sprig of Lily of the Valley for Stéphanie.*

■ A group of irregular verbs ending in -**ir** have the -**ir** removed and also the preceding consonant removed to form the stem for the first three persons in the singular – except in the case of **courir** (*to run*). The following endings are added:

-**s**, -**s**, -**t**, -**ons**, -**ez**, -**ent**.

The stem does not change in the plural:

courir *to run*	cours, cours, court,	courons, courez, courent
dormir *to sleep*	dors, dors, dort,	dormons, dormez, dorment
mentir *to lie*	mens, mens, ment,	mentons, mentez, mentent
partir *to leave*	pars, pars, part,	partons, partez, partent
sortir *to go out*	sors, sors, sort,	sortons, sortez, sortent

Le vendredi soir Mark et Stéphanie *On Friday nights Mark and Stéphanie*
sortent à Aberdeen. *go out in Aberdeen.*

■ Two -**ir** verbs are highly irregular:

tenir *to hold*	tiens, tiens, tient,	tenons, tenez, tiennent
venir *to come*	viens, viens, vient,	venons, venez, viennent

Verbs with similar spelling such as **devenir** (*to become*), **revenir** (*to come back*), **retenir** (*to hold back*) etc. follow the same pattern.

Isabelle **tient** les cordons de *Isabelle holds the purse-strings.*
la bourse.

Les parents de Mark **viennent** *Mark's parents come from*
de Dundee. *Dundee.*

3 Prepositions in, at, to, with

Prepositions can accompany verbs, for example: **sortir de** (*to go out of* / *to come from*) but they mainly introduce adverbial phrases indicating *where*, *when*, *how*, *why* things happen. See **Résumé grammatical 4** below.

Here is a list of prepositions (both single words and groups of words) you have already met in examples in this book:

Prepositions and prepositional groups indicating place (*where*)

à	*to / in / at*	**contre**	*against*
à côté de	*beside / next to*	**dans**	*in*
à l'intérieur de	*inside*	**de**	*of / from / by*
après	*after*	**derrière**	*behind*
au bord de	*on / at the edge of*	**devant**	*in front of*
au coin de	*on / at the corner of*	**en**	*to / in / of*
		en face de	*opposite*
au-dessous de	*below / underneath*	**entre**	*between*
		loin de	*far from*
au-dessus de	*above*	**parmi**	*among*
autour de	*around*	**près de**	*near*
avant	*before*	**sous**	*under*
chez	*at / at the home of* (someone)	**sur**	*on*
		vers	*towards*

L'Abbaye se trouve **sur** la place **en face de** l'hôtel de ville.	*The Abbey is situated in the market place opposite the town hall.*
L'agence de voyages se trouve **au coin de** la rue, **à côté du** marchand de légumes **près de** l'Abbaye.	*The travel agency is situated on the corner of the street next to the greengrocer's near the Abbey.*
À St Amand il y a un marché **sur** la place tous les vendredis **de** 9 heures **à** 13 heures.	*In St Amand there is a market in the square every Friday from 9 to 13.00.*

Prepositions indicating time (*when*)

à	*at*	**jusque**	*until*
avant	*before*	**pendant**	*during*
après	*after*	**pour**	*for*
depuis	*since / for*		

Stéphanie habite à Aberdeen **depuis** six mois.	*Stéphanie has been living in Aberdeen for six months.*
Avant ça elle était à l'université de Lille **pendant** 2 ans.	*Before that she was at the University of Lille for two years.*
Elle va travailler à Aberdeen **jusqu'**à la fin de son stage, puis elle espère y trouver un autre emploi.	*She is going to work in Aberdeen until the end of her work placement and then she is hoping to find another job there.*

Other prepositions and prepositional groups showing *how* or *why*:

afin de	*in order to*	**par**	*by / through*
à cause de	*because*	**pour**	*in order to*
au lieu de	*instead of*	**presque**	*almost*
avec	*with*	**sans**	*without*
comme	*like, such as*	**sauf**	*except*
d'après	*according to*	**selon**	*according to*
de façon à	*in order to*	**suite à**	*following*

Stéphanie travaille **comme** stagiaire pour une compagnie pétrolière à Aberdeen.	*Stéphanie works as a trainee for an oil company in Aberdeen.*

| Elle travaille **avec** Mark. | *She works with Mark. In his opinion* |
| *Selon lui, elle est très douée et elle se débrouille très bien dans son emploi. | *she is very gifted and is doing very well in her job.* |

Mark a tous les cadeaux **sauf** un   *Mark has all his presents except*
pour son meilleur ami.   *one for his best friend.*

*As mentioned in Unit 1 **Résumé grammatical 8** and **Comment dit-on? 3**, when prepositions are followed by personal pronouns, stressed pronouns are used: **moi, toi, lui/elle/soi, nous, vous, eux/elles**. See also Unit 7 **Résumé grammatical 6**.

Tu viens **avec moi**?	*Are you coming with me?*
Elle va à la librairie **avec lui**.	*She is going to the bookshop with him.*
Selon toi, Mark, est-ce que Stéphanie va obtenir un emploi à temps complet à la fin de son stage?	*Mark, in your opinion, is Stéphanie going to get a full-time job at the end of her training period?*
Tu y vas **sans moi**?	*Are you going without me?*

4 Adverbs

Adverbs describe *where*, *when*, *how*, or *why* something happens. They work with words such as verbs, adjectives or other adverbs to change or explain the basic meaning.

There are two main groups of adverbs:

a) Short, frequently used adverbs such as:

b) Other adverbs which are formed from adjectives. You simply add -**ment**, usually to the feminine form of the adjective:

assez	*fairly / enough*
bien	*well*
moins	*less*
plus	*more*
souvent	*often*
toujours	*very*
très	*always*
trop	*too*
vite	*fast*
vraiment	*really / truly*

actif (m)	**active** (f)	acti**ve**ment
heureux (m)	**heureuse** (f)	heureuse**ment**
mondial (m)	**mondiale** (f)	mondiale**ment**
passif (m)	**passive** (f)	passive**ment**
principal (m)	**principale** (f)	principale**ment**
régulier (m)	**régulière** (f)	régulière**ment**

For adjectives which already end in -**e**, add -**ment** without any change:

simple (m, f)	simple**ment**
véritable (m, f)	véritable**ment**

c) The position of adverbs
Adverbs can accompany/modify **verbs**, **adjectives** or **other adverbs**.

■ When adverbs modify **verbs**, they usually come after the verb (or after the first part of the verb: **être** or **avoir** in the perfect tense, see Unit 13 **Résumé grammatical** *3e*):

Mark travaille **souvent** sur la plate-forme pétrolière.	*Mark often works on the oil platform.*
Il téléphone **régulièrement** à Stéphanie.	*He phones Stéphanie regularly.*
Il a **déjà** acheté un téléphone portable.	*He has already bought a mobile phone.*

■ When adverbs modify **adjectives**, they come directly before the adjective:

Mark trouve les parents de Stéphanie **vraiment** sympathiques.	*Mark finds Stéphanie's parents really friendly.*
Il est **très** heureux d'être en France.	*He is very happy to be in France.*

■ Short adverbs such as **trop**, **plus**, **très** can also modify **other adverbs** and are placed before them:

Certains Français roulent **trop** vite.	*Some French people drive too fast.*
Les Britanniques roulent **plus** prudemment.	*The British drive more cautiously.*

d) Using the present participle (*-ing* word) to say *why*. See Unit 3 **Pour aller plus loin** *3*.

In English you form the present participle from the infinitive of the verb by adding *-ing*:
> to drive → driving; to go → going

In French you find the stem of the verb and add -**ant**:

> **rouler** → roul- → roul**ant** (*driving*); **aller** → all- → all**ant** (*going*)

Se couch**ant** tard à cause de ses examens, Sandy est très fatiguée.	*Going to bed late because of her exams, Stéphanie is very tired.*

To show that one thing causes another (*by / in …ing*), in French you add the preposition **en** before the present participle (the -**ant** form of the verb):

En pren**ant** des cours du soir, les parents de Mark espèrent apprendre assez de français pour communiquer avec les Lemaire.	*By taking evening classes Mark's parents hope to learn enough French to communicate with the Lemaires.*

e) There are some frequently used adverbial phrases which are formed from a preposition + a **noun**:

avec plaisir	*with pleasure*
en ce moment	*at the moment*
en retard	*late*

George et Isabelle accueillent Mark *George and Isabelle welcome*
avec plaisir.   *Mark with pleasure.*

f) To say when something happened, there are some time phrases which do not start with a preposition in French, although they do in English:

le samedi soir	*on Saturday nights*
le dimanche matin	*on Sunday mornings*
le matin	*in the morning*
lundi	*on Monday*
le lundi	*on Mondays*

5 Superlatives: the least, the most

■ To say that something or someone is *the most...*, or for adjectives that end in *-est* in English (great*est*, old*est*, new*est*), you use: **le/la/les plus** + adjective. The adjective agrees in number and gender with the noun, and its position does not change.

Most adjectives go *after* the noun:

Nicolas est le cinéphile **le plus** passionné de toute la famille. *Nicolas is the keenest cinema enthusiast of the whole family.*

St Amand est une des villes **les plus** connues du nord, ayant participé plusieurs fois aux jeux d'Interville. *St Amand is one of the most famous cities in the north, having taken part in the Interville Games several times.*

L' eau de St Amand est une des eaux **les plus** riches en minéraux et en magnésium et c'est **la plus** consommée dans le nord. *St Amand water is among the richest in minerals and magnesium and is the one most people drink it in the north.*

Here are some examples of adjectives which go *before* the noun. See Unit 3 **Résumé grammatical 1d**.

Nicolas est **le plus grand** garçon de sa classe. *Nicolas is the tallest boy in his class.*

A la maison, il a **la plus petite** chambre.	*At home, he has the smallest bedroom.*

■ To say that something or someone is *the least* you use: **le/la/les moins** + adjective. The adjective agrees in number and gender with the noun:

Nicolas est **le moins** sportif de toute la famille.	*Nicolas is the least sporty of the family.*
L'eau de St Amand est aussi une des eaux minérales **les moins** chères.	*St Amand water is also one of the least expensive mineral waters.*

En contexte

In the following conversation, look for **expressions of time** and **of place**, and for verbs **expressing an immediate future:**

Isabelle parle de Paris à Mark. *Isabelle is talking to Mark about Paris.*

Isabelle	Mark, connaissez-vous Paris?	*Mark, do you know Paris?*
Mark	Non, mais j'aimerais beaucoup y aller un jour avec Stéphanie. Est-ce que vous allez souvent à Paris?	*No, but I would very much like to go there one day with Stéphanie. Do you go to Paris often?*
Isabelle	Environ une fois par an. J'ai des cousins qui vivent là-bas. Exceptionnellement, je vais y aller la semaine prochaine, afin de rendre visite à ma cousine Jacqueline. Elle est à l'hôpital suite à un accident de la route. Je pars mercredi matin.	*About once a year. I have some cousins who live there. Exceptionally, I'm going to go there next week, to pay a visit to my cousin Jacqueline. She is in hospital as the result of a road accident. I'm leaving on Wednesday morning.*
Mark	Est-ce que c'est très grave?	*Is it very serious?*
Isabelle	Assez grave. D'après les docteurs elle a vraiment de la chance d'être en vie. Sa voiture est complèment inutilisable. Elle a les deux jambes cassées et quelques blessures aux bras et au visage. Elle dort très mal et elle se sent plutôt déprimée. Je vais donc aller la voir.	*Fairly serious. According to the doctors she is very lucky to be alive. Her car is a complete write-off. Both her legs are broken and she has a few cuts to her arms and face. She is sleeping very badly and feels rather depressed. So I'm going to go and see her.*

Mark	Combien de temps allez-vous rester à Paris?	*How long are you going to stay in Paris for?*
Isabelle	Trois ou quatre jours seulement. Je vais en profiter pour faire quelques courses pendant mon séjour là. Je voudrais aller à la *Samaritaine*, près du Pont-Neuf. C'est le magasin le mieux situé et le plus populaire de Paris. C'est au coeur de Paris, près du musée du Louvre et pas très loin de Notre-Dame de Paris. Il est extrêmement populaire avec les touristes. On a la plus belle vue de Paris de la terrasse de la *Samaritaine*.	*Only three or four days. I'm going to take the opportunity to do some shopping during my stay there. I'd like to go to the* Samaritaine *near the Pont-Neuf. It is the most convenient and the most popular shop in Paris. It is in the centre of Paris near the Louvre, not too far from Notre-Dame. It is extremely popular with tourists. You have the best view of Paris from the roof-top of* Samaritaine.

Pour vérifier

1   Put the words in the following sentences in the correct order, adding capitals and punctuation as necessary:

    a)   vais St Amand je visiter de l'Abbaye

    b)   est-ce des vas cartes que postales tu acheter

    c)   le j' aller les sangliers aimerais bois dans voir les de St Amand

2   Make the verbs in brackets agree with their subject and add the correct prepositions in the following sentences:

    a)   Mark (écrire) des cartes postales ___ St Amand et les (envoyer) ___ sa famille ___ Dundee et ___ ses amis.

    b)   Les parents ___ Mark (vivre) ___ un quartier résidentiel ___ Dundee.

    c)   Mr. Dickson (prendre) le bus ___ se rendre au travail le matin.

    d)   Il est directeur ___ un supermarché ___ quelques kilomètres ___ centre ville ___ de la rivière Tay.

    e)   Il (partir) ___ 8 heures le matin et (revenir) ___ 18 heures, ___ le jeudi soir car il travaille ___ 21 heures.

3 Select adverbs from the boxed lists in **Résumé grammatical 4a** and **4b** above, and add them to the following sentences:

Dundee occupe une position _____ privilégiée sur la côte est de l'Écosse. Les deux collines, Balgay et Law, offrent une vue _____ superbe de la Tay et de la campagne. Dundee est une ville _____ connue pour le bateau *Discovery*, et l'observatoire de Balgay avec ses vues féériques. Dundee est une ville _____ accueillante pas très loin de St Andrews _____ célèbre pour le golf.

Pour aller plus loin

1 -ir / -re *reflexive verbs*

Most reflexive verbs are -er verbs. See Unit 3 **Résumé grammatical 3**. Some -**ir** / -**re** verbs can also be used as reflexives. The extra pronoun **se** which comes in front of the verb changes form according to the subject of the verb.

Here are a few examples of -**ir** and -**re** reflexive verbs:

s'asseoir *to sit down*	Tu t'assieds.
se comprendre *to understand one another*	Nous nous comprenons.
se conduire *to behave (oneself)*	Ils se conduisent bien.
se connaître *to know oneself / know each other*	Vous vous connaissez?
se dire *to tell oneself*	Je me dis …
s'écrire *to write to each other*	Nous nous écrivons.
se tenir *to stand / behave / hold*	Ils se tiennent bien.

Mark et Stéphanie **se tiennent** la main. *Mark and Stéphanie hold hands.*

Les Dickson et les Lemaires ne **se connaissent** pas encore. *The Dicksons and the Lemaires don't know each other yet.*

2 *Verbs followed by prepositions*

a) Prepositions are often used differently in English and French. This is most noticeable in **verb groups** (**s'habituer à, penser à, se contenter de**). For example the preposition **à** can be translated by *at / in* and it also means *to*:

Mark s'habitue **à** la vie française. *Mark is getting used to French life.*

à can also mean *of/about* in expressions such as:

penser à (*to think of/about*)

de can also mean *with* in expressions such as:

se contenter de (*to be satisfied with*)

par can mean with *in* expressions such as:

commencer par (*to begin with*),
remplacer par (*to replace with*)

Mark pense à écrire à ses amis. — *Mark is thinking of writing to his friends.*

Mark et Stéphanie se contentent de sortir le week-end. — *Mark and Stéphanie are satisfied with going out at week-ends.*

b) Many French verbs are almost always followed by a preposition, forming a **verb group**. It is important to remember the verb *with its preposition* and to look up the verb in a good dictionary whenever you are unsure.

Here is a list of French verbs followed by the preposition **à**:

aboutir à	*to lead to*
aider quelqu'un à	*to help someone to*
s'amuser à (+ inf)	*to amuse oneself* (+ verb + *ing*)
appartenir à	*to belong to*
chercher à	*to try to*
commencer à	*to begin to*
consentir à	*to consent to*
continuer à	*to continue to*
s'habituer à	*to become used to*
inviter quelqu'un à	*to invite someone to*
penser à	*to think of*
réussir à	*to succeed in*

Stéphanie s'habitue à vivre à Aberdeen. — *Stéphanie is getting used to living in Aberdeen.*

Elle cherche à rester en Ecosse. — *She is trying to stay in Scotland.*

The verbs in the boxed lists above and below are not always followed by a preposition, either in English or in French. Some can also be followed by a direct object.

s'arrêter de	to stop
(+ inf)	(doing something)
avoir l'air de	to look like
avoir besoin de	to need
avoir envie de	to be afraid of
se contenter de	to be satisfied with
se dépêcher de	to hurry to
douter de	to doubt
éviter de	to avoid
	(doing something)
s'excuser de	to apologise for
finir de	to finish
offrir de	to offer to
ordonner à quelqu'un de	to order someone to
parler de	to talk about
se passer de	to do without
se souvenir de	to remember

Here is a list of French verbs followed by the preposition **de**. As you can see, this preposition can be translated in many ways: *to, from, of, for, with.* Note that the equivalent English verb may not be followed by a preposition.

Reflexive verbs (**s'arrêter, se contenter, se dépêcher** ...) are followed by a preposition when they are followed by an infinitive. You would say:

Je me dépêche.	*I hurry up*
but	
Je me dépêche **de faire** quelque chose.	*I hurry to do something.*
` Mark se dépêche **de téléphoner** à Stéphanie.	*Mark rushes to phone Stéphanie.*

c) There are some verbs which are followed by a preposition in English, but not in French:

chercher	*to look for*
écouter	*to listen to*
entrer	*to come in*
regarder	*to look at*

| Nous cherchons St Amand-les-Eaux. | *We're looking for St Amand-les-Eaux.* |
| Nicolas écoute la radio. | *Nicolas is listening to the radio.* |

d) Only a few prepositions can be followed by a verb – usually the infinitive:

■ **à, de**
■ compound prepositions containing **de** such as: **loin de, avant de, au lieu de**
■ **pour, sans, par**
■ **après** can be followed by **avoir** or **être** (See Unit 15 **Pour aller plus loin** *3*):

> **Après avoir** acheté ses cadeaux,   *After buying his presents he doesn't*
> il ne lui reste plus beaucoup d'argent.   *have a lot more money left.*

3 More about adverbs

Cher

The adjective **cher** can become an adverb and remain invariable when it is used in the set expression **coûter cher**:

> Cette robe coûte **cher**.   *This dress costs a lot.*
> Ces logiciels coûtent **cher**.   *These software packages*
>   *are expensive.*

Vite

Vite is an adverb and not an adjective.

You say:

> Ces trains sont **rapides**.   *These trains are fast.*
> (adjective qualifying the noun **trains** masc. plural)

But if you use **vite**, it is invariable:

> Stéphanie roule **vite**.   *Stéphanie drives fast.*
> (adverb modifying the verb **roule**).

Mal

Mal is also an adverb, not an adjective, so it does not show agreement:

> Cela fait **mal**.   *It hurts.*
> La cousine d'Isabelle se sent   *Isabelle's cousin feels rather unwell.*
> plutôt **mal**.

Beaucoup trop

Note that you can say **beaucoup trop** (*far too much*).

> Mark aime **beaucoup trop**   *Mark likes sweet things*
> les sucreries.   *(far) too much.*

7 | WHO OWNS WHAT?

Thèmes   Les biens, le logement

Find out about the Lemaires' house
Stéphanie and Nicolas' little squabbles about their possessions

In this Unit you will learn to:

1 Speak about personal ownership
2 Ask who owns something

Structures grammaticales

1 More about possessive adjectives *my*, *your*, *her/his/its*
2 Possessive pronouns *mine*, *his*, *hers*
3 The preposition **de** to show possession
4 The preposition **à** to show belonging
5 Useful verbs for possession and ownership: **être** (*to be*); **avoir** (*to have*), **appartenir** (*to belong to*) in the present tense
6 Stressed pronouns after **à** and **de**

Pour aller plus loin

1 More about possessive adjectives and pronouns
2 More about possession

Avant de commencer

You have already met possessive adjectives which indicate ownership.
See Unit 2 **Résumé grammatical 6**.

Voilà l'appartement de **mes** amis.   *That is my friends' flat.*
Leur appartement est situé près des   *Their flat is situated near*
magasins.   *the shops.*

As you can see from the above examples, possessive adjectives always
come before the noun and agree in gender and number with the noun they
precede and **not with the owner**.

Stéphanie cherche **son** livre.   *Stéphanie is looking for her book.*
«Où est **mon** livre?»   *"Where is my book?"*
demande-t-elle à Nicolas.   *she asks Nicolas.*

1 You use possessive pronouns to avoid repeating a noun.

Leur appartement is replaced by **le leur**.
Mon livre is replaced by **le mien**.

Cet appartement est **le leur**.   *This flat is theirs.*
Ce livre est **le mien**.   *This book is theirs.*

2 In English possession can also be expressed by the use of *'s* or *s'*. In
French the preposition **de** is used to show ownership.

Les amis **de** mes parents ont   *My parents' friends have a*
une propriété sur la Côte d'Azur.   *property on the Côte d'Azur.*

3 In this Unit you will also meet the preposition **à** to show ownership,
useful verbs to show ownership and possession – **être** (*to be*), **avoir** (*to
have*), **appartenir** (*to belong to*) and will learn to ask questions about
ownership and possession: *Whose is it/this?, Who do they/these belong
to?*

C'est **à** Nicolas? Non, c'est   *Is it Nicolas'? No, it*
à Stéphanie   *is Stéphanie's.*

4 As mentioned in Unit 6 **Résumé grammatical 3**, if a preposition is
followed by a personal pronoun, the stressed pronoun is used: **moi, toi,
lui/elle/soi, nous, vous, eux/elles**.

The other grammatical structures you will find useful to express
possession are:

- Demonstrative adjectives (Unit 2 **Résumé grammatical** 5)
- Demonstrative pronouns (Unit 5 **Résumé grammatical** 2)

Ce livre est à moi. Est-ce que **celui-ci** est à toi?	*This book is mine. Is this one yours?*

Comment dit-on?

The following examples show the different structures used in French to express possession. Look at them and check with the English translation if necessary before going on to the **Résumé grammatical**.

1 Showing personal ownership

Voici la maison **de** la famille Lemaire.	*This is the Lemaires' house.*
Leur maison est individuelle.	*Their house is detached.*
La chambre **de** Stéphanie est la plus grande.	*Stéphanie's room is the biggest.*
Voici la chambre **de son** frère.	*This is her brother's bedroom.*
Sa chambre est toujours en désordre.	*His bedroom is always untidy.*
Isabelle et George ont la chambre la plus spacieuse. **La leur** a un balcon et une salle de bains complète.	*Isabelle and George have the most spacious room. Theirs has a balcony and an en suite bathroom.*
Nicolas trouve **la sienne** trop petite.	*Nicolas thinks his is too small.*
Comment est **la tienne**?	*What is yours like?*

2 Asking who owns something

A qui est cette chambre?	*Whose is this bedroom?*
A qui appartient la plus grande chambre?	*Who does the biggest bedroom belong to?*
Tu **as** la plus grande chambre?	*Do you have the biggest bedroom?*
C'est l'ordinateur **de qui**?	*Whose computer is it?*
À qui sont ces logiciels?	*Who do these computer programmes belong to?*
Est-ce que ces logiciels **appartiennent à** Nicolas?	*Do these computer programmes belong to Nicolas?*

Résumé grammatical

1 More about possessive adjectives

As possessive adjectives must agree in both gender and number with the noun they accompany, there are more variations in French than in English.

mon, ma, mes	*my*
ton, ta, tes	*your*
son, sa, ses	*his/her/its*
notre, nos	*our*
votre, vos (plural and formal)	*your*
leur, leurs	*their*

Nicolas, est-ce que c'est **ta** chambre ou celle de **ta** soeur?
Nicolas, is this your bedroom or your sister's?

Stéphanie ne trouve pas **son** album de photos.
Stéphanie can't find her photo album.

Nos livres sont dans le bureau en bas.
Our books are in the office downstairs.

Leurs voisins se plaignent souvent du bruit.
Their neighbours often complain about the noise.

2 Possessive pronouns (mine, his, hers, ours, ...)

As you can see from the possessive pronouns in bold in the examples below (**la mienne**, **la sienne** etc.), they also agree in number and gender with the noun they replace. They *agree* in both number and gender *with whatever is owned* – not with the owner as in English. They are like nouns because they are accompanied by the definite articles **le / la / les**, which also vary according to the gender and number of the thing owned.

Forms of the possessive pronoun				
masc. sing.	fem. sing.	masc. plural	fem. plural	
le mien	la mienne	les miens	les miennes	*mine*
le tien	la tienne	les tiens	les tiennes	*yours* (informal)
le sien	la sienne	les siens	les siennes	*his/her/its*
le nôtre	la nôtre	les nôtres	les nôtres	*ours*
le vôtre	la vôtre	les vôtres	les vôtres	*yours* (plural, formal)
le leur	la leur	les leurs	les leurs	*theirs*

A qui est cette radio?	*Whose radio is this?*
C'est **la mienne**.	*It's mine.*
Nicolas emmène **la sienne** au lycée.	*Nicolas takes his to the secondary school.*
Ce disque n'est pas **le tien**.	*This record is not yours.*
Nos voisins se plaignent souvent.	*Our neighbours often complain.*
Comment sont **les vôtres** (plural)?	*What are yours like?*

3 The preposition de to show possession or ownership

Very often in French **de** is used, particularly with a person's name, to show that someone owns something. There is no equivalent structure to the English '*s, s*'.

La chambre **de** Stéphanie est toujours très bien rangée.	*Stéphanie's room is always very tidy.*
Celle **de** Nicolas est toujours en désordre.	*Nicolas' is always untidy.* (i.e. the one of ...)
La chambre **de** leurs parents offre une jolie vue sur la campagne.	*Their parents' room has a lovely view over the countryside.*

4 The preposition à to show belonging

In French the preposition **à** is used in questions to ask *Whose is ...?* or *Whose are ...?* **À qui est ...?**, **À qui sont ...?** as shown in these examples. It is also used to say to whom something belongs.

À qui sont ces magazines?	*Whose are these magazines?*
À qui est cette vidéo-ci?	*Whose is this video?*
Ces logiciels ne sont pas **à toi**.	*These computer programmes are not yours. They belong to your friend.*
Ils sont à ton ami.	
À qui est la nouvelle voiture garée devant la maison de nos voisins?	*Whose is the new car parked in front of our neighbours' house?*

5 Useful verbs for possession and ownership

■ **Avoir**: as with the English verb *to have*, **avoir** can be used to show ownership or possession:

Nicolas **a** deux disques de *Boyzone*.	*Nicolas has two* Boyzone *albums.*
Mark **a** aussi leur dernier disque.	*Mark also has their latest album.*

■ **Être + à**: can be used to show possession. See **Résumé grammatical** *4*.

C'est **à** qui?   *Whose is it?*
C'est **à** Nicolas.   *It's Nicolas'.*

■ **Appartenir + à** + noun: this can be used in similar situations to **être à**:

La voiture garée juste en face de la   *The car parked right in front of*
maison **appartient aux*** parents   *the house belongs to Stéphanie's*
de Stéphanie.   *parents.*

*Note that, as usual, **à** + **les** contract to make **aux**.

6 Stressed pronouns after à

If you want to indicate possession using **à** + a pronoun, you use the
stressed form of the pronoun: **toi, moi, lui/elle** etc. See Unit 1, **Résumé
grammatical** *8*; Unit 6 **Résumé grammatical** *3*.

Cette voiture est **à eux**.   *This car belongs to them.*
Est-ce que ce disque est **à toi**?   *Does this record belong to you?*
Non, c'est **à lui**.   *No, it belongs to him.*
Stéphanie a sa voiture bien **à elle**,   *Stéphanie has her very own car but*
mais elle n'est pas assurée en   *it is not insured at present.*
ce moment.

En contexte

Look for **possessive adjectives** and **possessive pronouns** in the following
conversation between Stéphanie and Nicolas.

Stéphanie cherche son album de photos pour le montrer à Mark.
Stéphanie is looking for her photo album to show it to Mark.

Stéphanie	Où est mon album de photos? Il n'est pas à sa place habituelle. Je me demande si Nicolas l'a. Nicolas, as-tu mon album de photos?	*Where is my photo album? It isn't in its usual place I wonder if Nicolas has it. Nicolas, have you got my photo album?*
Nicolas	J'ai un album mais c'est le mien.	*I've got an album but it is mine.*
Stéphanie	Mais non, ce n'est pas le tien, c'est le mien.	*No, it isn't yours, it's mine.*

	Le tien est sûrement enfoui	*Yours is probably buried under*
	sous un tas de vêtements.	*a pile of clothes. You are*
	Tu es si désordonné! Et ça?	*so untidy! And this?*
	Ce n'est pas à toi non plus.	*This doesn't belong to you either.*
	C'est mon logiciel.	*It is my computer programme.*
Nicolas	Non, tu te trompes. Ce n'est	*No, you're wrong. It is not*
	pas le tien. C'est celui de	*yours. It is my friend*
	mon copain, Claude. Le tien	*Claude's. Yours is probably*
	est sûrement bien rangé	*put away neatly on your*
	sur ton étagère.	*shelf.*
Stéphanie	Mark, est-ce que tu veux	*Mark, do you want to see*
	voir des photos amusantes	*some funny pictures*
	de Nicolas?	*of Nicolas?*

Pour vérifier

1   Replace the expressions in bold (**possessive adjectives + nouns**) with
the corresponding possessive pronouns in the following sentences.

Example: C'est **leur maison**. C'est **la leur**.

Où se trouve **votre maison**?	Où se trouve _____?
Andrew ne trouve pas **ses**	Andrew ne trouve pas _____.
disques compacts.	
Il prend **mes disques**.	Il prend _____.
J'oublie souvent de rendre	J'oublie souvent de
tes disques.	rendre _____.

2   Complete the following sentences with the words in the box.

> de, les nôtres, appartient, toi, eux, la leur, à, le mien, leurs, toi, leurs

C'est le dictionnaire ___ Sandy.
Ce magazine appartient ___ Sandy.
Ce livre n'est pas à ___. C'est _____.
_____ voisins sont plus aimables que _____.
Ce catalogue *La Redoute* _____ à Sandy.
«Est-ce qu'il y a des photos de ___ dans ce catalogue?», demande
Andrew.
La voiture garée en face de la maison des Dickson est à ___.
La nouvelle Peugeot 405 n'est pas _____. C'est celle de _____
voisins.

Pour aller plus loin

1 More about possessive adjectives and pronouns

a) Possessive adjectives and pronouns agree with *what is owned* and *not* the owner, so that some sentences can be ambiguous in French, as it is not clear who the owner is.

This is usually made clear by the context or situation, since the listener / reader would automatically know who the possessor was.

Son logiciel est le même que **le sien**.	*His/her computer programme is the same as his/hers.* = *Nicolas' friend's computer programme is the same as Stéphanie's.*

See **En contexte** above.

Votre can either refer to several owners or to one owner addressed in a formal way:

Où est **votre** voiture?	*Where is your car?*

Here again the context will show who the owner(s) is/are.

Possessive adjectives (**son, sa, ses**) and possessive pronouns (**le sien, la sienne, les siens, les siennes**) can also be used in a general sense to mean *one's, your* or *everyone's*:

On a besoin de **son** lecteur laser pour écouter **ses** disques compacts.	*You need your CD player to listen to your CD's.*

b) To make clear who the owner is, especially in spoken French, you can add the preposition **à** with a stressed pronoun:

Ce sont **ses** baskets **à elle**.	*These are **her** trainers.*
Mark a **son** appartement **à lui**.	*Mark has his **own** flat.*
Son dessin **à elle** a gagné le premier prix.	*Her drawing won first prize.*

A similar situation can arise with the possessive adjective *their* in English, and with **leur** and **leurs** in French. French can make matters clearer by using **à eux** or **à elles**.

Voici leur appartement **à eux**.	*Here is their flat.* (at least two people, one or both of whom are masculine)
Voici leurs photos **à elles**.	*Here are their photos.* (the girls')

c) Number agreements with the possessive adjective **leur / leurs** and the possessive pronouns **le (la) nôtre / les nôtres**, **le (la) vôtre / les vôtres**, **le (la) leur / les leurs** can sometimes cause a problem for English speakers. This is because in English we add an *-s* to change the adjective into the pronoun. (*your book* → *yours*; *our magazine* → *ours, their television* → *theirs*).

The possessive agrees with the owner in English, so you tend to think of *their* as always plural. In French, you add an **s** only when the thing owned is plural. Note the spelling in the following examples.

Possessive **adjective** + noun	Possessive **pronoun**
Voici leur platine laser et leurs disques compacts. *This is their CD player* (one) *and their CD's* (several).	**Voici la leur (platine laser).** *This one is theirs.* but **Ce sont les leurs (disques)?** *Are they theirs?* (several).

Les copains de Nicolas écoutent souvent **leurs** disques compacts.	*Nicolas' friends often listen to their CD's.*
S'ils n'apportent pas **leur** platine laser, ils peuvent se servir de **la nôtre.**	*If they do not bring their CD player they can use ours.*
Ils peuvent aussi écouter **les nôtres.**	*They can also listen to ours. (our CD's).*

2 More about possession

a) Possession with parts of the body

Possessive adjectives are used in English with parts of the body (*my* hand, *your* head etc). In French the definite article is preferred especially in written and more formal French:

Elle a une bague **au** doigt.	*She's got a ring on her finger.*
Il a mal **au** pied droit.	*His right foot hurts.*
J'ai mon sac à **la** main.	*I've got my bag in my hand.*

b) *Saying* of mine, of yours, of his, of theirs *etc.*

The preposition **à** followed by a stressed pronoun (**moi, toi**) or a name (Nicolas) is also used to express possession in this way in French. See **Résumé grammatical 6**.

Ce sont des copains **à moi**.	*They are friends of mine.*
Non. Ce sont des copains **à Nicolas**.	*No. They're friends of Nicolas'.*
J'ai trouvé des livres **à toi**.	*I found some books of yours.*

c) Appartenir à (*to belong to*)

Ce livre **appartient** à Stéphanie.	*This book belongs to Stéphanie.*

If the object of the verb **appartenir** is a pronoun, the pronoun comes before the verb:

Il **lui** appartient.	*It is hers/belongs to her.*

See Unit 9 **Résumé grammatical 3**.

8 | WHAT CAN YOU DO?
WHAT DO YOU WANT TO DO?
WHAT DO YOU HAVE TO DO?

Thème   Mark et Stéphanie en France

Life in St Amand and the Lemaires' occupations and plans
The Lemaires are planning a trip to the seaside
Mark and Stéphanie plan to go horse-riding

In this Unit you will learn to:

1   Talk about what you can do
2   Giving and refusing permission
3   Talk about what needs to be done
4   Give orders and instructions

Structures grammaticales

1   Verbs followed by an infinitive: **pouvoir** (*to be able to*), **savoir** (*to know, to know how to*), **vouloir** (*to want to*), **devoir** (*to have to*)
2   Impersonal expressions: **il faut** (**falloir** *to need something/to be necessary*), **il pleut** (pleuvoir *to rain*)
3   Other verbs ending in -**oir**: **valoir** (*to be worth*), **voir** (*to see*), **recevoir** (*to receive*), **s'asseoir** (*to sit down*)
4   Expressions with **avoir**

Pour aller plus loin

1   The difference between **savoir** and **connaître**
2   **Devoir** (*to have to*) or (*to owe*)

Avant de commencer

1 You have already met the structure **aimer** + infinitive (*to like doing something*) in Unit 2, **Résumé grammatical 3**.

Nous **aimons jouer** aux échecs.   *We like to play chess.*
J'**aime faire** du sport.   *I like to do/I am keen on sport.*

and the immediate future **aller** + infinitive (*to be going to do something*) in Unit 6 **Résumé grammatical 1**.

Je **vais acheter** des cadeaux.   *I am going to buy presents.*

In this Unit you will meet similar structures, i.e. verbs followed by infinitives which are used to say what:

- you *can do / are able to*: **pouvoir** + infinitive
- you *are allowed to*: **pouvoir** + infinitive
- you *are able / have the knowledge to*: **savoir** + infinitive
- you *want to do*: **vouloir** + infinitive
- you *must do / have to do*: **devoir** + infinitive

Georges **doit** se lever tôt pour aller travailler, car il commence à 8h00.	*Georges has to get up early to go to work, because he starts at 8 o'clock.*
Il **peut** rentrer plus tôt le soir, s'il n'y a pas de travail urgent et il **peut** faire soit du ball-trap soit du jardinage pour se distraire.	*He can come home earlier in the evening if there is no urgent work and he can enjoy himself clay-pigeon shooting or gardening.*
Il **doit** souvent travailler le samedi et Isabelle ne **sait** jamais à quelle heure il va rentrer.	*He often has to work on Saturdays and Isabelle never knows at what time he is going to come home.*
Isabelle **sait** très bien cuisiner et fait souvent de la pâtisserie pour l'église de la Croix du Petit Dieu.	*Isabelle is a very good cook and and often bakes cakes for the Croix du Petit Dieu Church.*
Elle travaille bénévolement pour une entreprise caritative car elle **veut** aider les défavorisés.	*She works on a voluntary basis for a charity, because she wants to help the underpriviliged.*

2 In this Unit you will also meet the impersonal way of saying what you need, what is necessary, what must be done or has to be done.

Il faut beaucoup d'adresse et de précision pour faire du ball-trap.	*You need a lot of skill and accuracy to do clay-pigeon shooting.*
Il faut beaucoup s'exercer pour gagner les premiers prix.	*You must train a lot to win the first prizes.*

3 You will meet other **-oir** verbs which are also irregular.

Georges aime faire les concours de ball-trap mais quand **il pleut** on ne **voit** pas très bien les assiettes et les concours sont annulés.

Georges likes clay-pigeon shooting competitions but when it rains you cannot see the plate very well and the competitions are cancelled.

4 In this Unit you will also learn a few set expressions with **avoir**:

Quand Georges va à la chasse il prend de la boisson et de la nourriture pour faire un pique-nique. Quand il **a soif** ou quand il **a faim** il peut s'arrêter et casser la croûte.

When Georges goes shooting he takes food and drink for a picnic. When he is hungry or thirsty he can stop and have a snack.

Comment dit-on?

1 Saying what you can do

Les Lemaire ne **peuvent** pas partir en vacances cette année car ils ont beaucoup de dépenses.

The Lemaires cannot go on holiday this year because they have many expenses.

Ils **peuvent** se distraire dans la région car il y a beaucoup de choses à faire, des randonnées en forêt, à la campagne …

They can enjoy themselves in the area because there are many interesting things to do, walks in the forest, in the country …

Ils **peuvent** se rendre à la mer, à Malo-les-bains ou à St Omer en un peu plus d'une heure.

They can go to the seaside to Malo-les-bains or St Omer in just over an hour.

Est-ce que Georges **peut** faire du ball-trap toute l'année?

Can Georges go clay-pigeon shooting all the year around?

Oui, mais il ne **peut** chasser que durant une période limitée.

Yes, but he can only shoot during a limited period.

2 Giving and refusing permission

Nicolas a envie d'aller faire du camping avec quelques amis. «Est-ce que je **peux** aller camper avec des copains?» demande-t-il à Isabelle.

Nicolas feels like going camping with some friends. "Can I go camping with some friends?" he asks Isabelle.

«Oui, tu **peux** si ton père veut bien.» *"Yes, you can if your dad agrees."*
«Vous **pouvez** emprunter notre tente.» *"You can borrow our tent."*

3 What needs to be done

Avant de partir, Nicolas **doit** ranger sa chambre.	*Before leaving Nicolas must tidy his bedroom.*
Isabelle veut aller à la mer avec Stéphanie et Mark. Georges **doit** travailler.	*Isabelle wants to go to the seaside with Stéphanie and Mark. Georges has to work.*
Elle **doit** préparer toutes les affaires de plage. Elle ne **doit** pas oublier le paravent.	*She must prepare all the beach things. She must not forget the wind break.*
Avant de partir, ils **doivent** vérifier la pression des pneus et le niveau d'huile.	*Before leaving they have to check the tyre pressure and the oil level.*

4 Giving orders and instructions

Nicolas, tu **dois** ranger tes affaires.	*Nicolas, you must tidy your things.*
Il faut aussi ranger tes vêtements.	*You must also tidy your clothes.*
Tu **dois** prendre soin de la tente.	*You must take care of the tent.*
Il faut la déplier et l'aérer avant de l'emporter.	*You have to unfold it and air it before taking it.*

Résumé grammatical

1 Verbs followed by an infinitive

These are known as *modal verbs* and are followed by an infinitive. They are irregular and the spelling of the stem changes in the **nous** and **vous** forms.

a) **Pouvoir:** just as in English, **pouvoir** (*to be able to*) can mean both *to have the ability to* and *to have permission to* do something. The exact meaning is indicated by the context.

pouvoir *to be able to*
je **peux**
tu **peux**
il/elle/on **peut**
nous **pouvons**
vous **pouvez**
ils/elles **peuvent**

Stéphanie **peut** conduire la voiture de ses parents.	*Stéphanie can drive her parents' car.*

Pouvoir either means *to be able to* or *to be allowed to* in the above example. Only the context will determine the exact meaning.

Stéphanie **peut** conduire la voiture de ses parents car la voiture est assurée.	*Stéphanie is able to drive her parents' car because it is insured.*

For other examples refer to **Avant de Commencer 1**.

Stéphanie **peut** conduire leur voiture car ils savent que c'est une bonne conductrice.	*Stéphanie is allowed to drive their car because they know she is a good driver.*

See other examples in **Comment dit-on? 2**.

b) **Savoir** or **pouvoir**: in French you use **savoir** and not **pouvoir** if you want to stress the fact that you *have the knowledge / the ability to* do something, and that you *know how to* do something:

> **savoir** *to know*
>
> je **sais**
> tu **sais**
> il/elle/on **sait**
> nous **savons**
> vous **savez**
> ils/elles **savent**

Alison **sait** cuisiner.	*Alison knows how to cook.*
Stéphanie **sait** bien conduire.	*Stéphanie can (knows how) to drive well.*
Est-ce qu'elle **sait** aussi bien conduire en Écosse? Ses parents ne le s**avent** pas.	*Can she drive as well in Scotland? Her parents do not know.*

c) **Vouloir**: this verb forms the present tense like **pouvoir**.

> **vouloir** *to wish/want*
>
> je **veux**
> tu **veux**
> il/elle/on **veut**
> nous **voulons**
> vous **voulez**
> ils/elles **veulent**

It is used:

■ in the **present tense** to say that someone *would like* something / *would like to do* something or to ask if they *would like* something/*would like to do* something:

Nicolas, **veux**-tu venir avec nous demain? Nous allons à St Omer.	*Nicolas, would you like to come with us tomorrow? We are going to St Omer.*
Non, je ne **veux** pas y aller.	*No, I don't want to go there.*
A quelle heure **voulez**-vous partir?	*What time do you want to leave?*
Mark **veut** visiter la région.	*Mark wants to visit the area.*

■ in the **conditional tense** (see Unit 18, **Résumé grammatical 3**) to say that you *would like* something in a less direct and more polite way.

You have already met **vouloir** in expressions such as: **je voudrais** (*I would like*).

Refer back to Unit 4 **Résumé grammatical 1**.

Mark, où **voudrais**-tu aller?	*Mark, where would you like to go?*
Je **voudrais** bien aller sur la côte.	*I'd like to go to the coast.*

d) **Devoir**: in English there is a choice between *have to* and *must* to express the necessity or the moral obligation to do something. In French there is only one verb, **devoir**.

devoir *to have to*
je **dois**
tu **dois**
il/elle/on **doit**
nous **devons**
vous **devez**
ils/elles **doivent**

Nicolas **doit** montrer le respect à ses parents et **doit** être poli. Georges est très strict.	*Nicolas must show respect to his parents and be polite. Georges is very strict.*
Lorsque Stéphanie conduit en France elle **doit** se souvenir des priorités à droite.	*When Stéphanie drives in France she has to remember to give way on the right.*

2 Impersonal expressions

a) Falloir / Il faut (one must/one has to)

Falloir is called an impersonal verb. It is only used with the subject pronoun *il*.

It can be used in different tenses. See verb tables page 232. It is used as follows:

■ To say that something is needed: **Il faut** is followed by a noun with a definite, indefinite or partitive article **le, la, les, un, une, des, du, de la, de l', d'**. See Unit 4 **Résumé grammatical** 2.

Il faut de la nourriture pour la route, le plan de St Omer et un guide touristique.	*We need food for the road, the street map of St Omer and a tourist guide.*

■ To say that you need something or that someone needs something:

Il me faut un plan de la ville.	*I need a street map of the city.*
Est-ce **qu'il vous faut** des directions précises?	*Do you need precise directions?*

In this case **il faut** is used with the indirect object pronoun, which is placed between **il** and **faut**. See Unit 9 **Résumé grammatical** 3.

■ To say that something *has to / must be* done. **Il faut** can also be followed by an infinitive:

Mark, **il faut** se lever de bonne heure demain matin.	*Mark, we must get up early tomorrow morning.*
Il faut partir avant l'heure de pointe.	*We must leave before the rush hour.*

b) Pleuvoir (to rain)

This is another impersonal verb used only with *il*.

Et s'**il pleut** beaucoup, qu'est-ce qu'on fait?	*If it rains a lot, what do we do?*
Stéphanie, comment dit-on: *"It's raining cats and dogs"* en français?	*Stéphanie how do you say: "…" in French?*
On dit:	*You say:* «Il pleut des cordes / des hallebardes.»

3 Other verbs ending in -oir

a) Valoir (to be worth)

Valoir is usually used with the third person singular or plural subject pronouns (**il/elle/ils/elles**) or with **ça/cela** (*this, that*) or with a noun.

Combien est-ce que **ça vaut**?	*How much is that worth?*
Combien **valent** ces plans de	*How much do these street plans of*
St Omer?	*St Omer cost?*
Ils **valent** 15F chacun.	*They cost 15F each.*
S'il pleut **cela** ne **vaut** pas la peine	*If it rains it's not worth going.*
de partir.	

b) Voir (to see)

■ This verb is conjugated like **croire**.
See Unit 6 **Résumé grammatical 2a**.

> **voir** *to see*
>
> je **vois**
> tu **vois**
> il/elle/on **voit**
> nous **voyons**
> vous **voyez**
> ils/elles **voient**

Quand il pleut beaucoup on ne **voit**	*When it is raining you don't see*
pas bien la route et il y a plus de	*the road well and there is more*
risques d'accident.	*risk of an accident.*

■ Other verbs, which are formed by adding a prefix to the verb **voir**, have the same endings as **voir**, but alter the stem when they are conjugated:

apercevoir *to notice*	lose **-ev** in the singular forms of
concevoir *to conceive*	the present tense:
décevoir *to deceive*	
percevoir *to cash in, to perceive*	a cedilla is added to the **c** (**c → ç**)
recevoir *to receive*	for pronunciation purposes.

Stéphanie se lève et **aperçoit** des	*Stéphanie gets up and notices*
nuages menaçants. Deux minutes	*threatening clouds. Two minutes*
plus tard, il pleut à verse. Un tel	*later it is pouring down. Such*
temps **déçoit** vraiment!	*weather is really disappointing!*

Stéphanie **reçoit** souvent des nouvelles de France.	*Stéphanie often receives news from France.*

c) S'asseoir (to sit down)

The verb **s'asseoir** is a highly irregular reflexive verb which you can see in full in the Verb Tables, page 232.

Mark **s'assied** à côté de Stéphanie et regarde la carte de France pour voir où se trouve St Omer.	*Mark sits down next to Stéphanie and looks at the map of France to see where St Omer is.*

4 Expressions with avoir

a) Expressions where avoir corresponds to to have in English

■ **avoir rendez-vous**

Isabelle **a rendez-vous** chez le coiffeur.	*Isabelle has an appointment at the hairdresser's.*

■ **avoir mal à la tête**

Elle **a mal à la tête** et elle prend deux aspirines.	*She has a headache and takes two aspirins.*

■ **avoir le courage de**

Georges **a le courage de** ses opinions.	*Georges has the courage of his convictions.*

b) Expressions where avoir + noun corresponds to to be + adjective in English

You have already come across some phrases using **avoir** which would not translate as *have* in English:

J'ai faim.	*I am hungry.*
J'ai soif.	*I am thirsty.*
J'ai 21 ans.	*I am 21.*

Other expressions

avoir de la chance	*to be lucky*
ne pas avoir de chance	*to be unlucky / unfortunate*
avoir la chance de	*to be lucky / fortunate (enough) to*
avoir du courage	*to be courageous*
avoir peur/avoir peur de	*to be afraid / afraid of*
avoir l'habitude de	*to be used to*
avoir honte/avoir honte de	*to be ashamed / ashamed of*
en avoir marre de	*to be fed up with*
avoir sommeil	*to be tired*

c) Expressions where avoir *is translated without using to be or to have in English:*

avoir besoin de	*to need*
avoir envie de	*to feel like*

Stéphanie, Mark and Isabelle **n'ont pas de chance** car le temps est affreux.

Stéphanie, Mark and Isabelle are unlucky because the weather is awful.

Isabelle **en a marre de** ce temps variable. Elle voudrait habiter dans un pays chaud.

Isabelle is fed up with this changeable weather. She would like to live in a hot country.

En contexte

From this stage you should feel confident enough to read and understand the French in the dialogues in **En contexte**. If you have any problems, look up unknown words or expressions in your dictionary. If you are completely at a loss, look at the transcriptions, pp.221–226.

In this conversation between Mark and Stéphanie, look for **verbs followed directly by an infinitive**, the modal verbs **pouvoir** and **devoir**.

Mark et Stéphanie prévoient de faire de l'équitation.

Stéphanie   Qu'est-ce que tu veux faire demain, s'il ne pleut pas? Tu veux faire de l'équitation ou des randonnées?

Mark	Je ne sais pas monter à cheval.
Stéphanie	Tu peux apprendre; ce n'est pas difficile.
Mark	Est-ce qu'il y a des centres équestres à St Amand?
Stéphanie	Il y en a plusieurs, mais je peux monter chez mon amie Monique, qui a plusieurs chevaux. Tu vois les pâtures, là-bas? Ce sont les siennes. On aperçoit les chevaux d'ici.
Mark	Il faut porter des vêtements spéciaux?
Stéphanie	Oui et non. Tu peux porter un jean et des baskets, mais tu dois porter une bombe. Mon père peut te prêter la sienne. Je vais téléphoner à Monique pour voir si nous pouvons monter demain. Au fait, quand tes parents veulent-ils venir?
Mark	Ils peuvent venir en juillet. Ils veulent visiter le nord et peut-être aller passer quelques jours à Paris.

Pour vérifier

1 Add the missing verbs and/or expressions in the following sentences: You will need **savoir, devoir, pouvoir**, **avoir envie de, vouloir**

S Je vais demander à mes parents s'ils _____ rester chez nous à ce moment-là. Je crois que Papa ne _____ pas travailler le 14 juillet car c'est férié. Est-ce que tu _____ combien de temps ils _____ rester?

M Je ne _____ pas exactement. Une quinzaine de jours. Ils _____ inviter tes parents à venir en Écosse l'année prochaine. Est-ce que tu crois que tes parents _____ venir à Dundee?

S Oui, j'en suis sûre. Cette année ils ne _____ pas partir en vacances.

2 Ask questions about the following phrases using the pronouns and verbs in brackets. Example: Chanter (tu, savoir) – Est-ce que tu sais chanter?

Parler français (vous, savoir)
Aller au cinéma (tu, vouloir)
Rentrer tard (il, pouvoir)
Ranger nos affaires (nous, devoir)

Pour aller plus loin

1 The difference between savoir and connaître

These two verbs often create problems as they both mean *to know*. **Savoir** means *to have knowledge of, to know how to* and **connaître** means *to be acquainted with, to be familiar with*.

Je **connais** le chemin.   *I know* (am familiar with) *the way.*

Je **sais** quel chemin prendre.   *I know which way to go.*

The idea of *having the knowledge of* is introduced in this second sentence.

You use **connaître** when talking about people:

Est-ce que Mark **connaît** les amis   *Does Mark know* (is he acquainted
de Stéphanie?   with) *Stéphanie's friends?*

2 Devoir (to have to), (to owe)

Devoir does not always mean *to have to / must*, it can also mean *to owe*.

The meaning will only be made clear by the context. When **devoir** means *to owe*, it is not followed by an infinitive. Notice the difference between these two examples:

Isabelle **doit** acheter une bouteille   *Isabelle must buy a bottle of*
de shampooing chez le coiffeur.   *shampoo at the hairdresser's.*

Je vous **dois** combien, s'il vous plaît?   *How much do I owe you, please?*

9 TELLING PEOPLE WHAT TO DO!

Thèmes   Les directions; Les projets des Dickson

Mark gives his parents directions for their trip to France
Alison tells Andrew what to do, and what not to do when they are away

In this Unit you will learn to:

1 Ask for and give directions
2 Advise and tell someone to do / not to do something

Structures grammaticales

1 Verbs to give directions: **continuer** (*to continue*), **tourner** (*to turn*),
   prendre (*to take*) and useful expressions such as **il faut**, **vous devez /
   tu dois** (*you need to / you have to*)
2 Using imperatives to give directions **prenez** (*take*)
3 Indirect object pronouns **me**, **te**, **lui** (*to me, to you, to her/him*)
4 The pronoun **y** (*there, about this*)

Pour aller plus loin

1 **Aller** and **donner** in the imperative
2 Functions of object pronouns
3 The difference between **y** and **en**

Avant de commencer

1 Useful verbs to give directions

a) The present tense, which you met in Units 1, 3, 5, 6, is used to give directions. Look back at these Units if you are not sure of verb endings, especially those of irregular verbs such as **prendre** (*to take*) (See Unit 6 **Résumé grammatical 2a**. You will also need to look back at ordinal numbers: **le premier / la première** (*the first*) etc. (Unit 3 **Résumé grammatical 4**) and at prepositions of place (Unit 6 **Résumé grammatical 3**) **à côté de** (*next to*), **près de** (*near*), **en face de** (*opposite*).

Vous **prenez** la première à droite.	*You take the first on the right.*
Vous **continuez** tout droit et vous **tournez** à gauche.	*You go straight ahead and you turn left. It is near here.*
C'**est** près d'ici.	
L'abbaye **est** sur la place en face de l'hôtel de ville.	*The abbey is in the market place opposite the town hall.*

b) The impersonal expression **il faut** (*one must/one has to /one needs to*) (Unit 8 **Résumé grammatical 2**) is also useful when giving directions and telling people what to do:

Il faut tourner à droite.	*You'll need to turn right.*
Il faut prendre la quatrième rue à gauche.	*You'll need to take the fourth street on the left.*

c) Another useful verb for giving directions is the verb **devoir** (Unit 8 **Résumé grammatical 1**):

Vous **devez** continuer tout droit, traverser la rue et continuer jusqu'à la rue de Lille.	*You have to go straight ahead, cross the road and continue as far as the rue de Lille.*

2 To give directions, you can use a form of the verb called the **imperative**. The imperative will be covered in more depth in Unit 12 **Résumé grammatical 1**. In this Unit, you will only learn how to use some imperatives to give directions.

Prenez à droite.	*Take a right-hand turn.*
Prends la première à droite.	*Take the first on the right.*
Continuez / continue tout droit.	*Go straight ahead.*

3 Finally, to give directions *to someone*, you need to learn different personal pronouns. You have already met *subject pronouns* and *stressed pronouns* in Unit 1 **Résumé grammatical 8.**

Je ne sais jamais donner les directions.	*I never know how to give directions.*
Et **toi**, tu sais donner les directions?	*Do you know how to give directions?*

You met **direct object pronouns** in Unit 5 **Résumé grammatical 3,** answering the question *what?*:

Je **le** prends.	*I take it. (I take **what?**)*
Je **l'**aime.	*I like him/her/it.*
Je sais **les** donner.	*I know how to give them* (directions).

The pronouns you need to answer the question *to whom?* are called **indirect object pronouns.** You will meet these pronouns in this Unit:

Je **lui** donne des directions précises.	*I give him/her precise directions.*
Un homme demande les directions pour aller à la gare.	*A man asks the way to the station.*
Stéphanie **lui** indique le chemin.	*Stéphanie shows him the way.*
Un couple **lui** demande le chemin pour aller à la mairie. Elle **leur** dit de continuer tout droit et de prendre la première rue à droite.	*A couple asks her the way to the town hall. She tells them to go straight on and to take the first on the right.*

Comment dit-on?

1 Asking for and giving directions

Excusez-moi, Monsieur, où **se trouve** le chemin de l'Empire, s'il vous plaît?	*Excuse me, where is the chemin de l'Empire, please?*
Ce n'**est** pas loin d'ici.	*It's not far from here.*
Vous **continuez** tout droit et juste après le pont vous **prenez** la première à gauche.	*You go straight on and just after the bridge you take the first on your left.*
Vous **allez** jusqu'au bout de la rue Salengro, puis vous **tournez** à gauche.	*You go right down to the end of the rue Salengro, then you turn left.*
Vous **êtes** au chemin de l'Empire.	*And you are at the chemin de l'Empire.*

Et pour **aller** au gîte Le Luron?	*And to go the gîte Le Luron?*
C'est dans la forêt de St Amand.	*It is in the St Amand forest.*
Du chemin de l'Empire, **prenez la**	*From the chemin de l'Empire you*
première à droite. **Continuez** tout	*take the first right. Go straight*
droit, **traversez** la rocade du Nord.	*ahead, cross the northern bypass.*
Ensuite **il faut continuer** tout droit	*Then you'll have to go straight ahead,*
jusqu'au bout de la rue Basse.	*right to the end of the rue Basse.*
Vous **arrivez** place du Mont	*You arrive at Mont des Bruyères*
des Bruyères.	*square.*
Là vous **continuez** tout droit.	*There you go straight on.*
Prenez la rue Transvaal et vous	*Take the rue Transvaal and you are*
êtes à la forêt de St Amand.	*at the forest of St Amand.*
Le gîte Le Luron **est** à votre droite.	*The gîte Le Luron is on your right.*

2 Advising someone to do/not to do something

Andrew, si tu veux rester à Dundee	*Andrew, if you want to stay at a*
chez un copain, tu dois être	*friend's in Dundee you must be*
raisonnable.	*sensible.*
Tu **dois** t'occuper de la maison.	*You must look after the house.*
Il faut sortir la poubelle le	*You must take the dustbin out on*
mardi matin.	*Tuesday mornings.*
Il faut te lever de bonne heure pour	*You must get up early to go to your*
aller en classe.	*classes.*
Il ne faut pas trop te servir du	*You must not use the telephone too*
téléphone.	*often.*
Si tu as des problèmes tu **dois**	*If you have any problems you*
contacter ton oncle. Tu **lui**	*must contact your uncle.*
téléphones et tu **lui** dis	*Give him a ring and tell him to*
de venir te chercher.	*come and fetch you.*
Il peut **nous** passer un coup de fil si	*He can give us a ring if necessary.*
nécessaire. Toi aussi, tu peux **nous**	*You can also keep in touch.*
donner de tes nouvelles.	

Résumé grammatical

1 Verbs for giving directions

a) Irregular verbs: aller (*to go*), être (*to be*) (Unit 1), prendre (*to take*) (Unit 6)

b) Regular verbs: continuer (*to continue*), descendre (*to go down*), remonter (*to go up*), tourner (*to turn*), traverser (*to cross*).

To give information and/or advice to someone formally these verbs are used with **vous**:

Vous continuez tout droit, **vous** tournez à gauche, puis **vous** prenez la deuxième à gauche. **Vous y êtes.**	*You go straight on, turn left, then you take the second on the left. You are there.*

To give information to someone you know well or to direct someone in an informal way, you would use the pronoun **tu** (Unit 1 **Résumé grammatical 5**):

Tu traverses la rue de Tournai et **tu** remontes le chemin du Corbeau.	*You cross the rue de Tournai and go up le chemin du Corbeau.*

c) falloir and devoir

You met both these verbs in Unit 8 **Résumé grammatical 1, 2.**

■ **Falloir**: this impersonal structure **Il faut** is often followed by verbs of direction in their infinitive form but could also be followed by **que** + verb in the subjunctive. You will meet expressions like these in Unit 16 **Résumé grammatical 2.**

Il faut tourner à droite et prendre la quatrième à gauche.	*You'll need to turn right and to take the fourth on the left.*
Il ne faut pas tourner à gauche car c'est un sens interdit.	*You must not turn left, as it is a one-way street.*

■ **Devoir**: this modal verb is used to tell people what they *have to do* to get to the place they are inquiring about. Unlike **il faut** which cannot be used with other pronoun subjects, **devoir** can be used with any of the subject pronouns. (See Unit 8 **Résumé grammatical 1**).

Vous devez vous arrêter aux feux, puis vous tournez à gauche.	*You must stop at the traffic lights, then you turn left.*
Tu dois remonter la rue de Condé jusqu'au rond-point.	*You have to go back up the rue de Condé as far as the round-about.*
Nous devons prendre un bus sur la place?	*Do we have to catch a bus in the market place?*

2 Using imperatives to give directions

This is the easiest and the most commonly used way of giving directions. You just use the verbs *without* a subject pronoun, i.e. instead of saying *you continue* **vous continuez**, you just say *continue* **continuez**. Instead of saying **tu continues**, you just say **continue**.

Note that for **-er** verbs, including the verb **aller**, you drop the **-s** when **tu** is the subject:

Continuez tout droit, **prenez** à gauche, **passez** devant la mairie et c'est à votre gauche.	*Go straight ahead, turn left, pass the town hall and it is on your left.*
Continue, **prends** à droite, **va** un peu plus loin et c'est à droite.	*Go straight on, go right, go a bit further and it is on the right.*

Here are the imperative forms of the verbs you have just met to give directions:

Tu form	Vous form	
va	**allez**	aller
continue	**continuez**	continuer
descends	**descendez**	descendre
passe	**passez**	passer
prends	**prenez**	prendre
remonte	**remontez**	remonter
tourne	**tournez**	tourner
traverse	**traversez**	traverser

Prenez la première à gauche. **Allez** jusqu'au carrefour. Au carrefour **continuez** tout droit jusqu'aux feux et **prenez** la première à droite.	*Take the first on the left. Go to the crossroads. At the crossroads go straight ahead to the traffic lights and take the first right.*

If you are speaking in an informal or friendly way you say:

Prends la première à gauche. **Va** jusqu'au
carrefour. Au carrefour **continue** tout
droit jusqu'aux feux et **prends** la première
à droite.

3 Indirect object pronouns

a) Here is a list of the **personal pronouns** you have already met:

- subject pronouns   Unit 1 **Résumé grammatical** *1*
- reflexive pronouns   Unit 3 **Résumé grammatical** *2*
- direct object pronouns   Unit 5 **Résumé grammatical** *3*

In the fourth column below you will find **indirect pronouns** – the
pronouns used to answer the question *to whom?* Where the direct and
indirect objects are different, the indirect objects are in italic:

subject	reflexive	direct object	indirect object
je	**me**	**me**	**me**
tu	**te**	**te**	**te**
il/elle/on	**se**	**le/la**	*lui*
nous	**nous**	**nous**	**nous**
vous	**vous**	**vous**	**vous**
ils/elles	**se**	**les**	*leur*

As you can see, object pronouns only differ in the third person singular
(**il/elle/on**) and plural (**ils/elles**). In the case of indirect pronouns, you use
lui and **leur** whether you are speaking about a male or a female person:

Les Dickson demande les directions   *The Dicksons ask for directions to*
pour aller chez les Lemaire.   *go to the Lemaires'.*
Mark va **leur** donner un plan de   *Mark is going to give them a street-*
St Amand à son retour.   *map of St Amand on his return.*
Il va aussi **leur** écrire pour   *He is also going to write to them to*
confirmer qu'ils sont les   *confirm that they are welcome at*
bienvenus chez les Lemaire.   *the Lemaires'.*
Les Dickson vont venir en juillet.   *The Dicksons are going to come in*
Isabelle demande à Georges si cela   *July. Isabelle asks Georges if this*
lui convient.   *is acceptable to him.*

Stéphanie **lui** explique que les Dickson souhaitent venir le 7 juillet.	*Stéphanie explains to him that the Dicksons wish to come on the 7th of July.*

You will find out about the use of two object pronouns in Unit 12 **Résumé grammatical 6**.

b) Here are some verbs which take indirect object pronouns:

appartenir à quelqu'un Cela **m'**appartient.	*to belong to someone* *This belongs to me.*
apporter quelque chose à quelqu'un Le facteur **nous** apporte le courrier à 7h.	*to bring someone something / to bring something to someone* *The postman brings us the mail / the mail to us at 7 o'clock.*
quelque chose donner/à quelqu'un Il **te** donne beaucoup de cadeaux.	*to give someone something / to give something to someone* *He gives you a lot of presents.*
écrire à quelqu'un Il **lui** écrit souvent.	*to write to someone* *He often writes to her/him.*
envoyer quelque chose à quelqu'un Il **vous** a envoyé un courrier électronique?	*to send someone something / to send something to someone* *Did he send you an E-mail?*
expliquer quelque chose à quelqu'un Il **leur** explique la situation clairement.	*to explain something to someone* *He explains the situation clearly to them.*
montrer quelque chose à quelqu'un Il **lui** montre le chemin.	*to show someone something/ to show something to someone* *He shows him the way.*
offrir quelque chose à quelqu'un Mark **lui** offre des fleurs.	*to present someone with something* *Mark presents her with some flowers.*
poser des questions à quelqu'un Elle **me** pose souvent la même question.	*to ask someone questions* *She often asks me the same question.*

4 The pronoun y

This pronoun means *there* in examples such as: Vous **y** êtes. (See
Résumé grammatical *1a*)

Vous **y** allez quand?   *When are you going there?*

Y also means *about this.*

J'**y** pense souvent.   *I often think about it.*

Y comes before the verb except when the verb is in the imperative.

Restez-**y**.   *Stay there.*

En contexte

From this discussion about Mark's parents and their visit to France, make
a list of the **instructions** and identify the **indirect object pronouns**.

Mark demande à Stéphanie si ses parents peuvent venir en juillet.

Mark   Stéphanie, ma mère vient de me demander si elle et papa
               peuvent venir chez vous le 7 juillet. Est-ce que cela convient
               à tes parents?

Stéphanie Je vais leur poser la question tout de suite et tu peux lui
               retéléphoner plus tard pour lui donner la réponse.

Stéphanie appelle sa mère et elle lui donne la nouvelle.

Stéphanie Maman, est-ce que les parents de Mark peuvent venir chez
               nous le 7 juillet? Ils aimeraient passer trois ou quatre jours
               chez nous, puis visiter la région et aussi Paris.

Isabelle   Bien sûr, avec plaisir. Ton père peut peut-être prendre
               quelques jours de congé. Comment vont-ils voyager?

Stéphanie Ils vont prendre l'avion de Glasgow à Paris et louer une
               voiture à l'aéroport. Mark va leur donner une carte routière
               et un plan de St Amand pour les aider.

Voici les instructions que Mark va donner à ses parents:

               Vous arrivez à l'aéroport Roissy-Charles de Gaulle et vous
               prenez l'autoroute du nord, la A1, jusqu'à Péronne.
               Ensuite prenez la A2 jusqu'à la sortie Cambrai/
               Valenciennes. Quittez la A2 à Valenciennes et continuez
               jusqu'à la Sentinelle. Là, vous devez prendre la A23 jusqu'à
               la sortie St Amand / Lille.

Quittez la A23 à l'entrée de St Amand et prenez la voie rapide jusqu'à la forêt de Raismes. Au deuxième rond-point, tournez à gauche et vous êtes au chemin de l'Empire.

Pour vérifier

1   Mark's instructions at the end of **En contexte** are given in the **vous** form as he is talking to his parents. Give them in the **tu** form.

2   Make up 4 instructions using the **vous** forms of the imperative and the vocabulary given below. The verbs are in bold.
For example: **Passez devant la mairie.**

tourner	à	la première	continuer	Lille
droite	**prendre**	à	gauche	
tout	devant	droit	**passer**	
descendre	la	jusqu'	mairie	
au	coin	de	rue	

3   Replace the expressions in bold below with the appropriate pronouns.
a)   Tu dis **à tes parents** que c'est d'accord.
b)   Tu téléphones **à Andrew** pour dire quand tu vas revenir.
c)   Tu donnes les directions **à Alison et Patrick**.
d)   Patrick demande les directions exactes **à Mark**.

Pour aller plus loin

1 Aller *and* donner *in the imperative*

For **-er** verbs, including **aller**, in the imperative you drop the **-s** from the **tu** form. **Va vite!** (*Go quickly!*) However you retain the **-s** before vowels or vowel sounds to make it easier to pronounce:

Vas-y!   *Go!* (there).
Donnes-en un peu!   *Give a bit/some of it!*

2 Functions of object pronouns

a) Reflexive and object pronouns

If you look back to indirect pronouns in the **Résumé grammatical 3**, you can see that **me, te, nous, vous** can serve different functions. They can be used as **reflexives, direct objects** or **indirect objects:**

Je **me** pose des questions.	*I am asking **myself** questions.* (to myself)
Il **me** regarde.	*He is looking at/watching **me**.* (me)
Il **me** pose des questions.	*He is asking **me** questions.* (to me)

To identify what type of pronoun it is, you ask the following questions:

- Are the subject and the object the same person?
- Does the pronoun answer the question *who (whom) / what?*
- Does the pronoun answer the question *to whom?*

b) Use of indirect object pronouns

Learners often have difficulty in using **indirect object pronouns** in French because English and French verbs are sometimes different in this respect. See Unit 12 **Avant de commencer 3**. Note particularly the following verb structures:

demander à	*to ask*
téléphoner à	*to phone*

Nous **leur** demandons les directions. *We ask them directions.*

Il **leur** téléphone.   *He rings them up.* (telephones to them)

You can choose the correct pronoun by identifying the verb and asking *who (whom)/what?* or *to whom?* after it. In the sentence **je le donne**, le answers the question *what?*:

verb = **donne; donne** *what?* → **le**; therefore **le** is a **direct object.**

In **je *lui* donne, lui** answers the question *to whom?*:

verb = **donne; donne** *to whom?* → **lui**; therefore **lui** is an **indirect object.**

3 The difference between y and en

They both mean *of this* but **y** replaces **à** + noun.

J'**y** pense souvent. = Je pense **à cela**. *I often think of/about this.*

whereas **en** (see Unit 5 **Résumé grammatical 3**) replaces **de** + *noun.*

J'**en** mange = Je mange **de cela**.   *I eat some (of it).*

10 | PROCESSES AND PROCEDURES

Thème   Projets de vacances

The Dicksons prepare for their visit to the Lemaires in France
The Lemaires decide to meet the Dicksons at the airport and get ready
to welcome them

In this Unit you will learn to:

1 Describe and ask about a process or a procedure that involves several stages
2 Describe and ask about a series of actions and events
3 Ask and say why something happened

Structures grammaticales

1 Expressions of time: **hier** (*yesterday*), **aujourd'hui** (*today*), **demain** (*tomorrow*)
2 Structuring adverbs: **d'abord** (*first*), **ensuite** (*then*), **finalement** (*finally*)
3 Time prepositions: **pendant** (*during*), **avant** (*before*), **après** (*after*), **depuis** (*since*)
4 Cause and effect: **parce que** (*because*), **donc** (*so*), **car** (*for*)

Pour aller plus loin

1 More about time expressions
2 Speaking impersonally:
   (a)   impersonal expressions: **Il faut** (*It is necessary*), **Il est important** (*It is important*), **Il est difficile** (*It is difficult*)
   (b)   the present passive: **ils sont invités par ...** (*they are invited by ...*), **l'invitation est envoyée par ...** (*the invitation is sent by ...*)

Avant de commencer

1 To talk or write about a series of events or actions, you use words such as **d'abord** (*first*), **ensuite** (*then*), **finalement** (*finally*). These words are adverbs of time (you have already met some of them in Unit 6) and they are used to make the sequence of events clear.

D'abord, tu organises le voyage, **ensuite** tu achètes les billets. **Puis** tu prépares les valises et **enfin** tu prends un taxi pour aller à l'aéroport.	*First you plan the trip, next you buy the tickets. Then you pack and finally you get a taxi to go to the airport.*

2 You can also express the idea of a sequence of events using a preposition + a noun: **avant l'aube / 6 heures** (*before dawn/6 o'clock*), **après le coucher du soleil / 19 heures** (*after sunset/7p.m.*), **pendant l'après-midi** (*during the afternoon*). See prepositions of time in Unit 6 **Résumé grammatical 3.**

These expressions let you write and speak about things which usually take place in an established order.

3 Events are sometimes related by a process of cause and effect, rather than by time. To show this kind of relationship between events or stages in a process you need to use conjunctions, words such as **parce que** (*because*), **donc** (*so*), **car** (*for*).

La famille Dickson va en France **parce qu'**ils veulent rencontrer la famille de la copine de leur fils Mark. Ils pensent que Mark et Stéphanie vont bientôt se fiancer, **donc** ils veulent rencontrer ses parents et voir son pays. Les parents de Mark sont un peu inquiets, **car** ils ne connaissent pas bien Stéphanie.	*The Dickson family is going to France because they want to meet the family of their son Mark's girlfriend. They think that Mark and Stéphanie are going to become engaged soon so they want to meet her parents and see her country. Mark's parents are a bit worried, since they don't know Stéphanie well.*

4 If you want to know how events are related to one another, you will need to be able to ask questions.

■ For time relationships, you can use **quand?** (*when*) or questions such as **Qu'est-ce qui se passe d'abord / ensuite?** (*What happens first / then?*) with the adverbs you have already learned (Unit 6 **Résumé grammatical 4**).

■ For cause and effect, you can use questions beginning with **Pourquoi?** (*Why?*).

Quand souhaitent-ils y aller?	*When do they wish to go there?*
Qu'est-ce qui se passe d'abord?	*What happens first?*
Pourquoi veulent-ils aller en France?	*Why do they want to go to France?*

Comment dit-on?

1 Asking about several stages

Qu'est-ce qui se passe d'**abord** à l'agence de voyage?	*What happens first at the travel agency?*
Premièrement je dis que nous voulons aller en France.	*First of all I say that we want to go to France.*
Et **ensuite / après / puis**?	*And then?*
Il faut **ensuite** leur dire combien de personnes, l'âge de chacun et à quelle période nous voulons y aller.	*Then I'll have to explain how many of us there are, how old we are and when we want to go.*
Puis tu te renseignes sur les prix et les horaires et **finalement** tu fais la réservation.	*Then you obtain information on prices and times and finally you make the booking.*

2 Asking about a series of actions or events

Comment pouvez-vous vous payer des vacances en France?	*How can you afford a holiday in France?*
En décembre dernier nous avons gagné un peu d'argent à la loterie. Ta mère a **aussi** donné plusieurs cours particuliers **en février et en mars**. Ce mois-ci nous n'allons pas au restaurant et nous limitons les sorties coûteuses, **donc** nous faisons des économies. **De plus, le mois prochain** mon patron va me donner une augmentation.	*Last December we won a bit of money on the lottery. Your mother also gave several private lessons in February and March. This month we aren't eating out and we're cutting down on expensive outings, so we're saving money. In addition, next month my boss is going to give me a pay rise.*

Pas de problème donc pour payer le billet!

So, no trouble paying the fare!

3 Asking why something happened

Pourquoi est-ce que les Lemaire veulent rencontrer les Dickson à l'aéroport?

Why do the Lemaires want to meet the Dicksons at the airport?

Parce qu'il est très difficile de conduire à Paris en raison de la circulation intense.

Because it is very difficult to drive in Paris due to the heavy traffic.

Pour quelle raison les Dickson veulent-ils aller en France? Ils veulent y aller pour faire la connaissance des Lemaire. **Pourquoi** est-ce qu'ils veulent les rencontrer cet été?

Why (For what reason) do the Dicksons want to go to France? They want to go there to make the acquaintance of the Lemaires. Why do they want to meet them thi summer?

Mark et Stéphanie vont peut-être se fiancer cette année. **Par conséquent** ils pensent qu'il est important de les rencontrer le plus vite possible.

Mark and Stéphanie are maybe going to get engaged this year. So they think it is important to meet them as soon as possible.

Comme il y a de la place chez les parents de Stéphanie les Dickson vont y rester quelques jours. **Puisqu'**ils ont envie de connaître la région, ils vont aussi visiter différents endroits.

As there is room at Stéphanie's parents', the Dicksons are going to stay there for a few days. Since they are keen to know the area, they are also going to visit different places.

Résumé grammatical

1 Expressions of time

To say when one thing happened in relation to another, you need to be able to use time expressions such as **hier** (*yesterday*), **aujourd'hui** (*today*), **demain** (*tomorrow*), the adjectives **dernier** (*last*) and **prochain** (*next*) and the demonstrative adjectives – **ce, cet, cette, ces** (See Unit 2 **Résumé grammatical 5**). You will learn the tenses you need to use with these time expressions in Units 11, 13 and 14.

		past	present	future
matin	*morning*	hier matin	ce matin	demain matin
après-midi	*afternoon*	hier après-midi	cet après-midi	demain après-midi
soir	*evening*	hier soir	ce soir	demain soir
nuit	*night*	la nuit dernière	cette nuit	la nuit prochaine
semaine	*week*	la semaine dernière	cette semaine	la semaine prochaine
mois	*month*	le mois dernier	ce mois-ci	le mois prochain
été	*summer*	en été dernier	cet été	l'été prochain
année	*year*	l'année dernière	cette année	l'année prochaine

L'année dernière Stéphanie a débuté *Last year, Stéphanie started her*
son stage en Écosse. **Cette année** *work placement in Scotland.*
la famille Dickson va en France *This year the Dickson family is*
et **l'année prochaine** les parents de *going to France and next year*
Stéphanie passeront les vacances *Stéphanie's parents will spend*
d'été chez les Dickson. *the summer holidays at the*
Dickson's.

See also **Comment dit-on? 2**.

2 Structuring adverbs

Verbs show whether they refer to the present, past or future by their form:

Mark **rencontre** Stéphanie. *Mark **meets** Stéphanie.*
Mark **a rencontré** Stéphanie. *Mark **met / has met** Stéphanie.*
Mark **va rencontrer** Stéphanie. *Mark **is going to meet** Stéphanie.*
Mark **rencontrera** Stéphanie. *Mark **will meet** Stéphanie.*

To show more precisely where the verb comes in a series of events, you
can use an **adverb of time**. Adverbs usually tell us more about verbs so
they are often found near verbs: **Je la rencontre souvent** (*I often meet
her*). You can change the word order depending on what you want to
emphasise:

Je vais **d'abord** l'inviter à prendre *I'll invite her first of all to have*
un café. *coffee.*
D'abord, je vais l'inviter à prendre *First I'll invite her to have coffee.*
un café.
Je vais l'inviter à prendre un café, *I'll ask her to have a coffee first.*
d'abord.

Other time adverbs or adverbial phrases which can be used to structure a series of events are:

d'abord	pour commencer	en premier lieu	*first*
ensuite	deuxièmement	en deuxièmement lieu	*second / next*
après	puis / alors	en 3ème/4ème ... lieu	*then / after that*
enfin	finalement	en dernier lieu	*finally*

See also **Comment dit-on?** *1* and **En contexte**.

3 Time prepositions

To explain where in a sequence an event occurs, occurred or will occur, you can use a **time preposition** plus a noun:

Après les examens je vais aller plus souvent au cinéma.	*After the exams, I will go to the cinema more often.*
Avant les vacances, nous sommes toujours fatigués. **Pendant** les vacances nous nous reposons et **après** notre retour à la maison nous sommes en pleine forme.	*Before the holidays we are always tired. During the holidays we rest and after coming home we are in top form.*
Je dois étudier sérieusement **avant** les vacances.	*I have to study seriously before the holidays.*

Prepositions showing the order of a series of events (**avant, après, jusqu'à**) can be followed by the time instead of a noun:

Je téléphone souvent à mes parents **après 9 heures** et nous parlons **jusqu'à 10h**.	*I often phone my parents after 9 o'clock and we talk until 10.*
L'avion de Londres arrive **avant 18 heures**, puis il part pour Berlin.	*The London plane arrives before 18.00, then it leaves for Berlin.*
Sandy travaille **jusqu'à 10 heures**. Ensuite elle se couche.	*Sandy works until 10 o'clock. Then she goes to bed.*

4 Cause and effect

Events can also be related through the effects they produce. The simplest way to show this is by using the expression **parce que** (*because*). You can ask a question to find out about cause and effect using **pourquoi?** (*why?*).

Pourquoi choisissez-vous de prendre l'avion?	*Why do you choose to go by plane?*

Parce que c'est plus rapide.	*Because it's quicker.*

Other **linking expressions** can be used to show the effect or the result of something:

L'avion va plus vite que le train, **donc** nous le prenons pour aller en France.	*The plane goes quicker than the train, so we will take it to go to France.*
Comme l'avion est plus rapide que le train, nous avons décidé de le prendre pour aller en France.	*Since the plane is faster than the train, we decided to fly to France.*
C'est parce que l'avion est plus rapide que le train, **que** nous avons décidé de le prendre pour aller en France.	*It's because the plane is faster than the train that we decided to fly to France.*
Puisque l'avion va plus vite que le train, nous avons décidé d'aller en France en avion.	*As the plane is faster than the train, we decided to go to France by plane.*

See also **Comment dit-on? 3.**

En contexte

Look particularly for **structuring adverbs** and **expressions of cause and effect**.

Les Lemaire se préparent à recevoir les Dickson.

Isabelle   Comment les choses vont-elles se passer? D'abord ils vont louer une voiture à l'aéroport. Ensuite il y a deux heures de route avant d'arriver chez nous. Puis il faut dîner, ...

Georges   Qu'est-ce qu'on fait d'habitude quand on a des invités? On leur montre la ville et puis on visite un peu la région. Les Dickson vont sûrement s'intéresser aux environs de St Amand. On peut donc les conduire en forêt et à Valenciennes. Et on peut aussi leur présenter nos amis.

Isabelle   Oui, bien sûr, mais on prend des vacances pour se reposer! Il faut leur laisser le temps de se détendre et ne pas essayer de faire trop de choses. D'ailleurs, comme c'est la première fois qu'ils viennent en France, il faut leur montrer ce qui est typiquement français.

Georges	Il est difficile de décider ce qui est intéressant pour des Écossais parce que nous ne connaissons pas l'Écosse.
Isabelle	Il est préférable donc de leur demander ce qu'ils veulent voir – la campagne, la mer, les villes, ...
Georges	Et puis, il est important de leur présenter des amis de Stéphanie car ils veulent sûrement mieux la connaître.

Pour vérifier

1 Check the **Résumé grammatical** *1*, *2*, *3*, *4* and identify the expressions of time, and of cause and effect in the extracts below. Then put the 10 elements in the correct order to make a brief story entitled **Les Vacances**.

- nous essayons de nous lever le plus tard possible.
- Il est donc midi et nous n'avons pas pris une décision.
- car nos parents commencent à se fâcher.
- Pendant les vacances, nous voulons nous reposer, mais nos parents préfèrent être très actifs.
- Après avoir mangé, il faut accepter de sortir.
- Finalement, tout le monde est prêt, et nous pouvons enfin partir.
- Puis nous prenons une douche et nous nous habillons très lentement.
- C'est pour cette raison que ...
- Alors nous discutons interminablement le programme du jour.
- D'abord nous mangeons un petit déjeuner copieux.

Pour aller plus loin

1 More about time expressions

Expressions such as **avant** (before), **après** (*after*), **pendant** (*during*) (see **Résumé grammatical** *3*), are not only found in sentences where the present tense is used. They are also used when talking about past, recently past and future events.

Avant mon stage en Grande-Bretagne je ne m'intéressais pas à l'histoire écossaise. J'ai téléphoné à Stéphanie ce matin **après** 9h et nous nous sommes rencontrés **avant** 10h.	*Before my work experience in Great Britain, I wasn't interested in Scottish history.* *I phoned Stéphanie after 9 o'clock and we met before 10 o'clock.*

Pendant notre séjour nous ferons beaucoup de randonnées en forêt. *During our stay we'll take a lot of walks in the forest.*

■ Exception: **depuis**

To indicate how long something has been going on, or when it started, you can use: **depuis** (*for / since*).

Les Lemaire **attendent** les Dickson depuis plus de deux heures. *The Lemaires have been waiting for the Dicksons for more than two hours.*

Depuis 1990 nous **allons** tous les ans à Annecy en juillet. *We've been going to Annecy in July every year since 1990.*

The verb tenses in English and French are different here – in French the present is used (see Unit 15 **Pour aller plus loin** for more information on **depuis**).

2 Speaking impersonally

It is useful to be able to speak about events without necessarily using the personal forms of the verb. There are two main ways of doing this: a) using **impersonal expressions** and b) using a form of the verb called the **passive**. The passive is based on the verb **être** (see Unit 1 **Résumé grammatical 2**).

a) Impersonal expressions

Some of these were used in earlier sections of this Unit in **En contexte**:

> **il faut dîner, ...**
> **Il faut leur laisser le temps de se détendre.**
> **il faut leur montrer ce qui est typiquement français.**
> **Il est difficile de décider**
> **Il est préférable donc de leur demander**
> **Il est important de leur présenter**

■ **Il faut** (*It is necessary*) is followed directly by an infinitive:

Il faut apprendre le français avant les vacances. *We'll have to* (it is necessary to) *learn French before the holidays.*

■ Other impersonal expressions are followed by **de** and an infinitive:

Il est difficile de comprendre Nicolas, car il parle très vite. *It's hard to understand Nicolas because he speaks very fast.*

Il est préférable de prendre vos vacances en été.	*It's better to take your holidays in the summer.*
Il est facile de voir pourquoi Mark aime Stéphanie.	*It's easy to see why Mark likes Stéphanie.*
Il est important de connaître les parents de Stéphanie.	*It's important to know Stéphanie's parents.*
Il est ridicule de refuser de parler français.	*It is stupid to refuse to speak French.*

b) The present passive

Another way of speaking impersonally or indirectly is to say that something *is done by someone.* This is called the **passive voice**. You need to be able to use **être** + the past participle of another verb, followed by the preposition **par** (*by*):

Les Dickson **sont accueillis par** les Lemaire.	*The Dicksons are welcomed by the Lemaires.*
Les valises **sont faites par** Alison parce que les autres n'aiment pas les faire.	*The packing is done by Alison because the others don't like doing it.*

Notice that the past participle acts like an adjective and agrees with the person(s) or thing(s) it is telling you about:

> Les Dickson (masc. plural) sont accueill**is**.
> Les valises (fem. plural) sont fait**es**.

The past participles of regular verbs are formed in the following way:

-er verbs		**-ir** verbs		**-re** verbs	
infinit.	past part.	infinit.	past part.	infinit.	past part.
donner	**donné**	**accueillir**	**accueilli**	**vendre**	**vendu**
inviter	**invité**	**atterrir**	**atterri**	**rendre**	**rendu**

For more information on past participles, see Unit 13 **Résumé grammatical *1*** and **Pour aller plus loin *1*.**

Here are some examples of the use of the **present passive** (for the past tenses of the passive, see Unit 15 **Résumé grammatical *4***).

Je **suis** toujours **accueilli** à la gare par mes parents.	*I'm always collected at the station by my parents.*

Tu **es invité(e)** par mes parents à venir dîner à la maison demain.	*You are invited by my parents to come and have dinner at home tomorrow.*
Il **est** très **attiré** par Stéphanie.	*He is very attracted by Stephanie.*
Cette voiture **est louée** par nos amis écossais.	*This car is hired by our Scottish friends.*
Nous **sommes invités** par les Lemaire.	*We are invited by the Lemaires.*
Vous **êtes** souvent **photographié** par votre copine.	*You are often photographed by your girlfriend.*
Les Dickson **sont invités** par les Lemaire à passer leurs vacances en France.	*The Dicksons are invited by the Lemaires to spend their holidays in France.*
Les valises **sont faites** par Alison.	*The packing is done by Alison.*

11 FUTURE PLANS AND EVENTS

Thèmes   Les projets des Lemaire; L'emploi

The Lemaires plan how they will entertain the Dicksons
Stéphanie, Mark, Alison and Georges talk about their work and their
future plans

In this Unit you will learn to:

1 Speak and write about the future
2 Ask about future events
3 Talk about your hopes and plans

Structures grammaticales

1 Regular verbs in the future tense (**le futur**)
2 Common irregular verbs in the future
3 Irregular verbs in -**er**: the future: **manger** (*to eat*), **appeler** (*to call*),
   acheter (*to buy*)
4 Time expressions and the future
5 Relative pronouns **qui** and **que**

Pour aller plus loin

1 The future: differences between French and English usage
2 Other time expressions and the future
3 Relative pronouns after **de**: **dont** (*of which / whom*)
4 Relative pronouns referring to people, after other prepositions: **avec
   qui**, **pour qui**
5 Relative pronouns referring to things, after other prepositions:
   lequel etc.

Avant de commencer

1 When you are speaking, you can often choose to use the present tense to refer to something you are going to do. If you do this, you will usually need to use a time expression as well, to show that you are referring to the future.

Je vais en France **cet été**.	*I'm going to France this summer.*
Tu vas au cinéma **ce soir**?	*Are you going to the cinema this evening?*
Il arrive demain matin **à 8 heures**.	*He's arriving tomorrow morning at 8 o'clock.*

2 You have already learned (Unit 6 **Résumé grammatical *1***) how to use **aller** (*to go*) with an infinitive to speak about the immediate future.

Je **vais acheter** un dictionnaire français-anglais.	*I'm going to buy a French-English dictionary.*
Mes parents **vont téléphoner** à Madame Lemaire ce soir.	*My parents are going to phone Madame Lemaire this evening.*
La semaine prochaine Mark **va commencer** à travailler sur une plate-forme Shell.	*Next week, Mark is going to start working on a Shell platform.*

Go back to Unit 6 and make sure you can use this form without any difficulty.

3 As well as learning to use the future tense in this Unit, you will also learn some of the time expressions you need so that you can talk about and ask questions about the future. Some of them you have already learned in Unit 10 **Résumé grammatical *1*, *2***. In the examples in **1** (above), these expressions are in bold. Locate the two time expressions in **Avant de commencer 2**.

4 The irregular verbs you have already covered

avoir	*to have*	**vouloir**	*to wish/want*
être	*to be*	**pouvoir**	*to be able*
aller	*to go*	**savoir**	*to know*
venir	*to come*	**devoir**	*to be obliged/have to*
faire	*to make/do*	**falloir**	*to be necessary*

use the same future endings as the regular verbs, but have an irregular stem.

Comment dit-on?

1 Speaking and writing about the future

Les parents de Mark **arriveront** à
l'aéroport Roissy-Charles-de-Gaulle
Là, ils **loueront** une voiture.
Les Lemaire les **rencontreront à**
l'aéroport et les Dickson les
suivront en voiture.
Ils **arriveront** à St Amand deux
heures plus tard.
Je leur **préparerai** un bon repas
français.
Je leur **ferai** une bonne mousse au
chocolat.
Ils n'**auront** peut-être pas faim à
cette heure-là.

*Mark's parents will arrive at
Roissy-Charles-de-Gaulle
airport. There they will hire a car.
The Lemaires will meet them at
the airport and the Dicksons
will follow them in the car.
They will arrive in St Amand two
hours later.
I will prepare them a good
French meal.
I will make them a nice chocolate
mousse.
Perhaps they won't be hungry at
that time.*

2 Asking about future events

À ton avis, qu'est-ce qu'ils **feront**
durant leur séjour?
Qu'est-ce qu'on leur **montrera**?
Seront-ils intéressés? **Voudront**-ils
visiter St Amand et ses environs?

Souhaiteront-ils rencontrer des
amis de Stéphanie?
Peut-être **auront**-ils déjà des
plans précis.
Nous leur **demanderons** ce qu'ils
veulent faire.
Ce **sera** la meilleure solution.

*What do you think they will do
during their stay?
What shall we show them?
Will they be interested? Will they
want to visit   St Amand and
its surroundings?
Will they want to meet some
of Stéphanie's friends?
Perhaps they'll have specific plans.
We'll ask them what they want
to do.
That'll be the best way.*

3 Talking about your hopes/your plans

J'espère qu'ils se **plairont**
chez nous.
Nous **ferons** tout notre possible
pour les mettre à l'aise.

*I hope (that) they'll enjoy
being here.
We'll do our best to put them
at their ease.*

Je ne sais pas comment nous **communiquerons**, mais nous **ferons** de notre mieux.		*I don't know how we will communicate, but we'll do our best.*

Je ne sais pas comment nous
communiquerons, mais nous
ferons de notre mieux.
J'**achèterai** un bon dictionnaire
demain ou bien j'**emprunterai**
celui de Nicolas.
J'espère que Nicolas nous **aidera**.
Nous **pourrons** toujours nous faire
comprendre par des gestes et
nous **demanderons** à Nicolas
d'être interprète.
Stéphanie **reviendra** peut-être en
France à ce moment-là.

*I don't know how we will
communicate, but we'll
do our best.*
*I'll buy a good dictionary
tomorrow or I'll borrow
Nicolas'.*
I hope that Nicolas will help us.
*We'll always be able to make
ourselves understood with gestures
and we'll ask Nicolas to be
our interpreter.*
*Stéphanie will perhaps come back
to France at that time.*

Résumé grammatical

1 Regular verbs in the future tense (le futur)

Subject pronoun	Stem (= infinitive)	Endings
j'	aimer-	AI
tu	finir-	AS
il	apprendr-	A
elle	visiter-	A
on	rencontrer-	A
nous	vendr-	ONS
vous	partir-	EZ
ils	grossir-	ONT
elles	entendr-	ONT

For regular verbs, and many irregular verbs, the stem for this tense is the infinitive – **aimer** (*to love*), **finir** (*to finish*). Regular verbs ending in -**re** – **entendre** (*to hear*), **apprendre** (*to learn*), **vendre** (*to sell*) – drop the **e** (**entendr-**, **apprendr-**, **vendr-**) before adding the endings. The endings are the same for all French verbs.

J'aimerai Stéphanie toute ma vie.
Tu finiras avant moi.
Il apprendra à faire de la planche à voile.
Isabelle **visitera** le musée avec
les Dickson.
On les **rencontrera** à l'aéroport.
Nous vendrons la BMW à
notre retour.

I'll love Stéphanie all my life.
You'll finish before me.
He'll learn to windsurf.
*Isabelle will visit the museum
with the Dicksons.*
We'll meet them at the airport.
*We'll sell the BMW when we
get back.*

Vous partirez tôt le matin.	*You'll leave early in the morning.*
Ils grossiront s'ils mangent trop.	*They'll get fat if they eat too much.*
Elles entendront de la musique française.	*They'll hear some French music.*

See **Comment dit-on?** *1, 2, 3*.

2 Common irregular verbs in the future

The stem of the future tense of these verbs is very irregular and has to be learned in each case.

Bonus: the same stem is used for the conditional tense – see Unit 18 **Résumé grammatical** *1* and Verb Tables page 232.

Although the stems are not the infinitives, they all end in -**r**.

avoir	*to have*
être	*to be*
aller	*to go*
venir	*to come*
faire	*to make/do*
vouloir	*to wish/want*
pouvoir	*to be able*
savoir	*to know*
devoir	*to be obliged/have to*
falloir	*to be necessary*

Infinit.	Stem	
avoir	**aur-**	aurai, auras, aura, aurons, aurez, auront
être	**ser-**	serai, seras, sera, serons, serez, seront
aller	**ir-**	irai, iras, ira, irons, irez, iront
venir	**viendr-**	viendrai, viendras, viendra, viendrons, viendrez, viendront
faire	**fer-**	ferai, feras, fera, ferons, ferez, feront
vouloir	**voudr-**	voudrai, voudras, voudra, voudrons, voudrez, voudront
pouvoir	**pourr-**	pourrai, pourras, pourra, pourrons, pourrez, pourront
savoir	**saur-**	saurai, sauras, saura, saurons, saurez, sauront
devoir	**devr-**	devrai, devras, devra, devrons, devrez, devront
falloir	**faudr-**	il faudra
voir	**verr-**	verrai, verras, verra, verrons, verrez, verront

Stéphanie

En 20.., j'**aurai** mon diplôme.	*In 200.., I will have my degree.*
Est-ce que j'**aurai** d'autres examens à passer?	*Will I have other exams to take?*
Non. Je ne **serai** plus étudiante et j'**irai** en Grande-Bretagne chercher du travail.	*No, I will no longer be a student and will go to Great Britain to look for work.*

Mark **viendra** me voir quand il ne **sera** pas sur la plate-forme de forage.	*Mark will come and see me when he is not on the oil-rig.*
Ferons-nous des promenades ensemble?	*Will we go for walks together?*
Nous **ferons** peut-être du sport.	*Perhaps we will take up sport.*
Il ne **voudra** pas m'accompagner à mes cours d'équitation mais on **pourra** aller à des matchs de foot ensemble.	*He will not want to accompany me to my horse-riding lessons, but we will be able to go to football matches together.*

Notice the **negative** form of the future: Il ne **voudra** pas; je ne **devrai** pas and also the **interrogative** forms: Est-ce que j'**aurai** … ? **Ferons**-nous … ?

Look for the irregular verbs in **Comment dit-on?** *1*, *2*, *3*.

3 Irregular verbs in -er in the future

Verbs spelt like **manger, appeler, acheter** follow the spelling rules you learned for the present tense (Unit 1 **Pour aller plus loin** *2*; Verb Tables p 232).

Quand nous serons en France, nous **mangerons** peut-être des escargots.	*When we are in France, maybe we'll eat some snails.*

(The **g** in **manger** remains soft because it is followed by **e**)

Je t'**appellerai** chez toi ce soir.	*I'll ring you at your place tonight.*

(To avoid two neutral **e**'s following one another, the consonant **l** is doubled.)

Mon père m'**achètera** le billet et je **viendrai** te voir en Écosse.	*My father will buy me the ticket and I'll come and see you in Scotland.*

(To avoid two neutral **e**'s following one another, a grave accent is added to the **e** in the second last syllable of the verb)

4 Time expressions and the future

When you use a verb in the future tense, you refer, either explicitly or implicitly, to a period of time after the moment at which you are speaking or writing.

a) Prepositions with time

In *2* (above) Stéphanie is talking about some years ahead (**En l'an 20**..).
As well as dates, you will find it useful to be able to use the names of days and months and expressions for telling the time (see Unit 2 **Comment**

dit-on? *3* and Unit 3 **Résumé grammatical** *4*). Note the **prepositions** used in the time expressions in bold below:

En 2000 le monde fêtera le commencement du troisième millénaire.	*In 2000 the world will celebrate the start of the third millennium.*
En été nous irons à la plage, mais **au printemps** nous serons dans le Massif central.	*In summer we shall go to the beach, but in spring we'll be in the Massif central.*
Elle viendra nous voir **en janvier**.	*She will come and see us in January.*
Nos amis les Dickson arriveront **lundi**.	*Our friends the Dicksons will arrive on Monday.*
Leur avion atterrira **à 13 h 15**.	*Their plane will land at 1.15 p.m.*

b) Prochain

You can also use the adjective **prochain** (*next*) (see Unit 10 **Résumé grammatical** *1*) with the names of months or days:

Vendredi **prochain** je terminerai mon stage et je rentrerai chez moi.	*Next Friday I'll finish my work placement and I'll go home.*

c) The future with dans and en

The prepositions **dans/en** are both used for future time. **Dans** is used in speaking about a point of time in the future:

Dans quinze jours mon patron sera en vacances et nous pourrons travailler plus calmement.	*In a fortnight's time my boss will be on holiday and we'll be able to work more calmly.*
Nous nous verrons **dans** huit jours et je te raconterai tout.	*We'll see one another in a week and I'll tell you everything.*
Je serai chez toi **dans** 10 minutes.	*I'll be at your place in ten minutes time.*

En is used to say how long it will take to do something:

Il viendra **en** moins de dix minutes.	*He'll come in less than ten minutes.* (i.e. it will take him less than 10 minutes)
Elle finira son doctorat **en** 4 ans.	*She'll finish her doctorate in four years.* (i.e. it will take her four years)

5 *Relative pronouns* qui *and* que

Relative pronouns are useful to make your French more polished. Like
other pronouns (e.g. personal pronouns, Unit 1 **Résumé grammatical *1***
and Unit 5 **Résumé grammatical *3***), they also make it possible for you
to avoid repetition and to construct longer sentences. They are particularly
useful in writing.

a) Qui

qui is a **subject** pronoun. It can replace people (*who*):

Mon chef, **qui** travaille souvent en France, sera très content de vous rencontrer.	*My boss, who often works in France, will be very pleased to meet you.*
Est-ce que tu connais le directeur **qui** m'a interviewée?	*Do you know the director who interviewed me?*

or things (*which / that*):

Je veux vous parler de votre CV **qui** m'intéresse beaucoup.	*I should like to talk to you about your CV which interests me very much.*
Vous travaillerez dans le bureau **qui** se trouve à côté du mien.	*You'll be working in the office (that is) beside mine.*

b) Que

que is an **object** pronoun which can replace people (*whom*):

J'ai attendu dans le bureau de la secrétaire **que** j'ai rencontrée la semaine dernière.	*I waited in the office belonging to the secretary (whom) I met last week.*

or things (*which / that*):

Je suis très contente de l'ordinateur **que** j'utilise pour mon travail.	*I'm very happy with the computer (that) I use for my work.*

Notice that in English, the relative pronoun is often not expressed:

the office (that is) beside mine
the secretary (whom) I met last week
the computer (that) I use for my work.

c) Some verbs are always followed by a preposition

téléphoner **à** quelqu'un (*to phone someone*)
demander **à** quelqu'un (*to ask someone*).

Where verbs like this are followed by a relative pronoun, **qui** (*whom*) is
used for people:

M. Monnoury est le nom de la   *Mr Monnoury is the person*
personne **à qui** j'ai téléphoné   *(whom) I phoned this morning.*
ce matin.

En contexte

In this passage, look for the **verbs in the future tense**, the **time
expressions** and the **relative pronouns**.

**Qu'est-ce que tu fais? Stéphanie, Mark, Alison et Georges parlent de
leur travail et de leurs projets d'avenir.**

Stéphanie   Le travail que je fais actuellement ne m'intéresse pas
beaucoup, mais après mon stage je pourrai trouver un
emploi quand je rentrerai en France. C'est mon chef, Mr
Williams, qui m'encourage à apprendre l'anglais et à me
perfectionner en informatique. «Vous utiliserez toujours
l'anglais et l'informatique» me dit-il.

Mark   A présent le poste que j'occupe m'oblige à passer beaucoup
de temps sur plate-forme. Mais j'aurai besoin de cette
expérience du forage en mer. C'est l'expérience pratique qui
sera nécessaire si je veux avoir plus tard un poste de cadre.

Alison   Le travail d'un professeur devient de plus en plus dur.
Pendant les vacances, qui passent toujours beaucoup trop vite
pour moi, on ne se repose pas. Il faut préparer les cours car il
est difficile de trouver le temps qu'il faut pendant le
trimestre. Ce soir, comme d'habitude, je corrigerai des copies
et je préparerai des polycopies que j'utiliserai demain.

Georges   Un plombier ne dort jamais tranquille car à tout moment le
téléphone peut sonner. Il faut toujours dépanner des gens qui
ont des problèmes – des problèmes qui n'arrivent que la nuit
ou pendant le weekend. J'espère que mon fils aura un emploi
qui lui permettra de bien dormir et de ne pas travailler à des
heures impossibles.

Pour vérifier

Change the **verbs** and the **time expressions** in the following passages to the future:

Stéphanie   Aujourd'hui je travaille au bureau. Je tape des lettres pour mon chef et j'assiste à une réunion des membres du département de ressources humaines. Est-ce que tu viens me chercher à 17 heures 30? On achète de quoi manger à *Marks et Spencer.*

Mark   Ce soir je mange avec Stéphanie. Mardi je ne suis pas ici car je prends l'hélicoptère et je recommence à travailler sur une plate-forme BP. Je règle l'appareil de forage et je le contrôle par ordinateur. Nous sommes sur plate-forme pour trois semaines. Je ne vois pas Stéphanie et elle me manque beaucoup.

Alison   Aujourd'hui à 4 heures nous avons une réunion de tous les enseignants. Elle dure au moins deux heures et demie et je ne rentre pas avant 19 heures 30. Vous préparez vous-mêmes le dîner - et il ne faut pas oublier de faire la vaisselle!

Georges   Est-ce que nous pouvons manger à 21 heures ce soir? La réparation du tuyautage chez Madame Vincent n'est pas terminée et je dois aussi remplacer les robinets dans sa salle de bains.

Pour aller plus loin

1 The future: differences between French and English usage

a) Using the future in place of the present

After:

quand *when* **lorsque** *when* **aussitôt que** *as soon as* **dès que** *as soon as*	French uses a verb in the future: Quand vous **arriverez** … but in English we use a verb in the present: *When you arrive* …

Nous les **accueillerons** quand ils **arriveront**.	*We'll welcome them when they arrive.*
Lorsque Mark **partira**, Stéphanie **se sentira** très triste.	*When Mark leaves, Stéphanie will feel very sad.*

Accueillir follows the same pattern as the verb **cueillir**. See Verb Tables page 232.

b) The future perfect

In French a tense called the **future perfect** (Quand **j'aurai terminé** mon travail) is used where in English you would use a past tense. This emphasises that one action will come after the other:

Je te téléphonerai quand j'**aurai terminé** mon travail.	*I'll ring you when I've finished work.*
Dès que j'**aurai réparé** le tuyautage de Madame Vincent, je rentrerai à la maison.	*As soon as I've repaired Madame Vincent's pipes, I'll come home.*

2 Other time expressions and the future

Some useful expressions are found in the table in Unit 10 **Résumé grammatical 1**. In addition, you may need:

après-demain   *the day after tomorrow*
le lendemain   *the following/next day*
demain en huit   *a week tomorrow/tomorrow week*
mercredi en quinze   *a fortnight on Wednesday*

3 Relative pronouns after de: dont

If you want to use a relative pronoun with expressions which always include the preposition **de**, for example **avoir besoin de** *to need*, **avoir peur de** *to be afraid of* or with verbs which can be followed by **de**, for example **parler de** *to speak about / of*, **rêver de** *to dream about*, the relative pronoun **dont** replaces **de** + **qui** (*of whom*; *of which*):

Les employés **dont** nous avons besoin sont difficiles à trouver dans cette région de l'Écosse.	*The employees we need are hard to find in this part of Scotland.*
Les résultats **dont** il a peur seront publiés la semaine prochaine.	*The results he's afraid of will be published next week.*

Je ferai ce soir les exercices **dont** le professeur nous a parlé.	*This evening, I'll do the exercises the teacher spoke about.*
La carrière en marketing **dont** je rêve me permettra de voyager partout en Europe.	*The career in marketing I dream of will allow me to travel all over Europe.*

Notice the word order in these sentences:

Noun		subject	verb
les employés	**dont**	nous	avons besoin
les résultats	**dont**	il	a peur
les exercices	**dont**	le professeur	a parlé
la carrière	**dont**	je	rêve

4 Relative pronouns referring to people, after prepositions

La collègue **avec qui** je viens au bureau habite près de chez moi.	*The colleague I come to work with (with whom I come to work) lives near me.*
Le client **pour qui** je fais des recherches veut améliorer ses logiciels.	*The client I'm doing research for (for whom I'm doing research) wants to improve his software.*

5 Relative pronouns referring to things, after prepositions

When they follow a preposition, relative pronouns referring to **things** have the following form. They agree with the word they replace in number and gender:

	Masculine	**Feminine**
Singular	lequel	laquelle
Plural	lesquels	lesquelles

As-tu vu l'ordinateur **sur lequel** je travaille? (ordinateur: masc. sing. → **lequel**)	*Have you seen the computer I work on* (on which I work)?
Les compagnies pétrolières **avec lesquelles** nous traitons sont rarement françaises. (compagnies: fem. plur. → **lesquelles**)	*The oil companies we work with* (with which we work) *are rarely French.*

12 GETTING THINGS DONE

Thème   La banque et l'argent

Mark and Stéphanie talk about money and financial problems
Getting money before and during your trip
Nicolas is trying to find money for a trip to Britain

In this Unit you will learn to:

1 Ask someone to do or not to do something
2 Give orders and instructions

Structures grammaticales

1 The imperative of regular verbs (**l'impératif**)
2 The imperative of irregular verbs
3 The present tense for giving instructions
4 The infinitive and giving instructions
5 Giving negative instructions
6 Two pronoun objects
7 The imperative with two pronoun objects

Pour aller plus loin

1 Other ways of giving orders
2 Polite requests

Avant de commencer

1 The imperative form of the verb is used for giving instructions (see Unit 9 **Résumé grammatical** *2*). To do this, you use parts of the present (indicative) tense. By now, you should have a secure knowledge of the present tense of regular and some irregular verbs. Check these in Units 1, 2, 5, 6, 8 and 9 and in your notebook.

2 In this Unit you will learn how to use verbs which have more than one pronoun object. You learned about direct pronoun objects in Unit 5 **Résumé grammatical** *3*, and indirect pronoun objects in Unit 9 **Résumé grammatical** *3*. You should revise them before beginning this Unit.

Alors, est-ce que tu **les** prends ou est-ce que tu ne **les** prends pas?

Well are you taking them or are you not taking them?

Stéphanie laisse tomber son carnet de chèques et Mark **le** ramasse.

Stéphanie drops her cheque book and Mark picks it up.

Mark **leur** téléphonera et **leur** dira que les Lemaire les **rencontreront** à l'aéroport.

Mark will phone them and tell them that the Lemaires will meet them at the airport.

3 The distinction between direct and indirect objects is sometimes difficult for English speakers. See Unit 9 **Pour aller plus loin** *2*. You can identify the **direct object** by asking *what?* or *whom?* after the verb:

I gave the teller the cheque. → verb = *gave* → gave **what?** → *the cheque* 'cheque'* is the **direct object**.

The **indirect object** is not related directly to the verb, but to a preposition, usually *to*. Because the preposition is often not expressed in English, it can take a moment to work out what is the indirect object.

You can decide whether an object is indirect by asking the question *to / for whom?* after the verb:

I gave the cheque → to / for whom? → *(to) the teller.* 'teller'* is the **indirect object**.

Study the following examples and ensure that you can recognise the difference between the two types of object in English.

Give him the money! → *'money'* = direct object: *'him'* = indirect object. *Give it to George!*

Let's buy them this book!
I'll give him the money.
Sandy brought her a cup of tea.

4 If you use the imperative without some kind of accompanying polite expression, it can be a very direct way of telling someone to do something or getting something done. For polite requests, you can use set expressions with **vouloir** (*to wish / want*). Some of the expressions given in Unit 4 **Résumé grammatical** *1* will help.

Comment dit-on?

1 Asking someone to do something

Est-ce que nous pouvons nous arrêter à la banque? J'ai besoin de retirer de l'argent.
Can we stop at the bank?
I need to draw some money.

Arrête s'il te plaît, car je voudrais acheter un petit cadeau pour Madame Lemaire.
Please stop, because I would like to buy a small gift for Madame Lemaire.

N'oublie pas les conseils de notre prof de français pour demander à quelqu'un de répéter quelque chose.
Don't forget our French teacher's advice for asking someone to repeat something.

Pourriez-vous répéter s'il vous plaît? *Could you repeat please?*

Pouvez-vous parler plus lentement s'il vous plaît?
Can you speak more slowly please?

2 Giving orders

Andrew, **occupe-toi** bien de la maison. *Andrew, look after the house well.*

Sors la poubelle le mardi matin. *Put the bin out on Tuesday mornings.*

Ne te lève pas trop tard. *Don't get up too late.*

Toi et tes amis, **n'utilisez pas** trop le téléphone.
You and your friends must not use the phone too much.

Contacte ton oncle si tu as des problèmes.
Contact your uncle if you have any problems.

Suivons les conseils de Mark. *Let's follow Mark's advice.*

Il ne **faudra** pas rouler pas trop vite car il est important de lire les panneaux routiers.
We mustn't drive too fast, as it is important to read the road signs.

Insérer la carte bancaire, taper le numéro personnel. **Choisir** le montant.	*Insert you bank card, key in your personal number. Select the amount.*
Retirer la carte avant d'obtenir l'argent.	*Take your card out before the money is issued.*

Résumé grammatical

1 The imperative of regular verbs

The verbs you have studied so far have been in the **indicative** (or standard) **mood**. It is used for making statements. See Unit 9 **Résumé grammatical 2**. The **imperative mood** is used for giving instructions or orders. In French, there are three forms of the imperative, depending on the situation the speaker is in:

a) speaking to a friend

b) speaking to someone you don't know well or to a group of people

c) speaking to a group of people in which you are included

Look back at **Comment dit-on?** and see if you can find examples of *a)* and *b)*.

In each of the situations described, *a)*, *b)* and *c)*, you can use part of the present tense of the verb (without a subject) to give an instruction:

a) speaking to a friend, use the tu form of the verb:

Donne* cet argent à ton frère!	*Give that money to your brother!*
Finis tes devoirs!	*Finish your homework!*
Viens ici!	*Come here!*

*Note that, for -**er** verbs only, the **s** of the **tu** form is dropped in the imperative: **Donne!** (*Give!*), **Achète!** (*Buy!*), **Chante!** (*Sing!*)

b) speaking to someone you don't know well or to a group of other people, use the vous form of the verb:

Insérez votre argent dans la fente à droite!	*Insert your money in the slot on the right!*
Protégez votre carte des regards indiscrets!	*Hide your card from prying eyes!*
Utilisez le service Cirrus pour obtenir des devises. C'est si pratique.	*Use the Cirrus service to get cash. It's so simple.*

c) speaking to a group of people in which you are included (Let's do something in English), use the nous form of the verb:

Allons à la banque ce matin!   *Let's go to the bank this morning!*
Essayons ma carte bancaire!   *Let's try my bank card!*
Apprenons à mieux parler français! *Let's learn to speak French better!*

■ *a)* and *b)* are more common than *c)* which, although it expresses a suggestion rather than an order, is thought of as an imperative in French.

In the boxes below, the imperative forms are in bold:

jouer *to play*	**finir** *to finish*	**rendre** *to give back*
je joue	je finis	je rends
tu **joue(s)**	tu **finis**	tu **rends**
il/elle/on joue	il/elle/on finit	il/elle/on rend
nous **jouons**	nous **finissons**	nous **rendons**
vous **jouez**	vous **finissez**	vous **rendez**
ils/elles jouent	ils/elles finissent	ils/elles rendent

Ne joue pas avec Pierre!   *Don't play with Pierre!*
Jouons le concerto No 3 ce soir! *Let's play the Concerto No 3 tonight!*
Jouez dans le jardin!   *Play in the garden!*

Finis tes devoirs!   *Finish your homework!*
Finissons le gâteau!   *Let's finish the cake!*
Ne **finissez** pas tout aujourd'hui! *Don't finish the lot today!*

Rends ton amie heureuse!   *Make your friend (f) happy!*
Rendons grâce à Dieu!   *(Let's) give thanks to God!*
Rendez ce livre à Andrew, s'il vous plaît. *Give this book back to Andrew please.*

2 The imperative of irregular verbs

a) Some irregular verbs such as **avoir** and **être** have special forms in the imperative:

avoir	Aie!	Ayons!	Ayez!
être	Sois!	Soyons!	Soyez!

b) Irregular -er verbs (Unit 1 **Pour aller plus loin** *2*) have an irregular **tu** form:

Achète trois livres de cerises!	*Buy three pounds of cherries!*
Appelle ce numéro à 8 heures!	*Phone this number at 8 o'clock!*
Jette ce papier dans la poubelle!	*Throw that paper in the bin!*
Lève-toi et marche!	*Arise and walk!*
Répète ce que je dis!	*Repeat what I say!*

Some of the irregular verbs in **-er**, e.g. **manger** (*to eat*), **placer** (*to place/put*), are also irregular in the **nous** form, if the pronunciation of the consonant becomes hard before the vowel **o**. This is avoided by inserting an **e** before the ending for verbs ending in -**ger** (e.g. **manger**) or by adding a cedilla to the **c** for verbs ending in -**cer** (e.g. **placer**):

Mangeons cette tarte!	*Let's eat this tart!*
Plaçons notre argent en lieu sûr!	*Let's invest our money in a safe place!*

c) Other irregular verbs

aller	Va!	Allons!	Allez!
faire	Fais!	Faisons!	Faites!
savoir	Sache!	Sachons!	Sachez!

3 The present tense for giving instructions

When you are speaking, you can use the present tense (including the subject – **tu** or **vous**) to give a direct order:

Tu ouvres un compte et **tu** y **verses** l'argent.	*You open an account and you put the money in.*
Tu prépares le terrain et **tu plantes** les fraises.	*You prepare the soil and you plant the strawberries.*
Tu tonds le gazon avant de sortir.	*(You) mow the lawn before you go out.*
Vous chantez tous ensemble.	*You all sing together.*
Vous rangez les bicyclettes et **vous nettoyez** vos baskets.	*(You) put the bikes away and (you) clean your trainers.*

4 The infinitive and giving instructions

In formal situations, where written instructions are given, the infinitive is sometimes used to issue a direct instruction:

Composer votre numéro personnel.   *Type in your PIN.*
Demander une liste de nos   *Ask for a list of our banking*
services bancaires.   *services.*
Retirer votre carte et votre argent.   *Take your card and your money.*
Se munir d'une pièce d'identité.   *Provide yourself with some ID.*
See **Comment dit-on?** *2.*

5 Giving negative instructions

The negative of the imperative is formed, as for the indicative, by using
ne and **pas** (see Unit 1). As in other tenses, **ne** precedes the verb and **pas**
follows it:

N'achète **pas** de devises!   *Don't buy foreign currency!*
Utilise plutôt des travellers!   *Instead, buy travellers' cheques!*
Ne mettez **pas** vos cartes de crédit   *Don't put your credit cards in your*
dans votre porte-monnaie!   *purse!*
Ne gaspillez **pas** votre argent!   *Don't waste your money!*
Ne dépensons **pas** sans réfléchir!   *Let's not spend without thinking*
   about it!

For negative commands using the infinitive (*4*, above), both **ne** and **pas**
come before the verb:

Ne pas utiliser la carte après la   *Do not use the card after the*
date d'expiration!   *expiry date!*

6 Two pronoun objects

You learned how to use direct pronoun objects in Unit 5 **Résumé
grammatical** *3*, and indirect pronoun objects in Unit 9 **Résumé
grammatical** *3*. A verb can sometimes have both a direct and an indirect
object. See above, **Avant de commencer 3.**

Je donnerai **un chèque** (direct object)   *I'll give a cheque to Mark.*
à Mark (indirect object).   *(I'll give Mark a cheque.)*

If both the objects are pronouns, they both go before the verb:

Je **le** (the cheque) **lui**   *I'll give it to him.*
(to Mark) donnerai.

There is a fixed order when two object pronouns are used. It is not related
to whether the pronouns are direct or indirect objects – you have to learn
the order in which the pronouns are used in French.

The grid below, which looks a bit like the placings for a football team, shows you the order to follow, from left to right, when you are using two pronoun objects. The most usual combinations are from columns 1 and 2:

Je **vous les** envoie.   *I'll send them to you.*

and from columns 2 and 3:

Mark **le lui** achète.   *Mark buys it for him/her.*
Les Dickson **les** (les cadeaux) **leur**   *The Dicksons take them* (the gifts)
  (aux Lemaire) apportent.   *to them* (the Lemaires).

subject	object pronouns				verb
Je	me te se nous vous se	le la les	lui leur	y en	envoie achète apporent

Here Je / Mark / Les Dickson are the subjects; envoie / achète / apportent the verbs.

7 *The imperative with two pronoun objects*

Using two pronoun objects with the direct imperative is simple. The objects follow the verb (as they do in English) and the direct object comes before the indirect object. The indirect object pronouns are: **moi**, **toi**, **lui**, **nous**, **vous**, **leur**, the same forms (except for **leur**) as the stressed pronouns (see Unit 1 **Résumé grammatical** *8*). The verb and the pronouns are joined by hyphens:

Envoie-**le-lui**!   *Send it to him/her!*
Apportons-**les-leur**!   *Let's take them to them!*
Achetez-**la-moi**!   *Buy it for me!*

If the imperative verb is in the negative, the rules given in *6*, above, apply:

Ne **le lui** envoyez pas!   *Don't send it to him/her!*
Ne **les leur** apportons pas!   *Let's not take them to them!*
Ne **me** l'achetez pas!   *Don't buy it for me!*

En contexte

In the conversation below, pick out the **verbs in the imperative** and the **object pronouns**.

Nicolas, son père et sa mère essaient de calculer comment il peut se permettre d'aller en Grande-Bretagne l'année prochaine.

Georges   Tu devrais changer complètement tes habitudes. Tu mets de l'argent de côté, tu ouvres un nouveau compte en banque, tu y verses au moins 1 000 francs par mois et tu ne dépenses rien!

Nicolas   C'est facile pour toi! Fais ceci! Fais cela! Ne fais pas ceci! Tu commandes et moi j'obéis. Mais pour moi, ce n'est pas facile. Imagine un peu! Je me prive de sorties, de vêtements, de livres, de cinéma. Pense à l'effet que tout cela aura sur moi!

Isabelle   Oui, écoute Georges! Aide-le! Ne lui donne pas d'ordres! Donne-lui plutôt des conseils!

Georges   C'est ce que j'essaie de faire. Je veux l'aider. Ne me le reprochez pas! D'ailleurs j'allais suggérer qu'on lui donne l'argent que nous avons mis de côté pour la nouvelle voiture. Donnons-le-lui! Il en a vraiment besoin.

Isabelle   Alors là, non! Ne nous affolons pas! Il a une année pour trouver cet argent. Il faut imaginer d'autres solutions parce que moi, je veux une nouvelle voiture!

Nicolas   Ne vous fâchez pas! Restons calmes. Je vous en prie, n'imaginez pas que je suis complètement stupide. Je me trouverai un petit boulot, je ferai du baby-sitting et bientôt j'aurai l'argent qu'il me faut.

Pour vérifier

1   Choose one word from each of the three lists below. Put the verb (Column 1) into the imperative (**tu** form) and make a list of five instructions for a friend going to France.

verbs	nouns	places
utiliser	**une carte Cirrus**	**la banque**
acheter	**une carte Visa**	**les restaurants**
changer	**vos travellers**	**les magasins**
	des devises	**un grand magasin**
	une ceinture porte-	
	monnaie	

Exemple: **Achetez une ceinture porte-monnaie dans un
grand magasin!**

2   In the same way, make a second list of five negative instructions using the imperative (**vous**) form:

verbs	nouns	places
ouvrir	**votre porte-monnaie**	**le métro**
changer	**vos travellers**	**l'hôtel**
laisser	**notre carte de crédit**	**votre chambre**
mettre	**votre argent**	
	votre passeport	

Exemple: **Ne laissez pas votre argent dans votre chambre!**

3   Look at the pronouns in bold in the following sentences, and imagine the nouns they might be replacing:

Exemple: Mark **les lui** achète → **Mark achète des roses à Stéphanie.**

Tu nous **le** donnes.
Il **la lui** apporte.
Nous **te les** offrons.

4   Answer the following questions, using two pronoun objects in your answer:

Exemple: **Mark, offre-t-il les fleurs à Stéphanie?** → Oui, il **les lui** offre.

Est-ce que tu donnes cet argent à notre fils?
Ces cadeaux, vous les apportez aux Lemaire?
Nous recommandons cet hôtel à nos amis?

Pour aller plus loin

1 Other ways of giving orders

As well as using the imperative, you can also give instructions using some
impersonal expressions such as **il faut** and **il est nécessaire / essentiel de**
followed by an infinitive. See Unit 9 **Résumé grammatical *1*** and Unit 10
Pour aller plus loin *2a*.

Il faut épargner quand on est jeune. *You have to save when you are young*
(It is necessary to save ...)

Il est nécessaire d'encaisser le   *You have to pay the cheque in*
chèque cette semaine.   *this week.* (It is necessary to pay ...)

See **Comment dit-on *2*?**

2 Polite requests

If you want to make a polite request, rather than give an order, you can use
set expressions based on the conditional tense of the verb **vouloir** (for
more information on the conditional see Unit 18 **Résumé grammatical *1, 3***).

Voudriez-vous fermer la fenêtre?   *Would you close the window please?*
Voudrais-tu me prêter quelques   *Would you lend me a few francs*
francs?   *please?*

To make an order or an instruction even more polite, you can add an
expression which makes it less direct:

n'est-ce pas?	Tu partages cet argent avec ton frère, n'est-ce pas?	*You're sharing that money with your brother, aren't you?*
s'il vous plaît **s'il te plaît**	Rends ce livre à Andrew, s'il te plaît.	*Give that book back to Andrew, please.*
je vous en prie **je t'en prie**	Je vous en prie, ne parlez pas de la crise économique!	*Please (I beg you), don't talk about the economic crisis!*

See **Comment dit-on?** *1*.

13 | TALKING ABOUT PAST EVENTS

Thème   Le voyage des Dickson

The Dicksons travel to France and talk about the journey
The Lemaires welcome them at the airport

In this Unit you will learn to:

1 Talk and write about past events
2 Talk and write about a series of events that happened in the past
3 Say that things took place over a period of time
4 Present events that happened in the recent past

Structures grammaticales

1 The past participle
2 The perfect tense with **avoir** (**le passé composé**)
3 The perfect tense with **être**
4 The immediate past: **venir de**
5 Other time expressions for sequencing events in the past

Pour aller plus loin

1 Agreement of the past participle
2 Uses of **il y a** (*ago*)

Avant de commencer

1 To form the perfect tense of most verbs, you use **a)** the present tense of **avoir** (Unit 1, **Résumé grammatical** 2) plus **b)** a past participle (**2** below). Notice the use of the present tense of **avoir** in the following examples:

Mark **a** rencontré Stéphanie à Aberdeen.	*Mark met Stéphanie in Aberdeen.*
Stéphanie **a** présenté Mark à ses parents.	*Stéphanie introduced Mark to her parents.*
Nous **avons** rendu visite aux Lemaire en France.	*We visited the Lemaires in France.*

2 To speak about the past, you will need to know the past participle of each verb. In earlier Units you learned a number of infinitives – the basic form of the verb – such as **donner, finir, vendre**. The past participle is formed from the infinitive:

donner	Il a **donné** un cadeau à sa mère.	*He gave his mother a gift.*
finir	Nous avons **fini** de dîner.	*We've finished eating.*
vendre	Vous avez **vendu** votre maison.	*You've sold your house.*

Check the irregular verbs you learned in Units 1, 5, 6, 8, 11, and those you have in your notebook. Sometimes the past participle of these verbs is irregular too:	pouvoir → **pu** vouloir → **voulu** savoir → **su** dire → **dit**

3 A small number of verbs do not use the present tense of **avoir**, but of **être**, to form the perfect tense. You have learned the present tense of **être** (Unit 1 **Résumé grammatical** 2), so you will easily recognise it when you find it as part of the perfect tense:

Nicolas **est** sorti à 20 heures.	*Nicolas went out at 8 o'clock.*
Il **est** allé voir son copain Pierre.	*He went to see his friend Peter.*
Ils **sont** montés dans la chambre de Pierre.	*They went up to Peter's room.*

4 In many ways past participles function as adjectives and follow the same rules for agreement.

■ If they are used with a noun, they agree with it in number and gender:

un rendez-vouz manqué (m. sing.)	*a missed meeting*
une lettre tapée (fem. sing.)	*a typed letter*
des bureaux partagés (m. plural)	*shared offices*
des réunions chargées (fem. plural)	*packed meetings*

■ If past participles are used with **avoir** or **être** to form the perfect tense, there are rules about agreement as these examples show:

J'ai rencontré votre secrétaire. Je l'ai rencontrée la semaine dernière. Elle s'est excusée et nous avons parlé du problème.	*I met your secretary. I met her last week. She apologised and we talked about the problem.*

You will gradually learn more about agreement of past participles.

5 In Unit 6 **Résumé grammatical *1*,** you saw how the present tense of **aller** + infinitive can be used to show that something is going to happen in the immediate future. In a similar way, the present tense of **venir** + **de** + an infinitive can be used to describe something in the immediate past – something which *has just* happened. (You learned the present tense of **venir** in Unit 6 **Résumé grammatical *2*.**)

Nicolas **vient de** rentrer. Il est 23 heures.	*Nicolas has just come in. It is 11 o'clock.*
Georges **vient de** se réveiller. Il n'est pas content. Isabelle **vient de** se coucher.	*Georges has just woken up. He isn't happy. Isabelle has just gone to bed.*
Ils **viennent de** se rendre compte que Nicolas grandit.	*They have just realised that Nicolas is growing up.*

6 In Unit 11, **Résumé grammatical *4*,** you met a set of time prepositions which are used to talk about the future. Similarly, there are prepositions – some of them the same – which are frequently used in speaking about the past:

Après le déjeuner, j'ai pris le bus pour aller en ville.	*After lunch, I got the bus to go to town.*
Avant le commencement du film, j'ai acheté des bonbons.	*Before the film started, I bought some sweets.*
Pendant le film, je me suis endormi.	*During the film, I went to sleep.*

7 Just as there are time expressions which are associated with the future (Unit 11 **Résumé grammatical 4**), there are time expressions which you will find useful for speaking about the past:

Nicolas? Je l'ai vu **hier**. Il m'a téléphoné **avant-hier** et **hier soir** je l'ai vu au cinéma.

La **semaine dernière** je l'ai rencontré en ville et nous sommes allés au parc.

Nicolas? I saw him yesterday. He phoned me the day before yesterday and last night I saw him at the cinema.
Last week I met him in town and we went to the park.

Comment dit-on?

1   Past events

Les Lemaire **ont décidé** d'aller accueillir les Dickson à l'aéroport.

L'avion **a atterri!** ... Les voilà! Dis donc! Ils **ont apporté** beaucoup de bagages! ... Comment allez-vous?
Avez-vous **fait** bon voyage?
Très bien, merci. Nous **n'avons pas eu** trop de problèmes.
Vous **êtes arrivés** à l'heure. Nous **avons laissé** la voiture dans le parking, car souvent l'avion est en retard.

The Lemaires decided to go and meet the Dicksons at the airport.

The plane has landed! ... There they are! Goodness! They've brought a lot of luggage! ... How are you?
Did you have a good trip?
Fine, thank you. We didn't have too many problems.
You arrived on time. We've left the car in the car park, because the plane is often late.

2   A series of events in the past

Avant le départ de l'avion, nous **avons pris** un café. Ensuite, nous **avons suivi** les indications pour la salle de départ.
Là nous **avons attendu** quelques minutes, et finalement ils **ont annoncé** le départ de l'avion.

Before the plane left, we had a coffee. Then we followed the signs to the departure lounge.
We waited there a few minutes, and finally they announced the departure of the flight.

3   Events that took place over a period of time

Le voyage **a demandé** beaucoup de préparation. Entre décembre et mars je **suis allée** plusieurs fois à l'agence de voyage. **J'ai téléphoné** souvent aussi. Mon mari **s'est occupé** de l'argent.	*The trip needed a lot of preparation. Between December and March I went to the travel agency several times. I phoned often as well. My husband looked after the money.*
Il **a** d'abord **commandé** des travellers, mais quand on lui **a expliqué** comment fonctionne la carte Cirrus, il **a décidé** de n'acheter ni travellers, ni devises.	*First he ordered some travellers' cheques, but when they explained how the Cirrus card works, he decided not to buy either travellers' cheques or currency.*

4   Events in the recent past

Le vol a été assez intéressant ... L'avion **vient de** décoller, quand un passager **se lève, sort** un pistolet, et **commence** à menacer l'hôtesse.	*The flight was quite interesting ... The plane has just taken off, when a passenger gets up, gets out a gun, and starts threatening the stewardess.*

Résumé grammatical

1   The past participle

The past participle is used as part of the **perfect tense** in both French and English. Examples in English are   I have **given**
they have **brought**
it has **landed**
we have **waited**.

a) Regular verbs and the past participle

For all regular French verbs, and for some irregular verbs such as **aller** (*to go*), **sortir** (*to go out*), **partir** (*to leave*), the past participle is formed from the infinitive, the part of the verb that ends in **-er**, **-ir**, **-re**:

apporter	*to bring*	→	**apporté**	*brought*
atterrir	*to land*	→	**atterri**	*landed*
attendre	*to wait*	→	**attendu**	*waited*

See also Unit 10, **Pour aller plus loin 2b**.

b) Irregular verbs and the past participle

For irregular verbs, you will have to learn the past participles, just as you learned them for irregular verbs in English: **gone, hung, ate**.

You should keep a list of irregular past participles in your notebook. Here are some of the most common, to add to those you have already noted in **Avant de commencer** above. You will find a more complete list of irregular verbs at the back of the book.

As you have seen (**4** above), there are rules about the agreement of past participles with subjects or objects. Some of the rules for agreement are given in **Pour aller plus loin 1**.

Infinitive		Past participle
avoir	to have	eu
écrire	to write	écrit
faire	to make/do	fait
mettre	to put	mis
prendre	to take	pris
suivre	to follow	suivi
venir	to come	venu
voir	to see	vu

2   The perfect tense with avoir (le passé composé)

Look back at **Comment dit-on?** The verbs in the perfect tense are in bold.

a) The perfect tense is used to speak about events that happened in the past. It is a **compound tense**, i.e. it is composed of more than one verb: the present tense of **avoir** (the **auxiliary verb**) and the past participle of a second verb (the **main verb**).

Most verbs in French form the perfect tense using the appropriate part of the present tense of **avoir** (Unit 1 **Résumé grammatical 2**) and the past participle.

Since you can already use the present tense of **avoir**, the formation of the perfect tense is not difficult:

J'**ai** acheté les billets.	*I have bought the tickets.*
Tu **as** préparé les valises.	*You did the packing.*
Elle **a** envoyé une lettre.	*She has sent a letter.*
Nous **avons** fini les préparatifs.	*We've finished the preparations.*
Vous **avez** choisi quelle agence de voyage?	*Which travel agency did you choose?*

Ils **ont** attendu l'arrivée de l'avion.   *They waited for the arrival of the plane.*

Now look again at the examples in **Avant de commencer 1** and **2** and **Comment dit-on?** *1* and *2*.

b) If you are using this tense in the **negative**, you put **ne** after the subject and **pas** after the auxiliary verb (the present tense of **avoir**):

Mon mari **n'**a **pas** acheté les billets.   *My husband hasn't bought the tickets.*

Nous **n'**avons **pas** téléphoné à   *We didn't ring Stéphanie.*
Stéphanie.

c) To ask more formal questions with inversion, reverse the order of the subject and the auxiliary verb (**avoir**):

As-tu envoyé la lettre?   *Did you send the letter?*

Pourquoi **ont-ils** attendu l'arrivée   *Why did they wait for the plane*
de l'avion?   *to arrive?*

3   *The perfect tense with* être

There are two groups of verbs which *do not* use **avoir** to form the perfect tense.

a) A group of verbs which express a change of state or movement

aller	**venir**	je suis allé(e)
arriver	**partir**	elle est arrivée
entrer	**sortir**	elle est descendue
monter	**descendre**	tu es entré(e)
naître	**mourir**	on est monté
tomber	**rester**	ils sont morts
		ils sont nés
		il est parti
		vous êtes resté(e)s
		tu es sorti(e)
		nous sommes tombé(e)s
		elle est venue

The negative and question forms are the same as those shown above for **avoir**:

Nicolas, **tu n'es pas arrivé** à l'heure.
    Nicolas, you didn't arrive on time.

Est-elle arrivée avec ses parents?
    Did she arrive with her parents?

b) Reflexive verbs

(See Unit 3 **Résumé grammatical 2.**)

All reflexive verbs form the perfect tense with **être**:

s'habiller	*to get dressed*	ils se sont habillés
se lever	*to get up*	nous nous sommes levé(e)s
se promener	*to go for a walk*	je me suis promené(e)

The negative and question forms of these verbs are formed in the same way as for the other verbs, but because of the reflexive pronoun object, they look different:

Nous **ne nous sommes pas levés** pour le déjeuner.
    We didn't get up for breakfast.

Se sont-ils habillés chaudement avant de sortir?
    Did they dress warmly before going out?

c) Agreements

As you can see from these examples, and from those in **Avant de commencer**, when the perfect tense is formed with **être** as the auxiliary verb, the past participle agrees in *number* and in *gender* with the *subject*. Check the examples above, and in **En contexte**, for this new type of agreement.

d) Both avoir and être form the perfect tense with avoir:

Isabelle n'**a** pas **eu** le temps de nettoyer la cuisine.
    Isabelle did not have time to clean the kitchen.

Patrick **a été** surpris quand Alison a commencé à parler français.
    Patrick was surprised when Alison started to speak French.

e) The position of adverbs with the perfect tense

Short adverbs can go between the auxiliary verb and the past participle:

Ils l'ont **vite** fait.	*They did it quickly.*
Il a **rarement** voyagé.	*He has seldom travelled.*
Il a **vraiment** été surpris.	*He was really surprised.*

Longer adverbs (Unit 6 **Résumé grammatical** *4*) normally go after the past participle:

Ils ont préparé leur voyage **méticuleusement.**	*They prepared their trip carefully.*
Ils ont appris les bases de la grammaire française **remarquablement vite.**	*They have learnt the basics of French grammar remarkably quickly.*

4 The immediate past: **venir de**

The present tense of **venir** (Unit 6 **Résumé grammatical** *2*) followed by **de** and an infinitive is used to say that something has just happened or has just been done:

Je **viens de descendre** de l'avion.	*I've just got off the plane.*
Nous **venons de rencontrer** les Lemaire.	*We have just met the Lemaires.*
Georges et Isabelle **viennent de** nous **accueillir.**	*Georges and Isabelle have just greeted us.*

Look back at **Comment dit-on** *4* for another example.

5 Other time expressions

To say when you did something in the past, you need to be able to use expressions to show when you did it. See Unit 10 **Résumé grammatical** *1*:

avant-hier *the day before yesterday*	**hier** *yesterday* **hier matin** *yesterday morning* **hier soir** *yesterday evening*	**aujourd'hui** *today*

Hier matin nous sommes allés à Lille.	*Yesterday morning we went to Lille.*

En contexte

In this conversation, identify the **verbs in the perfect tense** (with both **avoir** and **être**). Make a list of the **past participles** and add any that are new to yo to your list.

Isabelle raconte à une amie, Chloé, l'arrivée des Dickson à l'aéroport.

Isabelle Nous avons essayé d'apprendre un peu d'anglais. Heureusement que les Dickson ont appris le français avant d'arriver.

Chloé Est-ce qu'ils ont parlé français tout de suite?

Isabelle Non. Ils ont commencé par quelques mots en anglais, mais après, ils se sont souvenus de leurs cours de français.

Chloé Mais qu'est-ce que tu as fait? Vous ne vous êtes pas sentis un peu gênés?

Isabelle Si, Si. J'ai trouvé la situation très difficile. Des gens qu'on n'a jamais rencontrés, et des étrangers en plus. Et il ne faut pas oublier que Stéphanie a beaucoup insisté sur l'importance de cette visite! Quand ils sont descendus de l'avion, j'ai eu peur.

Chloé Je t'admire vraiment! Je n'ai jamais pu parler avec des gens que je ne connais pas, et comme je n'ai jamais appris l'anglais ...

Isabelle Le commencement n'a pas été facile. Mais avec de la bonne volonté on a réussi à communiquer. Ce sont peut-être les futurs beaux-parents de notre fille, après tout. Et ils ont été charmants avec elle. Ils l'ont accueillie chez eux et Alison, surtout, l'a beaucoup aidée. Nous nous sommes bien entendus finalement.

Pour vérifier

1 Imagine that you are Georges Lemaire. Write five sentences about what happened when you went to meet the Dicksons at the airport. (You will find some suggestions in **En contexte**.)

2 Fill in the appropriate auxiliary verb (**avoir** or **être**) in the following sentences:

Quel voyage! D'abord le taxi n'_____ pas arrivé à l'heure. Nous _____ téléphoné à la compagnie et ils _____ envoyé un autre taxi, mais nous _____ arrivés à la gare deux minutes avant le départ du train. Nous _____ couru et nous _____ attrapé le train de justesse. Avec des valises très lourdes et tous les paquets des enfants, nous _____ eu du mal à trouver des places. Finalement, nous nous _____ assis dans un wagon fumeurs. Naturellement ça m'_____ donné la migraine!

3 Write answers to the following questions:

Q Vous êtes parti(e)s en vacances cette année?	A Oui, nous...
Q Où êtes-vous allé(e)?	A Nous...
Q Qu'est-ce que vous avez vu?	A Nous...
Q Tu as acheté des souvenirs?	A Non, je...
Q Et ta soeur, elle en a acheté?	A Bien sûr que oui! Elle...

Pour aller plus loin

1   *Agreement of the past participle*

When the perfect tense is formed with **avoir**, the past participle agrees with the *direct object* if the object *comes before* the verb:

J'ai acheté les billets.	(Direct object = **les billets**. No agreement – it *follows* the verb.)
Je **les** ai achetés.	(Direct object = **les**, replacing **les billets**. It comes *before* the verb, so the past participle agrees.)

Où sont les valises? (fem. plural)	*Where are the cases?*
Mark les a mis**es** dans la voiture.	*Mark put them in the car.*
Et les passeports? (masc. plural)	*And what about the passports?*
Tu ne les as pas perdus, j'espère!	*You haven't lost them, I hope!*
Mais non! Quelle idée! Je les ai fourrés dans mon sac avec toutes les choses que nous avons préparé**es** pour le voyage.	*Of course not! What an idea! I shoved them in my handbag with all the other things we got ready for the trip.*

2   *Use of* **il y a** *(ago)*

To say how long ago something happened, you can use **il y a** (*ago*).

Ils sont arrivés **il y a** huit jours.	*They arrived a week ago.*
Nous sommes allés à Lille **il y a** cinq jours.	*We went to Lille five days ago*
Stéphanie a téléphoné **il y a** trois heures.	*Stephanie phoned three hours ago.*

14 | PAST HABITS AND ACTIVITIES

Thèmes   Souvenirs; Souvenirs d'enfance

Memories of earlier times; life and work before and after the children were born

The children talk about their childhood

In this Unit you will learn to:

1 Talk and write about past habits / things you used to do regularly
2 Discuss situations in the past which lasted for some time
3 Discuss single events in the past seen against a background
4 Say how often you did things, or how frequently things were done

Structures grammaticales

1 The imperfect tense (**l'imparfait**)
2 Time expressions used with the imperfect
3 Using the perfect and the imperfect together

Pour aller plus loin

1 Other time expressions used with the imperfect
2 More about the perfect and the imperfect used together
3 The use of the imperfect in direct and indirect (reported) speech

Avant de commencer

1   In Unit 13, you learned how to use the perfect tense. French has another
    past tense – the imperfect (**l'imparfait**) which is used to express other
    aspects of the past:

Quand il **était** jeune, Patrick   *When he was young, Patrick*
travaillait à Londres. Tous les   *worked in London. Every day he*
jours il **prenait** le métro.   *took the tube.*

2   The imperfect is used with some of the same time expressions as the
    perfect tense (Unit 13 **Résumé grammatical 5**). There are other time
    expressions which show that something was done frequently (**tous les
    week-ends**) or that a situation in the past lasted some time (**pendant
    cette**). The imperfect is the correct tense to use after these expressions:

Avant son mariage, Patrick ne   *Before he got married, Patrick*
s'intéressait pas au bricolage.   *wasn't interested in DIY. During*
Pendant cette période, il habitait un *that time, he lived in a horrible little*
petit appartement désagréable.   *flat. Every weekend he played*
Tous les weekends il faisait du   *sport. A that time he went out*
sport. **A cette époque-là**, il sortait   *a lot and on Saturdays, he*
beaucoup et **le samedi** il allait   *always went to the football match.*
toujours au match de foot.

3   Sometimes when you are speaking about the past, you have to choose
    whether to use the perfect or the imperfect, depending on what kind of
    past event you want to speak about. For single events (**s'est marié, est
    né, a cessé**) use the perfect (Unit 13 **Résumé grammatical 1, 2, 3**). For
    something that happened frequently (**il voyageait**) use the imperfect:

Patrick s'**est marié** avec Alison en   *Patrick got married to Alison in*
1970. Au début, il **voyageait**   *1970. At first, he used to travel a*
beaucoup, mais, quand Mark **est**   *lot, but, when Mark was born,*
né, il **a cessé** de voyager.   *he stopped travelling.*

4   When you are talking about the past, you use the imperfect for things
    which happened often. There are a number of time expressions you can
    use to show how frequently something happened:

Tous les jours Patrick allait à son   *Every day Patrick went to work.*

travail. **Le samedi**, il allait au match *On Saturdays, he went to the*
de foot. **Deux fois par mois**, il *football match. Twice a month,*
emmenait Mark et Alison au zoo. *he took Alison and Mark to the*
Une fois par an, ils prenaient des *zoo. Once a year they went on*
vacances. *holiday.*

Comment dit-on?

In the following passages, you will find examples of when to use the
structures in **Avant de commencer**. Note particularly the time
expressions that are followed by the imperfect.

1 Past habits / things you used to do regularly

Après la naisssance de Nicolas, *After Nicolas was born, we didn't*
nous **n'allions** plus au cinéma. *go to the cinema any more. On*
Le samedi, nous **prenions** le bus *Saturdays we used to get the bus*
pour aller chez mes parents et **le** *to go to my parents' place and*
dimanche nous nous **promenions** *on Sundays we went for a walk*
dans le parc près de chez nous. **Le** *in the park near our house. On*
vendredi soir, mes parents *Friday evenings, my parents*
gardaient Nicolas, et Georges et *looked after Nicolas, and Georges*
moi, nous **faisions** les courses. *and I did the shopping.*

2 Situations in the past which lasted for some time

Je me souviens des années 70. *I remember the seventies. We*
Nous n'**avions** pas beaucoup *didn't have much money but we*
d'argent mais nous **étions** fous de *were mad on rock music. It*
musique rock. Il n'**était** pas facile *wasn't easy to buy the records*
d'acheter les disques que nous *we wanted in St Amand and we*
voulions à St Amand, et nous ne *couldn't go to Lille every*
pouvions pas aller tous les *weekend.*
weekends à Lille.

3 Single events in the past seen against a background

Oui, la vie n'**était** pas facile à cette époque-là, et comme nous **voulions** acheter une voiture, il **fallait** faire des économies. Quand nous nous **sommes mariés**, mes parents nous **ont donné** de l'argent et c'est cet argent qui nous **a permis** d'acheter notre première maison.

Yes, life wasn't easy then, and as we wanted to buy a car, we had to save money. When we got married, my parents gave us some money and it was that money that made it possible for us to buy our first house.

4 Talking about how often you did things

Vous vous souvenez? Nous allions **tous les ans** à St Omer. Oui, c'était **chaque année**, en août, pendant les vacances scolaires. Il faisait beau **tous les jours** et **le matin**, nous allions nous promener sur la plage de bonne heure. Après, nous allions toujours nous baigner **plusieurs fois par jour. Une fois par semaine** il y avait un vieux film au cinéma. C'était **toujours** débile, mais on y allait quand même.

Do you remember? We used to go to St Omer every year. Yes, every year, in August, during the school holidays. The weather was good every day and in the morning we used to go for a walk on the beach early. Afterwards, we always went for a swim several times a day. Once a week there would be an old film at the cinema. It was always pathetic, but we used to go just the same.

Résumé grammatical

1 The imperfect tense (l'imparfait)

The imperfect tense of the verb is a single word, formed from a **stem**. You form the stem by taking the **vous** form (the second person plural) of the present tense (Unit 1). You take off the **-ez** ending:

	infinitive	vous form		stem
	avoir	vous avez	→	av-
	parler	vous parlez	→	**parl-**
	finir	vous finissez	→	**finiss-**
	prendre	vous prenez	→	**pren-**
Exception:	être		→	**ét-**

To the stem, you add the following endings:

-ais, -ais, -ait, -ions, -iez, -aient:

Quand nous étions petits:	*When we were little:*
Je te **détestais**.	*I hated you.*
Tu ne **cessais** pas de pleurer.	*You wouldn't stop crying.*
Notre père (il) t'**aimait** mieux que moi.	*Our father liked you better than me.*
Maman (elle) te **donnait** tout ce que tu voulais.	*Mum gave you everything you wanted.*
Toi et Papa (vous) **étiez** toujours ensemble.	*You and dad (you) were always together.*
Maman et moi (nous) **faisions** souvent la cuisine.	*Mum and I (we) were always doing the cooking.*
Nos parents (ils) ne **savaient** pas que tu me **battais**.	*Our parents didn't know that you used to hit me.*

The imperfect is used for:

- repeated actions or habits in the past

Tu me **battais tous les jours**.	*You used to hit me every day.*
Je me plaignais **souvent** à nos parents.	*I often used to complain to our parents.*

- situations which lasted a long time, or an indefinite time, in the past:

Nous **partagions** une chambre.	*We used to share a room.*
Nos parents n'avaient pas beaucoup d'argent.	*Our parents didn't have much money.*

Look back at **Comment dit-on?** and decide why the imperfect was used in each case.

2   Time expressions with the imperfect

a) Since this tense is used for things which were done frequently in the past, it is found with time expressions showing how often things were done:

souvent	*often*	**le samedi**	*every Saturday / on Saturdays*
fréquemment	*frequently*		
tous les jours	*every day*	**deux fois**	*twice a day*
tous les mois	*every month*	**par jour**	
tous les ans	*every year*	**cinq fois**	*five times a term*
		par trimestre	

Le samedi nous allions au cinéma.	On Saturdays, we used to go to the cinema.
J'allais **souvent** voir mes parents.	I often went to see my parents.
Tous les jours Patrick allait à son travail.	Every day Patrick went to work.
Il fallait passer un contrôle continu **deux fois par trimestre.**	There was continuous assessment twice a term.

b) The imperfect is also used with time expressions which refer to long periods or situations which lasted a long or indefinite time in the past. Look for some of these in **Comment dit-on?**

à cette époque	*at that time*
avant cet événement	*before that happened*
pendant cette période	*during that time*

A cette époque, nous étions plutôt pauvres.	*At that time, we were rather poor.*
Avant la naissance de ma soeur, mes parents pouvaient continuer à jouer au golf.	Before my sister was born, my parents could still play golf.
Tout le monde portait des vêtements bizarres **pendant les années 70.**	*Everyone wore weird clothes in the seventies.*

3 Using the imperfect and the perfect together

Both the perfect and the imperfect are used when talking about past time. Often you will need to make a choice between the two tenses. In the examples in **Avant de commencer 3** and in **En contexte**, you will find the two tenses used together.

Sometimes the imperfect is used to set the scene in the past, while the perfect is used for a single action or a series of actions (**Comment dit-on? 3, En contexte**):

| Oui! Je me souviens! Tu **étais** horrible. Tu **pleurais** tout le temps et Maman s'**occupait** de toi toute la journée. Je te **détestais.** Puis Andrew **est né** et tout **a changé.** | *Yes, I remember! You were awful. You cried all the time and Mum looked after you the whole day long. I hated you. Then Andrew was born and everything changed.* |

Je n'**étais** pas horrible! Tu ne **voulais** pas jouer avec moi et tu **prenais** tous mes jouets. Quand tu **as commencé** à l'école, tu **as cessé** de m'embêter.	*I was not awful! You didn't want to play with me and you used to take all my toys. When you went to school, you stopped bothering me.*

See also **Pour aller plus loin 2**.

En contexte

Make a list of all the **verbs in the imperfect** and another one of the **verbs in the perfect**. Can you explain why each one was chosen?

Isabelle parle à Alison de la jeunesse de Stéphanie

Isabelle Elle était très calme quand elle était petite et elle a appris à parler et à marcher plus tôt que Nicolas. Elle avait trois ans quand elle est allée à l'école maternelle et elle ne l'aimait pas beaucoup. Même très petite, elle chantait toujours juste et je n'ai pas été surprise quand, plus tard, elle a décidé de chanter avec la chorale *Les Quatre Vents*. Avant d'aller en Écosse, elle chantait avec la chorale deux fois par semaine.

Tous les enfants font des dessins à l'école, mais, pour Stéphanie, le dessin était très important. Elle adorait les couleurs vives et pour son anniversaire et à Noël elle demandait toujours des crayons ou des couleurs pour aquarelle. Et elle aimait beaucoup les musées d'art. On allait assez souvent voir des expositions, au moins deux ou trois fois par an. Je me souviens d'une exposition des impressionnistes à Paris, quand elle avait 12 ans. Elle a tant insisté que je suis allée à Paris avec elle, et nous avons vu l'exposition trois fois!

Pour vérifier

1 Using the verbs in the imperfect below, write five or six sentences about your childhood (real or imagined).

Nous habitions...
J'aimais...
Je n'aimais pas...
Mon père était...

Nous n'avions pas de...

Mes frères et mes soeurs étaient...

Ce qui nous amusait, c'était...

2 In the following paragraph, Nicolas is speaking about his memories of childhood. Identify the two time expressions which should be followed by the imperfect and the two usually followed by the perfect. Fill in the blanks with the appropriate tense (imperfect or perfect). See **Résumé grammatical 3**.

Nicolas: Tu te souviens, Stéphanie? Moi, j'(**être**) toujours plus petit que toi et pendant mon enfance, j'(**avoir**) honte, parce que ma soeur (**être**) plus grande que moi. Et puis, un jour, je (**remarquer**) que je (**mesurer**) quelques centimètres de plus que toi. Ce jour-là, je (**faire**) la fête!

Pour aller plus loin

1 Other time expressions used with the imperfect

- de (date) à (date)   *from* (date) *to* (date)

De 1990 à 1994, Stéphanie allait au collège.   *From 1990 to 1994, Stéphanie was at college.*

- entre (date) et (date)   *between* (date) *and* (date)

Nicolas était membre d'un club cinéma **entre septembre 1995 et juin 1996.**   *Nicolas was a member of a film club between September 1995 and June 1996.*

2 More about the perfect and the imperfect used together

See above, **Résumé grammatical 3**.

To say what the situation was, or what was going on, when something else happened, you use the imperfect for the background situation and the perfect for a single event:

Quand Stéphanie **est allée** à Aberdeen, elle **avait** 20 ans.   *When Stephanie went to Aberdeen, she was 20.*

Je lui **ai offert** de l'argent, parce qu'elle **était** sans le sou.   *I gave her some money because she didn't have a penny.*

Nous lui **avons ouvert** un compte en banque, car elle ne **savait** pas organiser ses finances.	*We opened a bank account for her, because she didn't know how to organise her money.*
Un soir, elle **a téléphoné** pendant que j'**étais** absente. Elle **voulait** me raconter ses problèmes. Elle **a rappelé** plus tard.	*One evening, she phoned while I was out. She wanted to talk to me about her problems. She phoned back later.*

3 The imperfect in direct and indirect (reported) speech

Notice how the tenses change when direct speech (the actual words spoken by the person) is reported and becomes indirect speech:

	Direct speech	**Indirect speech**
Georges	J'aime beaucoup le ball-trap mais je déteste l'équitation.	Georges a dit qu'il **aimait** beaucoup le ball-trap mais qu'il **détestait** l'équitation.
	'I like clay pigeon shooting very much but I hate horse-riding.	*Georges said that he liked clay pigeon shooting very much but (that) he hated horse-riding.*
Nicolas	Tous les soirs je m'amuse avec mon ordinateur. J'ai des amis partout dans le monde et on corrrespond par courrier électronique.	Nicolas m'a assuré qu'il **s'amusait** avec son ordinateur tous les soirs. Il a expliqué qu'il **avait** des amis partout dans le monde, et qu'ils **correspondaient** par courrier électronique.
	'Every evening I play with my computer. I have friends all over the world and we correspond by E-mail.'	*Nicolas told me that he played with his computer every evening. He explained that he had friends all over the world and that they corresponded by E-mail.*

15 GOING BACK IN THE PAST

Thèmes   L'informatique; Le voyage

Georges and Nicolas talk about computers
Alison writes home about their trip to France
The Dicksons visit the north of France

In this Unit you will learn to:

1 Relate various past events to one another
2 Say that something happened before or after something else
3 Write an account of past actions and events
4 Say that something was done by someone else

Structures grammaticales

1 The pluperfect tense (**le plus-que-parfait**)
2 Conjunctions of time
3 Complex sentences
4 The perfect passive

Pour aller plus loin

1 Other ways of expressing the passive
2 Saying how long something has been going on
3 Using the perfect infinitive
4 The infinitive after **avant de** (*before*)

Avant de commencer

1 If you want to go further back in time than the immediate past, you need to be able to use the pluperfect tense (**le plus-que-parfait**). This works just like the similar tense in English where we use the auxiliary verb *had*:

Before I began to learn French, I **had** already **learned** Spanish.

To form this tense, you will need to use the imperfect of **avoir** (Unit 14 **Résumé grammatical 1**) and use the appropriate past participles (Unit 13, **Résumé grammatical 1**).

Mon père m'**avait acheté** un ordinateur avant le développement de l'Internet. Je l'**avais utilisé** pour des jeux mais ensuite nous avons acheté la connexion Internet et maintenant, les jeux ne m'intéressent plus.

My father had bought me a computer before the expansion of the Internet. I had used it for games but then we bought the Internet connection and now, games don't interest me any more.

2 To use longer sentences explaining when one event happened in relation to another, and if you want to write more formal French, you will find there are a number of useful words which join parts of a sentence together. In Unit 10 (**Résumé grammatical 4**) you learned some conjunctions expressing cause and effect. Here you will learn some you can use in time sequences.

Nicolas et moi, nous avons décidé d'acheter la connexion Internet **après que** son professeur en avait parlé. Le soir, Nicolas envoyait des messages électroniques **pendant que** moi, je regardais la télé. Il est vite devenu expert et demande maintenant un nouvel ordinateur.

Nicolas and I decided to buy the Internet connection after his teacher had spoken about it. Nicolas used to send E-mails while I was watching TV. He quickly became an expert and now he's asking for a new computer.

3 You have already met the present passive in Unit 10, **Pour aller plus loin 2**. In this Unit, you will learn how to use the passive form when you are speaking about the past, to say that something *was done by someone*.

| L'ordinateur **a été acheté** par Georges pour Nicolas et à Noël, beaucoup de jeux informatisés lui **ont été offerts.** Les logiciels de base ont été développés par Microsoft. | *The computer was bought for Nicolas by Georges and at Christmas, he was given lots of computer games. The basic software was developed by Microsoft.* |

Comment dit-on?

1 Relating various past events to one another

| **Isabelle** L'année où nous sommes allés en Belgique – c'était en été 1996? Non, c'était avant. Nicolas **avait gagné** le prix au club cinéma en mars 1995 et c'est cette année-là que nous y sommes allés. | *The year we went to Belgium - was that in summer 1996? No, it was before. Nicolas had won the prize at the film club in March 1995 and that's the year we went.* |
| **Georges** Non. C'était l'année après, 1996, qu'il a gagné le prix et il a décidé d'aller à Paris pour visiter les studios de France 2. La Belgique, c'était donc en 1995. | *No. It was the year after, 1996, that he won the prize and he decided to go to Paris to visit the France 2 studios. So Belgium was in 1995.* |

2 Something happened before or after something else

| **Isabelle** Je me souviens d'un concert de la chorale de Stéphanie, *les Quatre Vents*, à Lille. Nous **avions réservé** une chambre à l'hôtel bien avant la date du concert. **Puis** ils ont changé la date. | *I remember a concert given by Stéphanie's choir, les Quatre Vents, in Lille. We had reserved a hotel room well before the date of the concert. Then they changed the date.* |
| **Georges** Non, tu n'**avais pas réservé** la chambre avant l'annonce de la nouvelle date! Tu **avais fait** la réservation au restaurant **d'abord**. **Ensuite**, ils ont annoncé le changement de date et nous avons eu du mal à trouver une chambre d'hôtel. | *No, you hadn't booked the hotel room before the new date was announced! You had made the restaurant booking first. Then they announced the change of date and we had trouble finding a hotel room.* |

3 Writing about past actions and events

Devoir d'Alison pour la classe de français – *Notre Visite en France*
(*Alison's homework for her French class* – Our Trip to France)

En septembre nous **avions décidé**   *In September we had decided to*
d'aller visiter les Lemaire en France. *visit the Lemaires in France. So I*
J'ai donc écrit à Isabelle Lemaire   *wrote to Isabelle Lemaire to ask*
pour lui demander de nous suggérer   *her to suggest some dates. We*
des dates. Nous **avions commencé**   *had started our French classes*
nos cours de français en octobre et   *in October and at the New*
au Nouvel An, nous **avions**   *Year, we had started to make*
commencé à préparer le voyage.   *preparations for the trip. At*
Au commencement du mois de   *the beginning of February I*
février j'ai écrit encore une fois à   *wrote again to Isabelle*
Isabelle Lemaire pour lui confirmer   *Lemaire to confirm the dates*
les dates de notre visite.   *of our visit.*

4 Something was done by someone else

Les cours de français **ont été**   *The French classes were*
organisés par le conseil de la ville. *organised by the town council. A*
Une salle **a été réservée** au lycée   *room was booked in the*
et les manuels et les dictionnaires   *secondary school and the textbooks*
français-anglais **ont été achetés**   *and the French-English*
par le professeur.   *dictionaries were bought by*
                                         the teacher.

Résumé grammatical

1   The pluperfect tense (le plus-que-parfait)

This is the tense of the verb you use to say that something **had** already happened before another event in the past, or to say that you **had** already done one thing before you did something else.

Like the perfect (Unit 13, **Résumé grammatical *1, 2, 3***), it is made up of two words, an auxiliary verb (**avoir** or **être**) and a past participle:

■   the auxiliary verb is in the imperfect (Unit 14, **Résumé grammatical *1***)

avoir	→	**j'avais** (+ past participle)
être	→	**j'étais** (+ past participle)

■ the past participles are the same as the ones you learned so that you could form the perfect (Unit 13 **Résumé grammatical *1***).

Avant d'aller en France:

J'	**avais écrit**	à Isabelle Lemaire.
Tu	**avais fait**	des économies.
Il (Georges)	**avait essayé**	d'apprendre l'anglais.
Nous	**avions appris**	le français.
Vous (G & I)	**aviez préparé**	votre itinéraire.
Ils (les enfants)	**avaient promis**	d'être sages.

2 Conjunctions of time

Some of the most useful conjunctions of time	
quand	*when*
après que	*after*
pendant que	*when/while*
puis/ensuite	*then*

In order to be able to tell a story, or speak or write about a number of past events, you need to use linking words called **conjunctions**. See also Unit 10 **Résumé grammatical *4***. These words allow you to situate the different happenings in relation to one another.

Quand Mark nous a parlé de Stéphanie, nous avons compris que c'était sérieux.

When Mark spoke to us about Stéphanie, we realised that it was serious.

Après que nous avons décidé de visiter les Lemaire, nous avons commencé à apprendre le français.

After we had decided to visit the Lemaires, we started to learn French.

Mark perfectionnait son français **pendant qu**'il parlait avec Stéphanie.

Mark was improving his French when he was talking to Stéphanie.

3 Complex sentences

When you are speaking or, more particularly if you are writing, about a series of events, you will need to be able to link different events and experiences together into longer sentences.

To do this, you use a variety of other conjunctions:

Simple link	Reason/ purpose	Time	Opposition
et *and*	**parce que** *because*	**après que** *after*	**mais** *but*
	car *because / for*	**pendant que** *while*	**pourtant** *however/ and yet*
	donc *thus*	**quand** *when*	**cependant** *however*

J'ai commencé à apprendre le français **et** Patrick veut l'apprendre aussi.

I started learning French and Patrick wants to learn too.

Nous avons acheté les cadeaux **après que** Stéphanie nous avait parlé de ses parents.

We bought the presents after Stéphanie had spoken to us about her parents.

La visite en France a été organisée **parce que** notre fils Mark a une partenaire française.

The trip to France was organised because our son Mark has a French partner.

Georges et Isabelle ne parlent pas anglais, **pourtant** nous avons réussi à communiquer avec eux.

Georges and Isabelle don't speak English, nevertheless we managed to communicate with them.

4 The perfect passive

In Unit 10 **Pour aller plus loin 2 b**, you learnt how to use the present passive (present tense of **être** + the past participle).

You will also need the passive to talk or write about past events. To do this, you use the perfect of **être**, followed by a past participle:

La visite en France **a été suggérée** par Mark.

The visit to France was suggested by Mark.

Les cours de français **ont été donnés** par un professeur du lycée.

The French classes were taken by a secondary teacher.

Les plans de St Amand et de sa région nous **ont été envoyés** par les Lemaire.

The maps of St Amand and the region were sent to us by the Lemaires.

En contexte

While you are reading this letter, make a note of the **verbs in the pluperfect tense** and the **conjunctions** or **linking words** Alison uses.

Alison écrit à son professeur de français en Écosse.

> *Cher Alain,*
>
> *Vous m'aviez demandé de vous écrire pendant notre séjour en France. J'avais donc commencé une lettre le jour de notre arrivée, mais nous avions trop de choses à faire et tout était si intéressant que je n'ai pas pu écrire plus tôt.*
>
> *Nous avions prévu de passer quelques jours chez les Lemaire et de visiter ensuite la région de St Amand. Plusieurs suggestions de choses à voir nous ont été offertes par Georges et Isabelle Lemaire, et nous allons maintenant quitter St Amand et visiter les sites des batailles de la première guerre mondiale dans le nord de la France. Nous irons ensuite à Paris.*
>
> *Pendant que Patrick parlait à Georges, Isabelle et moi avons bavardé de nos enfants, de sorte que je comprends mieux Stéphanie maintenant.*
>
> *Je n'y avais pas pensé, mais ma formation de professeur d'histoire et de géographie est très utile pour un voyage à l'étranger. Je me suis renseignée sur la situation géographique de St Amand et parce que j'ai lu plusieurs livres sur l'histoire de la France et de la première guerre mondiale, le nord de la France m'intéresse beaucoup.*
>
> *Nous vous remercions des excellents cours de français et nous espérons que vous passez des vacances très agréables. A bientôt!*
>
> *Avec notre meilleur souvenir,*
>
> *Alison Dickson*

Pour vérifier

1 In the following paragraph, the verbs are in bold. Re-write the paragraph one stage further back in the past, putting the verbs in the perfect tense into the pluperfect and the verbs in the present tense into the perfect:

Avant la première guerre mondiale, les Allemands **ont** bien **préparé** leurs armées, de sorte que les armées des alliés **perdent** des millions d'hommes dans des batailles dans le nord de la France. A Verdun, des millions de soldats **meurent** et les Allemands **traversent** facilement la ligne Maginot.

2 Using the conjunctions given, connect the sentences below into a single complex sentence:

a) Dans le nord de la France la terre est très plate.
Le paysage est quelquefois monotone.
Les villages sont agréables à voir.
Conjunctions: donc, mais

b) Les coquelicots poussent dans les champs de la Flandre.
On achète des coquelicots ce jour-là en Grande-Bretagne.
La guerre a cessé le 11 novembre.
On célèbre le jour de l'Armistice le 11 novembre.
Conjunctions: car, et, parce que

Pour aller plus loin

1 Other ways of expressing the passive

In French, the passive form of the verb (**être** + past participle) is used less often than in English. There are two other ways of expressing the passive (something being done to someone/something by someone/something else) in French:

a) using on as the subject of the sentence

On nous a priés de ne pas prendre de photos dans le musée.	*We were asked not to take photos in the museum.*
Quand nous avons visité les cimetières de guerre, **on** nous a expliqué la construction de la Ligne Maginot.	*When we visited the war cemeteries, the construction of the* Maginot Line *was explained to us.*

b) using a reflexive verb

Le guide a commencé par nous dire: «**Je m'appelle** Henri. Mon grand-père est mort à Verdun.»	*The guide began by saying: "I am called Henri. My grandfather died at Verdun"*

Le nombre de morts dans ces batailles **s'explique** par le manque de préparation des troupes alliées.	*The number killed in these battles is explained by the lack of preparation of the allied troops.*
Des livres d'histoire et des plans des sites intéressants **se vendent** en librairie.	*History books and maps of the interesting sites are sold in the bookshop.*

2 To say how long something had been going on

In French you use the word **depuis** (*since*, *for*), with the imperfect, to say that something *had been going on* for a certain time when something else happened:

J'attendais **depuis une heure** quand Stéphanie a enfin téléphoné.	*I had been waiting for an hour when Stéphanie finally phoned.*
Quand Nicolas est né, nous étions à St Amand **depuis** cinq ans.	*When Nicolas was born we had been in St Amand for five years.*

3 Using the perfect infinitive

To say that you did something after (**après**) something else, you can use **après** with a perfect infinitive. This is made up of the past participle of the main verb, with the infinitive form of **avoir** before it:

Après avoir quitté St Amand, nous avons visité le nord de la France.	*After leaving St Amand, we visited the north of France.*
Après avoir acheté un ordinateur, Georges a commencé à s'intéresser à l'Internet.	*After buying a computer, Georges started to get interested in the internet.*

4 The infinitive after avant de

You can use an infinitive after **avant de** to say something happened before something else:

Avant de quitter St Amand, nous avons remercié les Lemaire.	*Before leaving St Amand, we thanked the Lemaires.*
Georges s'est renseigné auprès d'un ami, **avant d'acheter** un ordinateur.	*Georges asked a friend for advice before buying a computer.*

16 | WISHING AND WANTING: PROBABILITY AND POSSIBILITY

Thème   Le tourisme

The Dicksons visit Paris

In this Unit you will learn to:

1 Talk about what you want and what you wish for
2 Envisage possibilities and probabilities
3 Construct longer and more complex sentences

Structures grammaticales

1 Using the subjunctive (**le subjonctif**)
2 Forming the present subjunctive: regular verbs
3 The subjunctive of irregular verbs
4 Verb 'signals' for the subjunctive
5 Other verb signals followed by the subjunctive: *wishing, wanting, fear, regret*
6 Impersonal expressions followed by the subjunctive: *necessity, importance, pity*
7 Relative pronouns **ce qui** and **ce que**

Pour aller plus loin

1 Probability and the subjunctive
2 Other verbs followed by the subjunctive
3 The subjunctive to express the future
4 **Lequel, laquelle** after the preposition **de**

Avant de commencer

1 There is another very useful form of the verb in French called the **subjunctive**. You have to use it in some common contexts. You will soon learn to recognise the most frequent of these:

Ma femme **veut que** nous **allions** à Paris, mais, avant d'y aller, **il faut que** nous **fassions** une réservation à l'hôtel.

My wife wants us to go to Paris, but before we go, we'll have to reserve a hotel room.

2 The subjunctive is used after certain expressions which function as 'signals'. Different signals are used to express wishes, to show doubt or approval and to give orders:

Les Lemaire **veulent que** nous passions la nuit à Arras.

The Lemaires want us to spend the night in Arras.

Ils **doutent que** nous trouvions un hôtel à Amiens.

They doubt we'll find a hotel in Amiens.

Ils **sont contents** que nous allions ensuite à Paris.

They are glad that we're going to to Paris afterwards.

Georges **insiste que** Patrick prenne la carte Michelin.

Georges insists that Patrick takes the Michelin map.

3 You have already learned a number of impersonal expressions in Unit 10, **Pour aller plus loin 2a**. In this Unit you will learn some to express probability and possibility:

Patrick n'a pas l'habitude de conduire en France. **Il est possible qu'**il ait des problèmes, mais **il est probable qu'**il s'y habituera facilement.

Patrick is not used to driving in France. It is possible that he will have some problems, but probably he will easily get used to it.

4 In Unit 11, **Résumé grammatical 5**, you met the relative pronouns **qui** and **que**. In this Unit, you will learn how to write more polished sentences using other relative pronouns:

Ce qui attire Alison, c'est surtout l'histoire de la Révolution française.

What interests Alison especially is the history of the French Revolution.

Patrick et Alison visiteront le musée Carnavalet **dont** la section sur la Révolution est très connue.	*Patrick and Alison will visit the Carnavalet Museum whose section on the French Revolution is well known.*
La Révolution est la période pendant **laquelle** les institutions politiques de la France moderne ont été créées.	*The Revolution is the period during which the political institutions of modern France were created.*

Comment dit-on?

1 What you want or wish for

Je veux que nous **visitions** le Musée Carnavalet et **j'aimerais que nous allions** aussi au Musée de l'Histoire de France. Patrick **souhaite** qu'on **ait** le temps de voir des stades de sport.	*I'd like us to visit the Carnavalet Museum and I'd like us to go to the Musée de l'Histoire de France too. Patrick hopes we have time to visit some sports stadiums.*

2 Envisaging possibilities

Avant d'arriver à Paris, **il est possible qu'**on **voie** la cathédrale à Beauvais. **Penses-tu que** nous **puissions** nous y arrêter?	*Before we get to Paris, we could see the cathedral at Beauvais. Do you think we could stop there?*
Je ne crois pas que nous **ayons** le temps de nous arrêter en route.	*I don't think we'll have time to stop on the way.*

3 Longer and more complex sentences

Les touristes à Paris ont un grand choix. Les grands monuments **dont** on parle dans tous les guides, les musées dans **lesquels** on trouve des expositions magnifiques, les attractions pour **lesquelles** la ville est connue, voilà **ce qu'**il faut voir!	*Tourists in Paris have a great choice. The big monuments all the guide books talk about, the museums in which there are magnificent exhibitions, the attractions for which the city is famous, that's what they have to see!*

Résumé grammatical

1 Using the subjunctive (le subjonctif)

Most of the verbs you know how to use are in what is called the **indicative mood** (Unit 12 **Résumé grammatical** *1*). This is the mood for statements and comments. There are two other important moods:

■ to express *commands* and *instructions*, you use the **imperative mood.** (Unit 12)

■ to express some feelings: *wishing, wanting, approval, disapproval, regret, doubt* etc. you use the **subjunctive mood.** (Units 16, 17)

The **subjunctive mood** (*If only he were here*; *Intelligent though she be* etc) has virtually disappeared from English but it is very frequently required in French.

Its use is always signalled by a word or expression (the 'signal') which comes before it in the sentence. There are two stages in learning to use it:

■ learning how to form the subjunctive (stem + endings)

■ learning to recognise the various 'signals' (Units 16, 17 and 18)

Look back at **Avant de commencer 1** and **2** and **Comment dit-on?** *1* and *2*, and see if you can identify some of the 'signals'.

2 Forming the present subjunctive

The present subjunctive (**le présent du subjonctif**) of both regular and irregular verbs is formed from the **ils/elles** (3rd person plural) part of the present tense. You are already familiar with this form (Unit 1).

To get the stem, you remove the -**ent** ending:

ils parlent	→	**parl-**
ils choisissent	→	**choisiss-**
ils mettent	→	**mett-**

To the stem you add the endings (you have met similar endings already in the present and the imperfect):   **-e, -es, -e, -ions, -iez, -ent.**

Avant de visiter Paris,

il faut	que	je		**lise**	un livre d'histoire.
	que	tu		**apprennes**	à conduire plus vite.
	qu'	il	nous	**prête**	un plan.
	que	nous		**trouvions**	un hôtel.
	que	vous	nous	**donniez**	des conseils.
	qu'	ils		**téléphonent**	à l'hôtel pour nous.

Virtually all the 'signals' of the subjunctive end in **que** (**il faut que**, **je veux que**) so, in grammar books, the forms of the subjunctive are always written with **que** (**que je lise**, **qu'ils téléphonent**) to remind you that **que** is part of the signal.

(**Que** also has many other functions in French. It is only followed by the subjunctive when it is part of one of the special subjunctive signals.)

Although the subjunctive of **-er** verbs looks very like parts of the present tense (**prête**, **téléphonent**) or the imperfect tense (**trouvions**, **donniez**), you can recognise that the subjunctive is being used once you are aware of the signalling expressions.

3 The subjunctive of irregular verbs

The verbs **être**, **avoir** and **aller** are irregular in the subjunctive:

être	**avoir**	**aller**
que je **sois**	que j'**aie**	que j'**aille**
que tu **sois**	que tu **aies**	que tu **ailles**
qu'il **soit**	qu'il **ait**	qu'il **aille**
que nous **soyons**	que nous **ayons**	que nous **allions**
que vous **soyez**	que vous **ayez**	que vous **alliez**
qu'elles **soient**	qu'elles **aient**	qu'elles **aillent**

Other irregular verbs: **faire**, **savoir**, **pouvoir**, have an irregular stem which is the same for all parts of the subjunctive:

infinitive	stem		
faire	**fass-**	fasse, fasses, fasse,	fassions, fassiez, fassent
savoir	**sach-**	sache, saches, sache,	sachions, sachiez, sachent
pouvoir	**puiss-**	puisse, puisses, puisse,	puissions, puissiez, puissent

4 Verb 'signals' for the subjunctive

The subjunctive *must be used* after a number of easily recognised 'signals'. The most common of these are verbs. The two most frequently used 'signals' are:

il faut que (see **Résumé grammatical 2** above)
vouloir que:

Alison **veut que** Patrick
l'**accompagne** au musée.
Nous **voulons que** Mark **réfléchisse**
avant de se marier.
Sandy et son frère **veulent que** leurs
parents **reviennent**.

*Alison wants Patrick to go with
her to the museum.*
*We want Mark to think carefully
before he gets married.*
*Sandy and her brother want their
parents to come home.*

5 Other verb 'signals' for the subjunctive

There are other groups of French verbs, usually expressing an *emotion* or a *condition*, which are followed by the subjunctive:

a) verbs for saying you wish or want something:

In addition to **vouloir que** (**Résumé grammatical 4**, above), this group includes:
désirer que
souhaiter que
aimer que (especially in the conditional tense – see Unit 18):

Je **désire que** tu m'accompagnes
au musée.
Je **souhaite que** ...
J' **aimerais que** ...

*I want you/I'd like you to come
to the museum with me.*

b) verbs expressing fear: avoir peur que, craindre que

Patrick **a peur que** les musées (ne)
soient ennuyeux.
Il **craint qu'**Alison (ne) passe trop
de temps dans la section sur
l'Occupation.

*Patrick is afraid the museums will
be boring.*
*He fears Alison will spend too
much time in the section on the
Occupation.*

Note that in formal French, there is a **ne** before the subjunctive which follows verbs expressing fear (**Il craint qu'Alison ne passe ...**). This **ne** has no negative meaning and in informal French it is sometimes omitted.

c) verbs expressing regret: **regretter que, être désolé/e que**

Patrick **regrette** qu'elle n'accepte pas de l'accompagner au Musée de l'Automobile.	*Patrick is sorry that she will not agree to go to the* Musée de l'Automobile *with him.*
Il **est désolé que** le Musée des Arts et Métiers soit fermé.	*He is disappointed that the* Musée des Arts et Métiers *is closed.*

6 Impersonal expressions and the subjunctive

Some impersonal expressions, such as **il** + verb + **que**, are followed by the subjunctive. The main ones are used to say that you feel something is *necessary*, *important*, or that it is *a pity*:

il faut / faudra que (see above, **Résumé grammatical *1***)
il vaut mieux que   it will be better if
il est préférable que   it is preferable that
il est important que   it is important that
il est dommage que   it is a pity that:

Il vaut mieux qu'Alison aille seule au Musée de la Libération à Montparnasse.	*It will be better for Alison to go to the Museum of the Liberation at Montparnasse by herself.*
Il est important qu'elle encourage Patrick à aller au Musée du Sport au Parc des Princes.	*It is important that she should encourage Patrick to go to the Museum of Sport at the Parc des Princes.*
Il est dommage qu'ils ne s'intéressent pas aux mêmes musées!	*It is a pity they are not interested in the same museums!*

7 The relative pronouns ce qui and ce que

When you are writing an account of events, or giving a formal oral presentation, you will find relative pronouns useful to help you to express yourself in a more structured way. See Unit 11 **Résumé grammatical *5*, Pour aller plus loin *3*.**

In addition to the relative pronouns you met in Unit 11, there are others you can use to give what you say or what you write a denser and more tightly knit structure, or to emphasise a particularly important point:

ce qui, ce que (*what/which*)

These relative pronouns, which refer only to *things*, can be used to emphasise a particular word or expression in the sentence.

■   **ce qui** is the **subject** of the verb in the clause it is in:

Ce qui intéresse Alison, c'est   *What Alison is specially interested*
surtout l'histoire de la France.   *in is the history of France.*

■   **ce que** is the **object** of the verb:

Ce qu'elle veut voir, c'est les   *What she wants to see is the*
musées historiques.   *historical museums.*

En contexte

In this passage, you should be able to find examples of various **'signals'** with **following subjunctive verbs**. Make a list of them and compare your list with **Résumé grammatical *1-6***.

> **Voici une description du quartier du Louvre, qu'Alison et Patrick ont visité à Paris.**
>
> Ce qui est remarquable dans ce quartier, c'est le grand nombre de monuments qui s'y trouvent. Il faut que les touristes voient non seulement le musée, mais aussi la Cour carrée, la Colonnade, la Pyramide et l'Arc de Triomphe du Carroussel.
>
> Le Palais du Louvre, dont l'architecture est très variée, a été aggrandi par Louis XIV. Il est peut-être dommage que la Pyramide, dont on a terminé la construction dans les années 80, soit si différente du reste du Palais.
>
> C'est le président François Mitterrand qui a ordonné qu'on construise une extension moderne au Louvre. Il a insisté que l'architecte soit de renommée internationale.
>
> Certains Français regrettent qu'il ait choisi un architecte étranger. Ils craignent que le contraste entre les bâtiments historiques et la Pyramide ne soit trop choquant. Il faut cependant que les gens s'habituent à de tels développements, s'ils veulent que les bâtiments historiques continuent à servir dans le monde moderne.

Pour vérifier

1 Identify the 'signals' and the accompanying verbs in the subjunctive in the following sentences:

Patrick est sûr qu'il faut qu'ils soient à l'aéroport à 7 heures du matin.

Sandy a peur que ses parents ne manquent l'avion, mais Nicolas a insisté qu'elle se calme.

Alison veut que Patrick soit assis à côté d'elle dans l'avion.

2 Complete these sentences, using an appropriate verb in the subjunctive:

Comme je veux apprendre le français, il faut que je...

Pour bien parler français, il est important que tu...

Je voudrais aller au cinéma ce soir, mais mon père insiste que nous...

Ma mère va au supermarché demain. Qu'est-ce que tu veux qu'elle...?

3 Put the words in the groups below in the correct order to form sentences:

■ Paris, visiter, femme, Tout, ma, musées, que, les, faire, ce, de, est, veut, c'

■ différence, Louvre, qui, Pyramide, est, Palais, intéressant, et, c', la, Ce, entre, le, la, est, du

■ que, faut, voir, il, Musée, c', du, le, Louvre, est, Ce

Pour aller plus loin

1 Probability and the subjunctive

There is a group of expressions used to talk about various degrees of probability.

a) The ones which indicate that something is likely or almost certain to happen are followed by the **indicative**. See above, **Résumé grammatical *1*:**

il est clair que
  certain que
  sûr que
  probable que
	+ verb in the indicative

Il est probable qu'Alison **ira** au   *Alison will probably go to the*
Musée Carnavalet.   *Musée Carnavalet.*

b) Those which mean that an event may not happen, or that it is doubtful,
are followed by the **subjunctive**:

il est possible que
    douteux que
    peu probable que   + verb in the subjunctive
    impossible que

Parce que Patrick n'aime pas la   *Since Patrick doesn't like music,*
musique, **il est peu probable qu'**ils   *they are unlikely to go to the*
aillent au Musée de la Musique   *Musée de la Musique at La*
à la Villette.   *Villette.*

Patrick et Alison ne passent que   *Patrick and Alison are only*
trois jours à Paris; **il est** donc   *spending three days in Paris,*
douteux qu'ils **voient** tous les   *so it is doubtful if they will*
monuments intéressants.   *see all the interesting monuments.*

2   *Other verbs with the subjunctive*

There are two other groups of verbs which signal a subjunctive in the
following verb:

a) verbs used to give orders or to make demands:

vouloir que   *to wish/want that* (see **Résumé grammatical 3**)
ordonner que   *to command that*
exiger que   *to demand that*
insister que   *to insist that*

Patrick et Alison **veulent que**   *Patrick and Alison want*
Sandy et Andrew **fassent** le ménage   *Sandy and Andrew to do the*
pendant leur absence. Patrick **a**   *housework while they are away.*
ordonné que la pelouse **soit**   *Patrick instructed them to mow*
tondue et Alison **a exigé que** les *the lawn and Alison demanded*
enfants **nettoient** la maison une   *that they clean the house once a*
fois par semaine. Sandy et Andrew   *week. Sandy and Andrew insisted*
ont insisté qu'Alison leur **prépare** *that Alison prepare frozen meals*
des repas congelés.   *for them.*

*b)*verbs used to say that you are pleased about something, or that you are
sorry:

être content(e) que	*to be happy that*
être ravi(e) que	*to be delighted that*
regretter que	*to be sorry that*

Sandy et Andrew **sont contents que**	*Sandy and Andrew are happy that*
leurs parents **reviennent.**	*their parents are coming home.*
Patrick **regrette qu'**il n'**ait** pas de	*Patrick is sorry that he hasn't got*
billet pour le match au Parc des	*a ticket for the match at the Parc*
Princes.	*des Princes.*

3   The subjunctive to express the future

In this Unit you have learned how to form and use the present tense of the
subjunctive. Although there is a past tense of the subjunctive (Unit 17),
there is no future. The present tense of the subjunctive can be used to talk
about future time:

Je suis contente que vous **preniez**	*I am glad you'll be taking the*
l'avion du matin. Il est possible que	*morning plane. It is possible that*
je **vienne** à l'aéroport mais	*I'll come to the airport, but I*
je ne pense pas qu'Andrew	*don't think Andrew will be able*
puisse venir.	*to come.*

4   Lequel / laquelle *after the preposition* de

Although **dont** (Unit 11 **Pour aller plus loin 3**) is usually used when a
relative pronoun follows **de**, there are some circumstances where it is
replaced by **de** + **lequel / laquelle** to speak about things, or **de** + **qui** if you
are speaking about people.

This happens if the noun being replaced by the relative pronoun (the
antecedent) comes after a preposition:

Nous avons décidé de téléphoner	*We decided to phone the hotel the*
à l'hôtel **duquel** les Lemaire nous	*Lemaires had spoken to us about.*
avaient parlé.	

Quand vous serez à Paris,	*When you are in Paris, you can*
vous pourrez téléphoner **aux** amis	*phone the friends we spoke about.*
de qui nous avons parlé.	

17 | HOW YOU FEEL ABOUT SOMETHING

Thème   L'avenir: vos désirs, vos anxiétés et vos projets

Isabelle, Georges and Nicolas reply to a questionnaire in three parts:
-ce que vous désirez
-ce que vous craignez
-vos projets pour l'avenir

In this Unit you will learn to:

1 Say what you intend to do and why
2 Restricting what people can do
3 Express your doubts
4 Talk about your hopes and fears

Structures grammaticales

1 Conjunctions followed by the subjunctive
2 More 'signals' followed by the subjunctive
3 The subjunctive or the indicative?
4 The subjunctive or an infinitive?
5 The present subjunctive and the perfect subjunctive (le subjonctif passé)

Pour aller plus loin

1 The subjunctive after superlatives
2 The subjunctive after expressions of time
3 The past historic (le passé simple)
4 The imperfect subjunctive (l'mparfait du subjonctif)

Avant de commencer

1 In Unit 16 (**Résumé grammatical 2, 3, 4, 5**), you learned some of the 'signals' for the subjunctive. You should make sure that you can form the present subjunctive and use these signals before continuing with this Unit. It is particularly important to be able to use **il faut que** and **vouloir que** (Unit 16, **Résumé grammatical 2**):

Georges, **il faudra** absolument **que** tu répondes aux questions dans ce sondage! Je **voudrais que** tous les membres de la famille y répondent. Comme ça, nous nous comprendrons mieux.

Georges, you'll absolutely have to answer the questions in this questionnaire! I'll want all the members of the family to reply. That way, we'll understand one another better.

2 The various ways of expressing doubt also involve the use of the subjunctive. You should now revise the present tense of **croire** and **dire** from your list of irregular verbs. These verbs will help you with saying you are doubtful about something:

Je ne crois pas que les réponses soient utiles. **Je ne dis pas que** ce soit une perte de temps, mais, ...

I don't think the answers are useful. I'm not saying it's a waste of time, but ...

3 Some aspects of the subjunctive in this Unit depend on your having a clear understanding of the difference between the indicative mood (all verbs in Units 1–15) and the subjunctive mood (Units 16 and 17). This is explained in Unit 16 **Résumé grammatical 1**. You will also need to be quick at identifying the subject of a verb and be able to use the infinitive.

4 Since you will meet the perfect subjunctive in this Unit, you should revise the perfect (Unit 13 **Résumé grammatical 1, 2, 3**) and the present subjunctive of **avoir** and **être** (Unit 16 **Résumé grammatical 3**):

Georges croit qu'il a déjà répondu à ces questions, mais Isabelle doute qu'il **ait donné** toutes les réponses.

Georges thinks he has already responded to these questions, but Isabelle doubts if he has answered all of them.

Comment dit-on?

1 What you intend to do and why

Isabelle: Je vais demander à tous les membres de la famille de répondre aux questions, **pour que** je **sache** ce qui les trouble et ce qu'ils attendent. Je répondrai moi-même d'abord, **de sorte qu**'ils **voient** que ce n'est pas difficile et **afin qu**'ils **puissent** voir que je n'ai rien à cacher.

I'm going to ask all the members of the family to answer the questions, so that I'll know what worries them and what they expect to happen. I'll answer myself first so that they see it's not difficult and that I've got nothing to hide.

2 Restricting what people can do

J'attendrai d'analyser les réponses **jusqu'à ce que** tout le monde ait répondu. **Bien que** les questions semblent faciles, il faut du temps pour y répondre. **Pourtant, à moins qu**'il n'y ait un problème, tout le monde aura terminé avant la fin de la semaine. Nous analyserons les réponses ensemble – **pourvu que** tout le monde soit d'accord.

I'll wait to analyse the answers until everyone has replied. Although the questions seem easy, they'll need time to reply. Unless there's a problem, everyone will have finished by the end of the week. We'll analyse the answers together, provided everyone agrees.

3 Expressing doubt

Tu sais, **je ne suis pas sûr que** ce sondage nous aide. **Je doute que** la personne qui l'a préparé **soit** sérieuse. **Penses-tu** vraiment qu'on **puisse** résoudre nos problèmes de cette façon? **Il est peu probable que** les enfants **répondent** de façon sérieuse et, de toute façon, **je ne trouve pas que** les questions **soient** intéressantes.

You know, I'm not sure that this questionnaire will help us. I doubt that the person who prepared it was serious. Do you really think that we can solve our problems in this way? It is unlikely that the children will answer seriously and, in any case, I don't think the questions are interesting.

4 Talking about hopes and fears

Georges replies to the question about the future of the family:

J'aimerais que les enfants restent dans la région et qu'ils ne quittent pas St Amand. **Je préfère qu'**ils soient près de nous, car, **je suis sûr que, quoi qu'**il arrive, on a toujours besoin de ses parents. **Je préférerais que** Stéphanie revienne en France après avoir terminé son stage, car **je doute qu'**elle puisse s'adapter à la vie en Écosse. **Je ne pense pas que** Mark ait trop de difficultés à s'habituer à la vie en France.

I'd like the children to stay in the area and not to leave St Amand. I prefer them to be close to us because I am sure that, whatever happens, you always need your parents. I'd prefer Stéphanie to return to France when she has finished her work placement, because I doubt that she will be able to adapt to life in Scotland. I don't think Mark would find it too difficult to get used to life in France.

Résumé grammatical

1 Conjunctions followed by the subjunctive

Unit 16 gave you examples of some of the verbs and impersonal expressions which are signals for the subjunctive.

There is another important group of 'signals' – certain types of **conjunctions**, joining parts of a sentence together. They are all followed by **que**. Some of the most common are in the box on the right:

bien que	*although*
pourvu que	*provided that*
pour que	*so that*
afin que	*in order that*
sans que	*without*
à moins que	*unless*

Identify the **verb in the subjunctive** that follows the **'signal'** in this passage:

Bien que Stéphanie aime l'Écosse, elle sera contente de revenir en France. Elle aimerait se marier avec Mark, **pourvu qu'**ils puissent vivre en France. Elle a l'intention de chercher un emploi à Paris

Although Stéphanie likes Scotland, she will be happy to return to France. She would like to marry Mark, provided they can live in France. She intends to look for a job in Paris or Lille

ou à Lille **pour qu'**ils aient de quoi
vivre **sans que** Mark soit obligé
de trouver un travail immédiatement.
Bien que son père **veuille qu'**elle
revienne à St Amand, elle
n'a aucune intention de le faire.

*so that they have enough to live
on, without Mark having to
find a job immediately. Although
her father wants her to come
back to St Amand, she has no
intention of doing so.*

2 More 'signals' followed by the subjunctive

a) There is a group of verbs used to express your opinion of something
which are *sometimes* followed by the subjunctive:

    croire que   *to believe that*
    penser que   *to think that*
    trouver que   *to think that*

    See also **Avant de commencer 2** and **Comment dit-on? 3**.

These verbs signal the need for a verb in the subjunctive when they are
used *in the negative*:

Nicolas répond à la question sur l'avenir:

Je ne crois pas que les matières
que j'étudie à l'école **soient** très
utiles pour ma carrière dans le
cinéma. Mes parents **ne pensent
pas** qu'une telle carrière **soit**
sérieuse, et mes professeurs **ne
trouvent pas qu'**on **puisse**
déjà, à mon âge, choisir son métier.

*I don't believe that the subjects
I am studying at school are very
useful for my career in the
cinema. My parents don't think
that such a career is serious
and my teachers don't think you
can already, at my age, choose
your job.*

b) Another group of
expressions can also signal
the subjunctive. These
involve *time* and *expectation*:

> **attendre que**   *to wait until*
> **s'attendre à ce que**   *to expect that*
> **jusqu'à ce que/en attendant que**   *until*
> **avant que (ne)** *before*

Identify the **verbs in the subjunctive** in the following sentences:

Isabelle **attendra que** Stéphanie
soit revenue pour analyser les
réponses.

*Isabelle will wait until Stéphanie
has come home to analyse the
answers.*

Elle **s'attend à ce que** les réponses de Stéphanie reflètent son indépendance, maintenant qu'elle a fait son stage en Écosse.	*She expects that Stéphanie's replies will reflect her independence, now that she has done her work placement in Scotland.*
Stéphanie restera en Écosse **jusqu'à ce qu'**elle ait terminé son rapport de stage.	*Stéphanie will stay in Scotland until she has finished the report on her work placement.*
Elle ne reviendra pas à St Amand **avant que** Mark (n')ait promis de passer ses vacances en France.	*She will not go back to St Amand before Mark has promised to spend his holidays in France.*

3 The subjunctive or the indicative?

a) To help you decide if a verb is followed by the subjunctive or not, you can study these two lists.

■ These verbs express *facts, certainty* and *probability*. They are followed by the **indicative**:

Isabelle …
   observe que
   remarque que les questions
                    sont faciles.

Georges …
   croit que
   pense que les questions
                sont stupides.

Nicolas …
   dit que
   déclare que sa mère
                   l'ennuie.

■ These verbs express *wishes, fears, commands* and *things which may never happen*. They are followed by the **subjunctive**:

Elle …
   souhaite que
   désire que
   aimerait que les autres
                    répondent
                    sérieusement.

Isabelle …
   a peur qu'
   craint qu' il (ne) réponde
                  pas.

Nicolas …
   veut que
   aimerait que sa mère
                    n'insiste pas.

b) The verbs **croire que, penser que, trouver que** (*2a*, above) are also followed by the subjunctive if they are *inverted to form a question*:

Georges ...

> **pense** que
> **croit** que
> **trouve** que le sondage est stupide.

Pense-t-il que le sondage soit sérieux?

c) Probability and possibility

Expressions of *probability* (**il est clair / certain que** i.e. likely to happen) are followed by the *indicative*:

Il est ...
  clair que
  certain que   Georges n'aime pas parler de lui.

Il est **probable** qu' il refusera de répondre.

Expressions of *possibility* (**il est peu probable que,** i.e. uncertain) are followed by the *subjunctive*:

Il est ...
  peu probable que Georges **veuille** parler de lui.

Il est **possible** qu'il **réponde** par des mensonges.

d) Note that **espérer que** is *always* followed by the *indicative*:

Isabelle espère qu'il n'y **aura** pas de conflit entre ses projets et ceux de Georges.

Isabelle hopes that there will not be a conflict between her plans and Georges'.

4 The subjunctive or an infinitive?

The subjunctive is usually used in compound sentences – sentences with at least two verbs. One is the 'signal'; the other is the verb in the subjunctive.

If the *subjects* of the two verbs are *different*, the **subjunctive** is used:

Georges (subject 1) regrette qu'Isabelle (subject 2) lui **ait demandé** de répondre aux questions du sondage.	*Georges is sorry that Isabelle has asked him to reply to the questions.*

If the **subject** is the same in each case, you use an **infinitive**:

Georges ne veut pas **répondre**.	*Georges doesn't want to reply.*
Isabelle a peur de **tomber** malade.	*Isabelle is afraid she will fall ill.*
Nicolas préférerait **étudier** le cinéma.	*Nicolas would prefer to study the cinema.*

5 Subjunctive: the present and the perfect

The subjunctive is most often used in its present tense form. Sometimes, however, if you are talking about a situation in the past, you need to use a past tense subjunctive - the perfect subjunctive. This is made up of the present subjunctive of the auxiliary verb (**avoir, être,** see Unit 16 **Résumé grammatical 3**) and a past participle (Unit 13 **Résumé grammatical 1**):

Isabelle a peur que Stéphanie **ait décidé** de rester en Écosse.	*Isabelle is afraid that Stéphanie may have decided to stay in Scotland.*
Bien qu'elle ne **soit allée** à Aberdeen que pour faire un stage, il est possible qu'elle **ait promis** à Mark d'y rester.	*Although she only went to Aberdeen for a work placement, it is possible that she may have promised Mark that she will stay there.*

En contexte

In this text from the questionnaire published in the magazine, identify the
seven verbs in the subjunctive and their 'signals'.

Le sondage du mois!

Vos voeux? Vos craintes? Vos projets?
Répondez à nos questions pour y voir plus clair!
Comparez vos réponses avec celles de vos proches!
Peut-être serez-vous surpris?

Les questions dans notre sondage ont été préparées pour que
vous puissiez analyser vous-mêmes les problèmes que vous
affrontez. Bien que vous ayez une vie de famille réussie, il est
possible que vos projets et ceux de vos proches ne soient pas
compatibles.

Vous ne croyez pas qu'un tel conflit puisse se produire? Nous
espérons que vous avez raison, et pourtant ... N'attendez pas
que les problèmes vous accablent!

■ La première section du sondage concerne vos voeux - vous
voulez voyager? Vous souhaitez changer d'emploi? Vous
aimeriez déménager? Qu'en pensent les autres?

■ Dans la deuxième section, vous allez faire face à vos
cauchemars. Avez-vous peur que la pollution nous tue?
Craignez-vous de prendre l'avion? Et pour vos amis, vos
collègues, votre famille? Pensez-vous que l'avenir leur réserve
de mauvaises surprises?

■ Finalement, nous vous donnons la possibilité de penser
sérieusement à vos projets d'avenir. Qu'est-ce que vous pouvez
faire afin de surmonter vos craintes et préparer un avenir rose?

Ne dites pas que ce soit trop difficile!

Il est certain que, si vous répondez sérieusement, vous pourrez
envisager avec sérénité les petits malheurs que la vie peut vous
réserver.

Pour vérifier

1 Write two sentences about your hopes (**espérer** + the indicative) and two about your fears (**avoir peur que, craindre que** + the subjunctive) for someone else (two different subjects, see **Résumé grammatical 4**).

Examples: J'espère que mon collègue sera promu.
J'ai peur que mon ami(e) aille vivre à l'étranger.

2 Write the same sentences, this time about yourself (both subjects the same, **Résumé grammatical 4**).

Examples: J'espère être promu(e).
J'ai peur d'aller vivre à l'étranger.

3 Imagine that you are going to change your job. What are the possible problems? Think of three and write three sentences based on the model below, using the conjunction **bien que**:

Bien que le traitement soit modeste, je vais changer d'emploi.

4 After answering the questionnaire, you have decided it would be a good idea to have a big family reunion. What could be a suitable occasion for doing this?

Imagine that you are announcing three of the possible occcasions to the rest of the family. Use the expressions **afin que**, **pour que** and **de sorte que** followed by the subjunctive (see **Résumé grammatical 1**):

Example: J'ai décidé de vous inviter à une grande réunion familiale **afin que** nous **puissions** fêter l'anniversaire de grand-père.

Pour aller plus loin

1   The subjunctive after superlatives

You have learned how to say something is *the most* or *the least* in Unit 6 **Résumé grammatical 5**. In some situations, you may need to follow a superlative by the subjunctive:

C'est le sondage **le plus stupide** que j'**aie** jamais **vu**.   *It's the stupidest questionnaire I've ever seen.*

La discussion sur les réponses au
sondage est **la plus intéressante**
que nous **ayons** jamais **eue**.

*The discussion about the answers
to the questionnaire is the most
interesting one we've ever had.*

2 The subjunctive after expressions of time

a) Some time expressions are used to speak about events that have not yet
taken (or may never take) place. They are followed by the subjunctive:

J'**attends que** ta soeur **soit** là pour
discuter les réponses aux questions.

*I'll wait until your sister is here
to discuss the answers to the
questions.*

Nous attendrons **jusqu'à ce qu**'elle
soit revenue, pour lui poser des
questions sur ses projets.

*We'll wait until she comes back to
ask her questions about her plans.*

The expression **s'attendre à ce que** (*to expect that*) is also followed by
the subjunctive:

Georges **s'attend à ce que**
Stéphanie **décide** de se marier.

*Georges expects that Stéphanie
will decide to get married.*

b) Note that, while **avant que** is followed by the **subjunctive** (an event
which has not yet happened), **après que** (an event which has happened
and is now over) is followed by the **indicative**:

Avant que Stéphanie (ne) **revienne**,
il faudra peindre sa chambre.

*Before Stéphanie comes home,
we'll have to paint her bedroom.*

Après que Stéphanie **est partie**,
je me suis sentie très seule.

*After Stéphanie left, I felt very
lonely.*

3 The past historic tense (le passé simple)

In formal written texts, you may meet, as well as the perfect and the
imperfect, another past tense called the past historic. The word **simple**
means it is made up of only one word – it is not a compound tense like
the perfect.

The past historic is used only in written French, to recount events in the
past which do not appear to have an on-going effect in the present. Like
the perfect, it is used with (and in contrast to) the imperfect (Unit 14
Résumé grammatical *3*).

The stem is usually formed from the infinitive, and endings are added as shown below:

donner		finir		vendre	
je donn-	**ai**	je fin-	**is**	je vend-	**is**
tu donn-	**as**	tu fin-	**is**	tu vend-	**is**
il/elle donn-	**a**	il/elle fin-	**it**	il/elle vend-	**it**
nous donn-	**âmes**	nous fin-	**îmes**	nous vend-	**îmes**
vous donn-	**âtes**	vous fin-	**îtes**	vous vend-	**îtes**
ils/elles donn-**èrent**		ils/elles fin-**irent**		ils/elles vend-**irent**	

The past historic of irregular verbs may be difficult to recognise, but the endings – apart from the vowel **a**, **i** or **u** – are always the same:

avoir	j'eus	**pouvoir**	je pus
être	je fus	**vouloir**	je voulus

Find the examples of the two tenses in the extract from Stéphanie's **Rapport de stage**. (A formal, written report):

Je **pris** l'avion avec tous les stagiaires qui allaient en Écosse, et nous **arrivâmes** à Aberdeen à 15 heures 30. Mon Directeur de stage, M. Robertson, m'**accueillit** et nous **allâmes** directement à l'entreprise où m'attendait Madame Wilson. Elle m'**expliqua** le travail que j'avais à faire et m'**emmena** ensuite chez Madame Rushton qui a plusieurs chambres qu'elle loue aux étudiants.

I caught the plane with all the other sudents who were going to Scotland and we arrived in Aberdeen at 3.30 p.m. My supervisor, Mr Robertson welcomed me and we went straight to the office where Mrs Wilson was waiting for me. She explained the work I would have to do and then took me to the home of Mrs Rushton who has several rooms which she lets to students.

4 The imperfect subjunctive (l'imparfait du subjonctif)

Another tense you will only need for reading and formal writing is the imperfect subjunctive.

In speaking, you usually use the present subjunctive or, less often, the perfect subjunctive. In formal writing, however, you will sometimes see the imperfect subjunctive.

The stem, and the main vowel, of this increasingly rare tense are found in the second person singular (the **tu** form) of the past historic (above, **Pour aller plus loin 3**):

donner	→	**donnas**	→	donn-
finir	→	**finis**	→	fin-
vendre	→	**vendis**	→	vend-

Although you are unlikely to meet all the forms of the imperfect subjunctive, you should be able to recognise them if necessary:

donner		**finir**		**vendre**	
que je donn-	**asse**	que je fin-	**isse**	que je vend-	**isse**
que tu donn-	**asses**	que tu fin-	**isses**	que tu vend-	**isses**
qu'il donn-	**ât**	qu'il fin-	**ît**	qu'il vend-	**ît**
que nous donn-**assions**		que nous fin-**issions**		que nous vend-**issions**	
que vous donn-**assiez**		que vous fin-**issiez**		que vous vend-**issiez**	
qu'ils donn-	**assent**	qu'ils fin-	**issent**	qu'ils vend-	**issent**

Note the forms for **avoir** and **être** which, as usual, are very irregular. The past historic will help you:

avoir   que j'**e-usse**   **être**   que je **f-usse**

In formal writing, the imperfect subjunctive **must** be used after certain tenses: the imperfect, the past historic and the conditional (Unit 18):

Madame Wilson **voulait que** ses locataires **payassent** le loyer au commencement de la semaine.

Mrs Wilson wanted her lodgers to pay the rent at the beginning of the week.

Monsieur Robertson **insista que** je **fusse** dans mon bureau à neuf heures moins le quart.

Mr Robertson insisted that I be (subjunctive in English) in my office at a quarter to nine.

18 | IMAGINING WHAT COULD HAPPEN

Thèmes   Les fiançailles et le mariage

Stephanie and Mark and their families make plans

In this Unit you will learn to:

1 Say what would happen if...
2 Say what would need to happen before something else could happen
3 Imagine how you would react to new or unknown circumstances
4 Say what you thought would happen

Structures grammaticales

1 The formation of the conditional tense (**le conditionnel**)
2 The conditional with **si**
3 The polite use of the conditional

Pour aller plus loin

1 The conditional to make suggestions
2 The conditional in reported speech
3 The conditional perfect
4 Giving doubtful information

Avant de commencer

1 Forming the conditional is like forming the future. Check back to Unit 11 **Résumé grammatical** *1*, *2*, *3*, for the stem of the future tense, especially of irregular verbs:

Stéphanie: Si mes parents sont d'accord, nous **pourrons** (future) nous marier au printemps.	*If my parents agree, we'll be able to get married in the spring.*
Si mes parents étaient d'accord, nous **pourrions** (conditional) nous marier au printemps.	*If my parents were in agreement, we could get married in the spring.*

You should also check Unit 14 **Résumé grammatical** *1*, for the endings of the imperfect.

2 You have already met some frequently used parts of the verbs **vouloir** and **aimer** in the conditional. Check back to Unit 4 **Comment dit-on** *1* (**voudrais**) and Unit 4, **Résumé grammatical** *1*, Unit 16 **Résumé grammatical** *5* (**aimerais**).

Remember that these verbs are often followed by the subjunctive:

Les Dickson **voudraient** que Mark et Stéphanie **puissent** vivre en Écosse.	*The Dicksons would like Mark and Stéphanie to live in Scotland.*
Mark **aimerait** que ses parents **sachent** que les Lemaire l'ont tout de suite accepté.	*Mark wants his parents to know that the Lemaires accepted him straight away.*

Comment dit-on?

1 Saying what would happen if...

Stéphanie Si mes parents pouvaient visiter l'Écosse, ils **comprendraient** vite pourquoi je l'aime. Mon père n'aime pas voyager, mais je suis convaincue que, s'il acceptait de venir en Grande-Bretagne, il **oublierait** qu'il n'aime pas les étrangers. D'ailleurs, il a vite accepté Mark - si seulement il pensait à moi, plutôt qu'à lui-même, il n'y **aurait** pas de problème!

If my parents could visit Scotland, they would soon understand why I like it. My father doesn't like travelling, but I am convinced that, if he agreed to come to Britain, he would forget that he doesn't like foreigners. In any case, he quickly accepted Mark – if only he thought of me, rather than himself, there would be no problem!

2 What would have to happen first?

Isabelle Pour que le mariage ait lieu au printemps, il **faudrait** vraiment que je commence à m'organiser. Si on n'invitait pas tous les membres de la famille, on **pourrait** envisager une cérémonie intime. On n'**inviterait** pas tous les cousins germains et on **expliquerait** que seulement la famille proche de Mark pourra venir.

So that the wedding can take place in spring, I'll really have to start getting myself organised. If we didn't invite all the members of the family, we could have a small wedding. We wouldn't invite all the second cousins and we could explain that only Mark's close family will be able to come.

3 How would you react in unknown circumstances?

Nicolas Si ma copine voulait se marier avec moi, je lui **dirais** tout de suite que je ne me marierai jamais. Je lui **expliquerais** qu'on n'a pas besoin de se marier pour vivre heureux. Je lui **demanderais**: «**Aimerais**-tu passer toute ta vie avec la même personne? Ne t'**ennuierais**-tu pas?» Je la **convaincrais** que la vie d'un couple marié manque de surprises et nous **continuerions** à vivre ensemble, heureux mais pas mariés.

If my girlfriend wanted to marry me, I'd tell her straight away that I'll never get married. I'd explain to her that you don't need to get married to be happy. I'd ask her: "Would you like to spend your whole life with the same person? Wouldn't you be bored?" I'd convince her that the life of a married couple has no surprises and we'd keep on living together, happy but not married.

4 What did you think would happen?

Sandy Je croyais que Mark **choisirait** une fille écossaise. Je n'avais jamais pensé qu'il **rencontrerait** une Française et **déciderait** de se marier avec elle. Qui **aurait** cru qu'il **préférerait** la France à la Grande-Bretagne? Mes parents pensaient qu'il **continuerait** à travailler sur des plate-formes dans la mer du nord.

I thought Mark would choose a Scottish girl. I had never thought that he would meet a French girl and decide to marry her. Who would have thought that he would prefer France to Britain? My parents thought he would continue working on oil platforms in the North Sea.

Résumé grammatical

1 The conditional tense (le conditionnel)

The conditional is a simple (one word / not compound) tense. It is made up of the same stem you use for the future (Unit 11) and the endings you learnt for the imperfect (Unit 14): **-ais, -ais, -ait, -ions, -iez, -aient**

For nearly all verbs, the stem is the infinitive (or, for **-re** verbs, the infinitive with the final **-e** removed):

se marier		choisir		attendre	
je me marier-	**AIS**	je choisir-	**AIS**	j'attendr-	**AIS**
tu te marier-	**AIS**	tu choisir-	**AIS**	tu attendr-	**AIS**
il/elle se marier-	**AIT**	il choisir-	**AIT**	elle attendr-	**AIT**
nous nous marier-	**IONS**	nous choisir-	**IONS**	nous attendr-	**IONS**
vous vous marier-	**IEZ**	vous choisir-	**IEZ**	vous attendr-	**IEZ**
ils/elles se marier-	**AIENT**	elles choisir-	**AIENT**	ils attendr-	**AIENT**

Remember the future stems of the irregular verbs:

aller → **ir-**
avoir → **aur-**
devoir → **devr-**
faire → **fer-**
falloir → **faudr-**
mourir → **mourr-**

pouvoir → **pourr-**
recevoir → **recevr-**
savoir → **saur-**
venir → **viendr-**
voir → **verr-**
vouloir → **voudr-**

2 The conditional with si

This tense is mainly used when in English you use *would* or *could*. It is frequently used in sentences where you imagine something:

Si Stéphanie m'invitait à son   *If Stéphanie invited me to her*
mariage, j'**accepterais** avec plaisir.   *wedding, I'd accept with pleasure.*

In sentences like this, where **si** is used, there are strict rules about the tenses you are allowed to use:

a) If the tense used after **si** is the **imperfect** (as in the example above):

Si Stéphanie m'**invitait** à son mariage...

the tense in the main clause must be the **conditional**:

j'**accepterais** avec plaisir.

Si Mark **voulait** vivre en France,   *If Mark wanted to live in France,*
il **faudrait** qu'il trouve un emploi.   *he'd have to find a job.*

Si les Lemaire **organisaient** le   *If the Lemaires were organising*
mariage, ils **voudraient** une   *the wedding, they would want a*
cérémonie à l'église, après le   *ceremony in the church after the*
mariage civil.   *civil marriage.*

Si le repas **avait** lieu dans un   *If the wedding breakfast were in*
restaurant, il y **aurait** plusieurs   *a restaurant, there would be*
plats et beaucoup de vins.   *several courses and a lot of wines.*

b) If the tense after **si** is the **present**:

Si Stéphanie m'**invite** à son mariage...

the tense in the main clause must be the **future**:

j'**accepterai** avec plaisir.

Si Mark **veut** vivre en France,   *If Mark wants to live in France,*
il **faudra** qu'il trouve un emploi.   *he'll have to find a job.*

Si Stéphanie se **marie**, elle ne   *If Stéphanie gets married,*
voudra pas cesser de travailler.   *she won't want to stop working.*

Le mariage civil **aura** lieu vendredi, *The civil ceremony will take*
s'ils se **marient** à l'église samedi.   *place on Friday if they are*
                                          married in the church on Saturday.

3 The polite use of the conditional

The conditional tense is used in French, especially with the verbs **vouloir**,
aimer (**mieux**) and **préférer**, to make a statement less direct, or less
brusque, than it would be if the present tense were used:

Georges **veut que** Stéphanie reste à St Amand.	*Georges wants Stéphanie to remain in St Amand.*
Georges **voudrait que** **aimerait mieux que** **préférerait que** Stéphanie reste à St Amand.	*Georges would like Stéphanie to remain in St Amand.*

The verb **devoir** can also be used in the conditional to make what you say
more polite:

Tu **dois** inviter Tante Alice au mariage.	*You must invite Aunt Alice to the wedding.*
Tu **devrais** inviter Tante Alice au mariage.	*You ought to invite Aunt Alice to the wedding.*
Selon la tradition britannique, les parents du marié **doivent** payer les boissons.	*According to the British tradition, the groom's parents have to pay for the drinks.*
Selon la tradition britannique, les parents du marié **devraient** payer les boissons.	*According to the British tradition, the groom's parents should pay for the drinks.*

A similar distinction can be made with **falloir**:

Il **faut** célébrer les fiançailles en Écosse et en France.	*The engagement must be celebrated in Scotland and in France.*
Il **faudrait** célébrer les fiançailles en Écosse et en France.	*The engagement should be celebrated in Scotland and in France.*
Tu **dois** te marier dans une robe très simple.	*You must get married in a very simple dress.*
Tu **devrais** te marier dans une robe très simple.	*You should get married in a very simple dress.*

En contexte

In this letter, Stéphanie uses many **verbs in the conditional**. Identify at least ten of them, with their **subject**.

Lettre de Stéphanie à sa cousine Jeannette:

Ma chère petite Jojo,

Il faudrait que tu t'assoies! Qu'est-ce qui t'étonnerait le plus? Pourrais-tu imaginer ta grande cousine mariée – et avec un étranger? Que dirais-tu d'un mariage au printemps?

Tu serais une des demoiselles d'honneur et l'autre serait ... une Écossaise! Car je me marie avec Mark, un Écossais que j'ai rencontré pendant mon stage.

Je sais que tu pensais que je ne me marierais jamais, car je voudrais poursuivre ma carrière. Je commence à penser qu'on pourrait faire les deux. On ne devrait pas accepter de rester à la maison, simplement parce qu'on est mariée. Je compte bien continuer à travailler – à quoi bon avoir fait ce stage en Écosse, si je ne peux pas profiter de tout ce que j'ai appris?

As-tu jamais pensé à faire un stage à l'étranger? Je t'assure que tu profiterais énormément de l'expérience – et peut-être rencontrerais-tu quelqu'un d'aussi merveilleux que Mark. Je pensais que je m'ennuyerais et que je trouverais très difficile de me séparer de ma famille, mais je me suis vite habituée à la vie et au travail dans un pays différent ...

Pour vérifier

1 Complete the verbs in the following sentences, using the **conditional tense** of the verb given in brackets:

Vous (pouvoir) acheter une grande maison, si vous aviez beaucoup d'argent.

Elle croyait que son frère (se marier) avec une Écossaise.

Nous pensions que le voyage (coûter) moins cher.

Si Mark se mariait en France, nous y (revenir) avec grand plaisir.

J'(aimer) célébrer mes fiançailles à Noël.

2 Following the example given, write two sentences to say what you would do in each of the situations described – see **Résumé grammatical 2a**:

Exemple: Si nous avions un château en Espagne, nous y passerions les vacances d'été.

Si j'avais un oncle très riche, ...
Si j'avais perdu les clés de la voiture, ...
Si les Martiens envahissaient la terre, ...

3 Make the following requests more polite (**Résumé grammatical 3**) by using the verb in bold in the conditional:

Je **veux** que tu me prêtes ta voiture.
Nicolas, je **préfère** que tu ne sortes pas ce soir.
Chéri, tu sais, **j'aime mieux** que tu rentres sans aller au bar.

Pour aller plus loin

1 The conditional to make suggestions

The conditional tense of **pouvoir** is used to suggest that something might happen, or that someone might do something:

Le mariage **pourrait** avoir lieu à Noël.	The wedding could take place at Christmas.
Nous **pourrions** réserver des chambres à l'hôtel pour les invités.	We could book rooms at the hotel for the guests.
Ne **pourriez**-vous pas attendre une année avant de vous marier?	Couldn't you wait a year before you get married?

Sometimes the impersonal expression **Il se peut/pourrait** is used with the subjunctive:

Il se **pourrait** que le mariage **ait** lieu à Noël.	*It is possible that the wedding could take place at Christmas.*

2 The conditional in reported speech

In Unit 14, **Pour aller plus loin 3**, you saw how the imperfect is used in indirect speech (reporting what other people said). When you are using indirect speech, a verb the speaker used in the future (**tuerai**) will be changed into the conditional (**tuerais**):

Je **tuerai** Nicolas s'il ne cesse pas de me taquiner.	*I'll kill Nicolas if he doesn't stop teasing me.*
Stéphanie a dit qu'elle **tuerait** Nicolas s'il ne cessait pas de la taquiner.	*Stéphanie said she would kill Nicolas if he didn't stop pestering her.*
Nicolas et moi, nous **irons** nous promener parce que nous ne voulons pas vous gêner.	*Nicolas and I will go for a walk because we don't want to get in the way.*
Georges a dit que lui et Nicolas **iraient** se promener parce qu'ils ne voulaient pas nous gêner.	*Georges said he and Nicolas would go for a walk because they didn't want to get in the way.*

3 The conditional perfect

The conditional tense of **avoir** or **être** + a past participle is used when speaking about conditions in the past – *would have* in English:

Je ne l'**aurais** jamais **cru**. On dirait que mes parents sont fous. C'est que ma soeur vient de se fiancer avec un Écossais. Tu te rends compte? Ils **auraient accepté** un Italien, un Allemand **aurait posé** peut-être un petit problème, mais un Écossais! Elle **aurait dû** choisir un Français. Si elle avait pensé à eux, elle se **serait mariée** avec un garçon de St Amand.	*I would never have believed it. You'd think my parents were mad. What's happened is that my sister has just got engaged to a Scot. Can you imagine? They would have accepted an Italian, a German would perhaps have caused a slight problem, but a Scot! She should have chosen a Frenchman. If she'd thought about them, she would have married a boy from St Amand.*

4 Giving doubtful information

To suggest that something might not be true, or to cast doubt on a source of information, you can use the conditional in French.

In newspapers and other public accounts of events, it is sometimes necessary to show that one's sources are not absolutely certain to be accurate. Where in English expressions such as *alleged* or *suggested* are used, in French the conditional conveys this nuance:

Le marié **aurait** volé l'alliance.   *The groom is supposed to have stolen the wedding ring.*

Le mariage **aurait** coûté   *It is alleged that the wedding cost*
FF 100 000.   *100,000 francs.*

TRANSCRIPTIONS –
EN CONTEXTE
(UNITS 8–18)

Unit 8

Mark and Stéphanie plan to go horse-riding.

S   What do you want to do tomorrow, if it isn't raining? Do you want to go horseriding or go for walks?

M   I don't know how to ride.

S   You can learn; it isn't difficult.

M   Are there riding schools in St Amand?

S   There are several, but I can ride at my friend Monique's; she has several horses. Can you see the pastures over there? They are hers. You can see the horses from here.

M   Do you have to wear special clothes?

S   Yes and no. You can wear jeans and trainers, but you have to wear a riding-hat. My father can lend you his. I'm going to phone Monique to see if we can ride tomorrow. By the way, when do your parents want to come?

M   They can come in July. They want to visit the north of France and perhaps go and spend a few days in Paris.

Unit 9

Mark asks Stéphanie if her parents can come in July.

M   Stéphanie, my mother has just asked me if she and dad can come to your house on July 7th. Is that all right with your parents?

S   I'm going to ask them the question straight away and you can phone her back later to give the answer.

Stéphanie calls her mum and gives her the news.

S   Mum, can Mark's parents come and see us on July 7th? They would like to spend three or four days with us, then visit the area and Paris as well.

I   Of course, with pleasure. Your dad can perhaps take a few days' holiday. How are they going to travel?

S   They're going to catch the plane from Glasgow to Paris and hire a car at the airport. Mark is going to give them a road map and a street-map of St Amand to help them.

Here are the instructions Mark is going to give his parents.

You arrive at the airport Roissy-Charles de Gaulle and you take the motorway to the north, the A1 up to Péronne.
Then go up the A2 right to the exit Cambrai / Valenciennes. Leave the A2 at Valenciennes and drive on to the Sentinelle. There you have to follow the A23 to the St Amand / Lille exit. Leave the A23 when entering St Amand and take the dual carriageway to the Raismes forest. At the second roundabout, turn left and you are at the chemin de l'Empire.

Unit 10

The Lemaires are planning how they will entertain the Dicksons.

I   What will happen? First they're going to hire a car at the airport. Then it takes two hours to get to our place. Then we'll have to have dinner, ...

G   What do we usually do when we have guests? We show them the town and then we visit some of the local area. The Dicksons will surely be interested in the area around St Amand. So we could drive them to the forest and to Valenciennes. And we could also introduce them to our friends.

I   Yes, of course, but people go on holiday to have a rest! We'll have to give them time to relax and not try to do too many things. In any case, as this is their first time in France, we'll have to show them things that are typically French.

G   It's hard to decide what is interesting for Scottish people since we don't know Scotland.

I   It's better to ask them what they want to see – the countryside, the sea, towns, ...

G   And then, it's important to introduce them to Stéphanie's friends because they will certainly want to get to know her better.

Unit 11

"What do you do?" Stéphanie, Mark, Alison and Georges speak about their work and their plans for the future.

S   The work I'm doing now doesn't interest me very much, but after my work placement I'll be able to find a job when I go back to France. It's my boss, Mr Williams, who is encouraging me to learn English and to improve my computing skills. "You'll always use English and computer skills" he tells me.

M   At the moment the job I have means I have to spend a lot of time off-shore. But I'll need this experience of drilling at sea. This is the practical experience which I'll need if I want to have a management post later on.

A   The work of a teacher is getting harder and harder. During the holidays, which always go too quickly for me, you don't rest. You have to prepare your classes because it's hard to find the time you need during the term. This evening, as usual, I'll be correcting homework and preparing the handouts I'll be using tomorrow.

G A plumber never sleeps peacefully because at any moment the telephone might ring. You always have to help out people who have problems – problems that only happen at night or at the weekend. I hope my son will have a job that will allow him to sleep well and not work at impossible hours.

Unit 12

Nicolas, his mother and father are trying to work out how he can afford to go to Britain next year with a group of friends.

G You ought to completely change your habits. You put money aside, you open a bank account, you deposit at least 1,000 francs each month and you don't spend anything!

N It's easy for you! Do this! Do that! Don't do this! You give the orders and I obey. But for me it's not easy. Just think! I deprive myself of outings, clothes, books, the cinema. Think of the effect all that will have on me!

I Yes, listen Georges! Help him! Don't give him orders. Better give him some advice.

G That's what I'm trying to do. I want to help him. Don't criticise me for that! In any case I was going to suggest that we give him the money we have put aside for the new car. Let's give it to him! He really needs it.

I Well really! No! Let's not do anything crazy! He's got a year to find the money. We'll have to think of other solutions because *I* want a new car!

N Don't get mad! Let's stay calm. Please don't think I'm completely stupid. I'll find a little job, I'll do some baby-sitting and soon I'll have the money I need.

Unit 13

Isabelle tells a friend, Chloé, about the Dicksons' arrival at the airport.

I We tried to learn a bit of English. Fortunately the Dicksons learnt French before they came.

C Did they speak French straight away?

I No. They started with a few words in English, but afterwards, they remembered their French lessons.

C But what did you do? Didn't you feel a bit embarrassed?

I Oh yes. I found the situation very difficult. People you've never met, and foreigners as well. And you must remember that Stéphanie made a great point of this visit! When they got off the plane, I was scared.

C I really admire you! I've never been able to speak to people I don't know, and as I've never learned English ...

I The beginning wasn't easy. But with good will we managed to communicate. They are perhaps our daughter's future in-laws, after all. And they were so nice to her. They welcomed her into their home and Alison especially helped her a lot. We got on well in the end.

Unit 14

Isabelle tells Alison about when Stéphanie was young.

I   She was very calm when she was small and she learned to talk and to walk earlier than Nicolas. She was three when she went to Nursery School and she didn't like it much. Even when she was very small, she always sang in tune and I wasn't surprised when, later on, she decided to sing in the *Quatre Vents* choir. Before she went to Scotland, she sang with the choir twice a week.

    All children draw at school, but for Stéphanie drawing was very important. She loved bright colours and for her birthday and at Christmas she always used to ask for colouring pencils or water colours. And she loved art galleries. We used to go fairly often to see exhibitions, at least two or three times a year. I remember an impressionist exhibition in Paris, when she was 12. She made such a fuss that I went to Paris with her and we saw the exhibition three times!

Unit 15

Alison writes to her French teacher in Scotland.

Dear Alan,

You asked me to write to you during our time in France. So I had started a letter the day we arrived, but we had too many things to do and everything was so interesting that I couldn't write sooner.

We had planned to spend a few days with the Lemaires and then to visit the area round St Amand. Several suggestion for things to see were given to us by Georges and Isabelle Lemaire and we are now going to leave St Amand and visit the battlegrounds from the First World War in the north of France. Then we'll go to Paris.

While Patrick was speaking to Georges, Isabelle and I chatted about our children, so now I understand Stéphanie better.

I hadn't thought about it, but my training as a History and Geography teacher is very useful for a trip abroad. I found out about the geographical situation of St Amand and because I've read several books about French history and the First World War, the north of France interests me very much.

We both thank you for your excellent French classes and we hope you're having a very enjoyable holiday. See you soon!

Best wishes from us both

Alison Dickson.

Unit 16

Here is a description of the area round the Louvre which Alison and Patrick visited in Paris.

What is remarkable in this area is the great number of monuments there are here. Tourists have to see not only the museum, but also the Cour carrée, the Colonnade, the Pyramide and the Arc de Triomphe du Carroussel.

The palace of the Louvre, whose architecture is very varied, was enlarged by Louis XIV. It is perhaps a pity that the Pyramide, the construction of which was completed in the 80s, should be so different from the rest of the palace.

It was President François Mitterrand who ordered a modern extension to be constructed at the **Louvre**. He insisted that the architect should have an international reputation.

Some French people find it regrettable that he should have chosen a foreign architect. They are afraid that the contrast between the historic buildings and the Pyramide will be too striking. However, people will have to get used to such developments if they want the historic buildings to continue to be used in the modern world.

Unit 17

Questionnaire of the month!

Your wishes? Your fears? Your plans?
Answer our questions to understand them all better!
Compare your replies with those of your family and friends!
Maybe you'll get a surprise?

The questions in our questionnaire have been prepared so that you can analyse the problems you are confronted with for yourself. Even though you may have a happy family life, it is possible that your plans and those of your nearest and dearest may not be compatible.
You don't believe such a conflict could arise? We hope you're right, however ...
Don't wait for the problems to overwhelm you!
■ The first part of the questionnaire is about what you want – you'd like to travel? You want to change your job? You'd like to move house? What do the others think?
■ In the second section, you will confront your nightmares.
Are you afraid that we'll all be killed by pollution? Are you scared to take a plane? And for your friends, your colleagues, your family? Do you think the future may have unpleasant surprises in store for them?
Finally, we give you the chance to think seriously about your future plans.
What can you do to overcome your fears and ensure a happy future?
Don't say it's too difficult! It's certain that, if you reply seriously, you will be able to think calmly about the unpleasant things life may have in store for you.

Unit 18

Extract from a letter from Stéphanie to her cousin Jeannette:

> My dear little Jojo,
>
> You'd better sit down! What would surprise you the most?
> Could you imagine your big cousin married – and to a foreigner? How would
> you feel about a spring wedding?
>
> You'd be one of the bridesmaids and the other one would be
> ... a Scottish girl! because I'm getting married to Mark,
> a Scots boy I met during my work placement.
>
> I know you thought I'd never get married, because I wanted to pursue my
> career. I'm starting to think that one could do both. You shouldn't agree to
> stay at home simply because you're married. I'm really determined to carry on
> working – what's the use of having done a work placement in Scotland if
> afterwards I can't take advantage of everything I've learnt?
>
> Have you ever thought about doing a work placement abroad?
> I assure you that you'd benefit enormously from the experience – and maybe
> you'd meet someone as wonderful as Mark. I thought I'd be bored and that I'd
> find it hard to leave my family, but
> I quickly got used to life and work in a different country. ...

POUR VÉRIFIER – KEY

Unit 1

1
a) Je vous **présente** Alison. Elle **a** 48 ans.
b) Elle **est** professeur d'histoire-géographie.
c) Voici Patrick. **Il a** 54 ans.
d) Il **est directeur** (de supermarché).
e) Ils **ont** trois enfants: Mark, Sandy, Andrew.
f) Andrew **ne** travaille **pas**. Il **est/va** à l'école.

2
a) Comment **s'appellent** les parents de Mark? Comment **vont** les parents de Mark?
b) Quel âge **a** Sandy?
c) **Est-ce que** Sandy travaille?
d) Les Dickson **habitent**-ils (à) Aberdeen?
e) Et Stéphanie? **Habite-t-elle** (à) Dundee?

3
a) Ils s'appellent Alison et Patrick. Ils vont bien.
b) Sandy a 20 ans.
c) Elle ne travaille pas. Elle est étudiante.
d) Ils n'habitent pas (à) Aberdeen. Ils habitent (à) Dundee.
e) Elle n'habite pas (à) Dundee. Elle habite (à) Aberdeen.

Unit 2

1
a) **Qu'**est-ce que **votre** maman fait comme passe-temps?
b) Elle aime **les** randonnées en montagne, **la** photographie et faire **du** ski.
c) Et **votre** père? **Quels** sports fait-il?
d) Il joue **au** golf.
e) **Où** est-ce qu'il joue au golf?
f) **Qui** est sur **la** photo?
g) C'est **mon** frère Andrew et ici c'est **ma** soeur Sandy.
h) **Qu'**est-ce qu'elle fait dans **la** vie?
i) Elle est étudiante. Elle fait **des** études de sciences humaines et de français.

2
Comment t'appelles-tu? / Comment tu t'appelles?/Tu t'appelles comment?
Où est-ce que tu habites? / Où tu habites?/Tu habites où?
Quand joues-tu au rugby? / Quand est-ce que tu joues au rugby?

3
Mon anniversaire est le *26 mai.*
Je suis né/e le *26 mai 1983.*
Aujourd'hui, la date est/c'est *le 25 février 1999/20--*
Aujourd'hui, nous sommes *le 25 février 1999/200-* C'est/nous sommes *le mercredi 25 février 1999/20--).*

Unit 3

1 a)
George est un homme **grand**. Il mesure **1.92m**.
Il est **blond**. Il a les cheveux **bouclés** et les yeux **bleus**.
Isabelle a les **cheveux bruns, mi-longs**. Elle est **mince** et **jolie**. Elle a les **yeux marron**. Ils ont la **quarantaine**.

b)
Stéphanie est **jolie**. Elle a les yeux **bleus**. Elle a les cheveux blonds, bouclés. Elle est blonde. Elle a les cheveux bouclés. Elle est mince.
Nicolas est blond. Il a les cheveux blonds. Il est grand et mince. Il mesure 1.90m. Il a les yeux noisette.

2
231 456: deux cent trente et un mille quatre cent cinquante-six
245 985: deux cent quarante-cinq mille neuf cent quatre-vingt-cinq
3 500 765: trois million cinq cent mille sept cent soixante-cinq

12-hour system	
	6.15: Il est six heures et quart.
	3.45: Il est quatre heures moins le quart.
	3.05: Il est trois heures cinq.

24-hour system
13.55: Il est treize heures cinquante- cinq.
22.35: Il est vingt-deux heures trente- cinq.
23.45: Il est vingt-trois heures quarante-cinq.

Unit 4

1

a) Je voudrais un kilo de belles pommes rouges.
b) Quelle taille vous désirez acheter?/Vous désirez acheter quelle taille?
Quelle taille désirez-vous acheter?
c) Je ne veux plus de viande, merci.
d) Nous voudrions acheter du parfum pour ma mère.
e) Laquelle de ces robes voudriez-vous?

2

a) Isabelle voudrait **du** pâté, **du** beurre, **du** fromage, **des** pommes de terre, **de la** limonade, **des** croissants.
b) Stéphanie a besoin de/d':
une bouteille de bordeaux.
un gros poulet.
un **kilo d'**oignons.
500 **grammes de** champignons.
une **livre** / une **plaquette de** beurre.
5 **kilos de** pommes de terre.

3

Je voudrais:
un pantalon	**Lequel** préfères-tu?
des bonbons	**Lesquels** préfères-tu
des cerises	**Lesquelles** préfères-tu?
du whisky	**Lequel** préfères-tu?

Unit 5

1

a) Je **choisis** une fleur. Je prends **celle-ci.**
b) Tu **choisis** un pot de confiture. Tu prends **celui-ci.**
c) Il/Elle/On **choisit** un stylo-plume.
Il/Elle/On prend **celui-ci.**
d) Nous **choisissons** un livre. Nous prenons **celui-ci.**
e) Vous **choisissez** des brochures. Vous prenez **celles-ci.**
f) Ils/Elles **choisissent** des biscuits.
Ils/Elles prennent **ceux-ci.**

2

a)
A St Amand nous **entendons** les cloches de l'Abbaye sonner tous les jours
Ils **entendent** leurs voisins partir très tôt.
Quand Mark joue au rugby il **salit** son maillot.
Mark **réfléchit** et **choisit** l'assiette en porcelaine pour sa voisine.
b)

A St Amand nous **les** entendons sonner tous les jours.
Ils **les** entendent partir très tôt.
Quand Mark joue au rugby il **le** salit.
Mark réfléchit et **la** choisit pour sa voisine.

3

Un hôtel quatre étoiles est **plus** luxueux **qu'**un hôtel deux étoiles.
Un hôtel deux étoiles est **moins** luxueux **qu'**un hôtel quatre étoiles.

La Tour Eiffel est **plus** haute **que** la Tour de Blackpool.
La Tour de Blackpool est **moins** haute **que** la Tour Eiffel.

Mark est **plus** âgé **que** Stéphanie.
Stéphanie est **moins** âgée **que** Mark. Elle est **plus** jeune **que** Mark.

Unit 6

1

a) Je vais visiter l'Abbaye de St Amand.
b) Est-ce que tu vas acheter des cartes postales?
c) J'aimerais aller voir les sangliers dans le bois de St Amand.

2

a) Mark **écrit** des cartes postales **de** St Amand et **les** envoie à sa famille à Dundee et à ses amis.
b) Les parents de Mark **vivent dans** un quartier résidentiel **de/à** Dundee.
c) Mr Dickson **prend** le bus **pour/afin de** se rendre au travail le matin.
d) Il est directeur **d'**un supermarché à quelques kilomètres **du** centre ville **près de/au bord de** la rivière Tay.
e) Il **part** à 8 heures le matin et **revient à** 18 heures, **sauf** le jeudi soir car il travaille **jusqu'à** 21 heures.

3

Dundee occupe une position **très / vraiment** privilégiée sur la côte est de l'Écosse. Les deux collines, Balgay et Law, offrent une vue **vraiment** superbe de la Tay et de la campagne. Dundee est une ville **très / principalement /** bien connue pour le bateau Discovery et l'observatoire de Balgay avec ses vues féériques. Dundee est une ville **toujours / très / vraiment** accueillante pas très loin de St Andrews, **mondialement / très** célèbre pour le golf.

Unit 7

1

Où se trouve votre maison? Où se trouve **la vôtre?**

Andrew ne trouve pas ses disques compacts.
Andrew ne trouve pas **les siens.**
Il prend mes disques. Il prend **les miens.**
J'oublie souvent de rendre tes disques.
J'oublie souvent de rendre **les tiens.**

2
C'est le dictionnaire **de** Sandy.
Ce magazine appartient **à** Sandy.
Ce livre n'est pas à **toi.** C'est **le mien.**
Leurs voisins sont plus aimables que **les nôtres.**
Ce catalogue *La Redoute* **appartient à** Sandy.
«Est-ce qu'il y a des photos de **toi** dans ce catalogue?», demande Andrew.
La voiture garée en face de la maison des Dickson est à **eux.**
La nouvelle Peugeot 405 n'est pas **la leur.**
C'est celle de **leurs** voisins.

Unit 8

1
S Je vais demander à mes parents s'ils **peuvent/veulent** rester chez nous à ce moment-là. Je crois que Papa ne **doit** pas travailler le 14 juillet car c'est férié. Est-ce que tu **sais** combien de temps ils **peuvent/veulent** rester?
M Je ne **sais** pas exactement. Une quinzaine de jours. Ils **veulent/ont envie d'**inviter tes parents à venir en Écosse l'année prochaine. Est-ce que tu crois que tes parents ont **envie de/veulent** venir à Dundee?
S Oui, j'en suis sûre. Cette année ils ne **peuvent** pas partir en vacances.

2 Est-ce que vous **savez** parler français?
Est-ce que tu **veux** aller au cinéma?
Est-ce qu'il **peut** rentrer tard?
Est-ce que nous **devons** ranger nos affaires?

Unit 9

1
Tu arrives à l'aéroport Roissy-Charles de Gaulle et **tu prends** l'autoroute du nord, la A1, jusqu'à Péronne.
Ensuite **tu prends** la A2 jusqu'à la sortie Cambrai/Valenciennes.
Quitte la A2 à Valenciennes et **continue** jusqu'à la Sentinelle. Là, **tu dois** prendre la A23 jusqu'à la sortie St. Amand/Lille.
Quitte la A23 à l'entrée de St Amand et **prends** la voie rapide jusqu'à la forêt de Raismes. Au deuxième rond-point, **tourne** à gauche et **tu es** au chemin de l'Empire.

2
Prenez la première à droite / à gauche.
Continuez tout droit jusqu'au coin.

Descendez la rue de Lille.
Tournez à gauche / à droite.

3
a) Tu **leur** dis que c'est d'accord.
b) Tu **lui** téléphones pour dire quand tu vas revenir.
c) Tu **leur** donnes les directions.
d) Patrick **lui** demande les directions exactes.

Unit 10

1 (model answer): Pendant les vacances, nous voulons nous reposer, mais nos parents préfèrent être très actifs.
C'est pour cette raison que nous essayons de nous lever le plus tard possible.
D'abord nous mangeons un petit déjeuner copieux.
Puis nous prenons une douche et nous nous habillons très lentement.
Alors nous discutons interminablement le programme du jour.
Il est donc midi et nous n'avons pas pris de décision.
Après avoir mangé, il faut accepter de sortir car nos parents commencent à se fâcher.
Finalement, tout le monde est prêt, et nous pouvons enfin partir.

Unit 11

Stéphanie Aujourd'hui je **travaillerai** au bureau. Je **taperai** des lettres pour mon chef et **j'assisterai** à une réunion des membres du département de ressources humaines. Est-ce que tu **viendras** me chercher à 17 heures 30? On **achètera** de quoi manger à **Marks et Spencer.**

Mark Ce soir je **mangerai** avec Stéphanie. Mardi je ne **serai** pas ici car je **prendrai** l'hélicoptère et je **recommencerai** à travailler sur une plate-forme BP. Je **règlerai** l'appareil de forage et je le **contrôlerai** par ordinateur. Nous **serons** sur plate-forme pour trois semaines. Je ne **verrai** pas Stéphanie et elle me **manquera** beaucoup.

Alison Aujourd'hui à 4 heures nous **aurons** une réunion de tous

les enseignants. Elle **durera**
au moins 2 heures et demie
et je ne **rentrerai** pas avant
7 heures 30. Vous **préparerez**
vous-mêmes le dîner – et il
ne **faudra** pas oublier de
faire la vaisselle!

Georges Est-ce que nous **pourrons**
manger à 9 heures ce soir?
La réparation du tuyautage
chez Madame Vincent ne
sera pas terminée et je
devrai aussi remplacer les
robinets dans sa salle de bains.

Unit 12

1 (model answer)
Utilise ta carte Cirrus à la banque.
Achète tes repas dans les restaurants
avec ta carte Visa.
Utilise tes travellers dans les magasins.
Utilise ta carte Visa dans les grands
magasins.
Change tes devises à la banque.
Achète une ceinture porte-monnaie.

2 (model answer)
N'ouvrez pas votre porte-monnaie dans
le métro!
Ne changez pas vos travellers à l'hôtel!
Ne laissez pas votre carte de crédit et
votre passeport dans votre chambre!
Ne laissez pas votre porte-monnaie dans
le métro!

3 (model answer)
Tu nous donnes ton numéro de
téléphone.
Il apporte la rose à Stéphanie.
Nous offrons les cadeaux à toi, Maman!

4
Oui, je **le lui** donne. Non, je ne **le lui**
donne pas.
Oui, je **les leur** apporte. Non, je ne **les
leur** apporte pas.
Oui, nous **le leur** recommandons. Non.
nous ne **le leur** recommandons pas.

Unit 13

1 Par exemple:
Nous **avons laissé** la voiture dans le
parking. Ma femme **a** tout de suite
reconnu les Dickson. Ils **ont appris** à
parler français, et ma femme leur **a
parlé** lentement.

2 Quel voyage! D'abord le taxi n'**est** pas
arrivé à l'heure. Nous **avons téléphoné**
à la compagnie et ils **ont envoyé** un
autre taxi, mais nous **sommes arrivés** à
la gare deux minutes avant le départ du

train. Nous **avons couru** et nous **avons
attrapé** le train de justesse. Avec des
valises très lourdes et tous les paquets
des enfants, nous **avons eu** du mal à
trouver des places. Finalement, nous
nous **sommes assis** dans un wagon
fumeurs. Naturellement ça m'**a donné**
la migraine!

3 (model answer)
Oui, nous **sommes parti(e)s** en
vacances en été.
Nous **sommes allé(e)s** à St Omer.
Nous **avons vu** la mer et beaucoup de
gens sur la plage.
Non, je **n'ai pas acheté** de souvenirs
parce que je n'ai pas d'argent.
Bien sûr que oui! Elle **a acheté** des
choses stupides – des animaux en
peluche et une assiette horrible.

Unit 14

1 (model answer)
Nous habitions San Francisco aux
États-Unis.
J'aimais le pont qui s'appelle le *Pont
d'or.*
Je n'aimais pas la brume.
Mon père était ingénieur et il travaillait
souvent dans d'autres villes.
Nous n'avions pas de famille à San
Francisco, car mes parents sont
français.
Mes frères et mes soeurs étaient très
contents de se trouver aux États-Unis.
Ce qui nous amusait, c'était de cacher
le chat dans la corbeille à linge.

2
imparfait – **tu te souviens; pendant mon
enfance**
passé composé – **un jour; ce jour-là**

Tu te souviens, Stéphanie? Moi, j'**étais**
toujours plus petit que toi et pendant mon
enfance, j'**avais** honte, parce que ma soeur
était plus grande que moi. Et puis, un jour,
j'**ai remarqué** que je **mesurais** quelques
centimètres de plus que toi. Ce jour-là, j'**ai
fait** la fête!

Unit 15

1 Avant la première guerre mondiale, les
Allemands **avaient** bien **préparé** leurs
armées, de sorte que les armées des
alliés **ont perdu** des millions d'hommes
dans les batailles dans le nord de la
France. A Verdun, des millions de
soldats **sont morts** et les Allemands **ont
traversé** facilement la Ligne Maginot.

2
a) Dans le nord de la France la terre est très plate, **donc** le paysage est quelquefois monotone, **mais** les villages sont agréables à voir.

b) On célèbre le jour de l'Armistice le 11 novembre **parce que / car** la guerre a cessé le 11 novembre **et** on achète des coquelicots ce jour-là en Grande-Bretagne, **car / parce que** les coquelicots poussent dans les champs de la Flandre.

Unit 16

1

'Signals'	Verbs
il faut que	**soient**
a peur que	**(ne) manquent**
a insisté que	**se calme**
veut que	**soit**

2 (model answers)
Comme je veux apprendre le français, il faut que je travaille beaucoup.
Pour bien parler français, il est important que tu assistes à toutes les classes.
Je voudrais aller au cinéma ce soir, mais mon père insiste que nous restions à la maison.
Ma mère va au supermarché demain.
Qu'est-ce que tu veux qu'elle achète?

3
■ Tout ce que ma femme veut faire c'est visiter les musées de Paris.
■ Ce qui est intéressant c'est la différence entre le Palais du Louvre et la Pyramide.
■ Ce qu'il faut voir, c'est le Musée du Louvre.

Unit 17

1 (model answer)
J'espère que mes parents aimeront les Lemaire.
J'ai peur qu'ils aient du mal à comprendre le français.

J'espère que mon père m'achètera un nouvel ordinateur.
Je crains qu'il n'ait pas suffisamment d'argent.

2 (model answer)
J'espère aimer les Lemaire.
J'ai peur d'avoir du mal à parler français.

J'espère acheter un nouvel ordinateur.
Je crains de ne pas avoir suffisamment d'argent.

3
Bien que j'aime bien mes collègues, je vais changer d'emploi.
Bien que mes enfants veuillent rester ici, je vais changer d'emploi.
Bien que ma femme soit contente ici, je vais changer d'emploi.

4 (model answer)
J'ai décidé d'inviter tous mes cousins britanniques à la réunion **afin que** nous **puissions** les rencontrer.
J'ai décidé de louer plusieurs chambres à l'hôtel **pour que** tout le monde **soit** ensemble.
J'ai décidé de faire une grande réunion familiale en été **de sorte que** tous nos parents **soient** libres au même moment.

Unit 18

1 Vous **pourriez** acheter une grande maison, si vous aviez beaucoup d'argent.
Elle croyait que son frère se **marierait** avec une Écossaise.
Nous pensions que le voyage **coûterait** moins cher.
Si Mark se mariait en France, nous y **reviendrions** avec grand plaisir.
J'**aimerais** célébrer mes fiançailles à Noël.

2 (model answers)
Si j'avais un oncle très riche, je lui **demanderais** de m'acheter une voiture.
Si j'avais un oncle très riche, il me **donnerait** des cadeaux merveilleux.
Si j'avais perdu les clés de la voiture, j'**irais** à la police.
Si j'avais perdu les clés de la voiture, je **serais** affolé(e).
Si les Martiens envahissaient la terre, nous **verrions** qu'ils ne sont pas verts.
Si les Martiens envahissaient la terre, tout le monde **aurait** peur.

3
Je **voudrais** que tu me prêtes ta voiture.
Nicolas, je **préférerais** que tu ne sortes pas ce soir.
Chéri, tu sais, j'**aimerais** mieux que tu rentres sans aller au bar.

VERB TABLES

Key irregular verbs in different tenses

pt.p = present participle
- = part in **bold** repeated
.. = past participle repeated

Present (Imperative)	Future	Conditional	Imperfect	Perfect (Past Historic)	Pluperfect	Present Subjunctive (Perfect Subjunctive)

Avoir *to have* Present participle: **ayant** Past participle: **eu/e/s**

Present (Imperative)	Future	Conditional	Imperfect	Perfect (Past Historic)	Pluperfect	Present Subjunctive (Perfect Subjunctive)
j'ai	aurai	aurais	avais	ai eu	avais eu	aie
tu as	auras	aurais	avais	as eu	avais eu	aies
il/elle/on a	aura	aurait	avait	a eu	avait eu	ait
nous avons	aurons	aurions	avions	avons eu	avions eu	ayons
vous avez	aurez	auriez	aviez	avez eu	aviez eu	ayez
ils/elles ont	auront	auraient	avaient	ont eu	avaient eu	aient
(aie, ayons, ayez)				(eus, eus, eut, eûmes, eûtes, eurent)		aie eu aies eu, etc.)

être *to be* Present participle: **étant** Past participle: **été/e/s**

Present (Imperative)	Future	Conditional	Imperfect	Perfect (Past Historic)	Pluperfect	Present Subjunctive (Perfect Subjunctive)
je suis	serai	serais	étais	ai été	avais été	sois
tu es	seras	serais	étais	as été	avais été	sois
il/elle/on est	sera	serait	était	a été	avait été	soit
nous sommes	serons	serions	étions	avons été	avions été	soyons
vous êtes	serez	seriez	étiez	avez été	aviez été	soyez
ils/elles sont	seront	seraient	étaient	ont été	avaient été	soient
(sois, soyons, soyez)				(fus, fus, fut, fûmes, fûtes, furent)		(aie été, aies été etc.)

s'asseoir *to sit down* — Present participle: **s'asseyant** — Past participle: **assis/e/s**

Present (Imperative)	Future	Conditional	Imperfect	Perfect (Past Historic)	Pluperfect	Present Subjunctive (Perfect Subjunctive)
je m'assieds	– assiérai	– assiérais	– asseyais	– suis assis(e)	– étais assis(e)	– asseye
tu t'assieds	– assiéras	– assiérais	– asseyais	– es assis(e)	– étais ..	– asseyes
il s'assied	– assiéra	– assiérait	– asseyait	– est assis(e)	– était ..	– asseye
nous nous asseyons	– assiérons	– assiérions	– asseyions	– sommes assis(es)	– étions ..	– asseyions
vous vous asseyez	– assiérez	– assiériez	– asseyiez	– êtes assis(es)	– étiez ..	– asseyiez
ils s'asseyent	– assiéront	– assiéraient	– asseyaient	– sont assis(es)	– étaient ..	– asseyent
(assieds-toi, asseyons-nous, asseyez-vous)				(– assis, – assis, – assit, – assîmes, – assîtes, – assirent)		(– sois assis(e), – sois assis(e) etc.)

Aller *to go* — Present participle: **allant** — Past participle: **allé/e/s**

Present (Imperative)	Future	Conditional	Imperfect	Perfect (Past Historic)	Pluperfect	Present Subjunctive (Perfect Subjunctive)
je vais	irai	irais	allais	suis allé(e)	étais allé(e)	aille
tu vas	iras	irais	allais	es allé(e)	étais ..	ailles
il va	ira	irait	allait	est allé(e)	était ..	aille
nous allons	irons	irions	allions	sommes allé(e)s	étions ..	allions
vous allez	irez	iriez	alliez	êtes allé(e)s	étiez ..	alliez
ils vont	iront	iraient	allaient	sont allé(e)s	étaient ..	aillent
(va, allons, allez)				(allai, allas, alla, allâmes, allâtes, allèrent)		(sois allé(e), sois allé(e) etc.)

Boire *to drink* — Present participle: **buvant** — Past participle: **bu/e/s**

Present (Imperative)	Future	Conditional	Imperfect	Perfect (Past Historic)	Pluperfect	Present Subjunctive (Perfect Subjunctive)
je bois	boirai	boirais	buvais	ai bu	avais bu	boive
tu bois	boiras	boirais	buvais	as bu	avais ..	boives
il boit	boira	boirait	buvait	a bu	avait ..	boive
nous buvons	boirons	boirions	buvions	avons bu	aviez ..	buvions
vous buvez	boirez	boiriez	buviez	avez bu	avions ..	buviez
ils boivent	boiront	boiraient	buvaient	ont bu	avaient ..	boivent
(bois, buvons, buvez)				(bus, bus, but, bûmes, bûtes, burent)		(aie bu, aies bu etc.)

Croire *to believe*   Present participle: **croyant**   Past participle: **cru/e/s**

Present (Imperative)	Future	Conditional	Imperfect	Perfect (Past Historic)	Pluperfect	Present Subjunctive (Perfect Subjunctive)
je crois	croirai	croirais	croyais	ai cru	avais cru	croie
tu crois	croiras	croirais	croyais	as cru	avais ..	croies
il croit	croira	croirait	croyait	a cru	avait ..	croie
nous croyons	croirons	croirions	croyions	avons cru	avions ..	croyions
vous croyez	croirez	croiriez	croyiez	avez cru	aviez ..	croyiez
ils croient	croiront	croiraient	croyaient	ont cru	avaient ..	croient
(crois, croyons, croyez)				(crus, crus, crut, crûmes, crûtes, crurent)		(aie cru, aies cru etc.)

Devoir *to have to/to owe*   Present participle: **devant**   Past participle: **dû/s/ due/s**

Present (Imperative)	Future	Conditional	Imperfect	Perfect (Past Historic)	Pluperfect	Present Subjunctive (Perfect Subjunctive)
je dois	devrai	devrais	devais	ai dû	avais dû	doive
tu dois	devras	devrais	devais	as dû	avais ..	doives
il doit	devra	devrait	devait	a dû	avait ..	doive
nous devons	devrons	devrions	devions	avons dû	avions ..	devions
vous devez	devrez	devriez	deviez	avez dû	aviez ..	deviez
ils doivent	devront	devraient	devaient	ont dû	avaient ..	doivent
				(dus, dus, dut, dûmes, dûtes, durent)		(aie dû, aies dû etc.)

Dire *to say*   Present participle: **disant**   Past participle: **dit/e/s**

Present (Imperative)	Future	Conditional	Imperfect	Perfect (Past Historic)	Pluperfect	Present Subjunctive (Perfect Subjunctive)
je dis	dirai	dirais	disais	ai dit	avais dit	dise
tu dis	diras	dirais	disais	as dit	avais ..	dises
il dit	dira	dirait	disait	a dit	avait ..	dise
nous disons	dirons	dirions	disions	avons dit	avions ..	disions
vous dites	direz	diriez	disiez	avez dit	aviez ..	disiez
ils disent	diront	diraient	disaient	ont dit	avaient ..	disent
(dis, disons, dites)				(dis, dis, dit, dîmes, dîtes, dirent)		(aie dit, aies dit etc.)

Dormir *to sleep* Present participle: **dormant** Past participle: **dormi**

Present (Imperative)	Future	Conditional	Imperfect	Perfect (Past Historic)	Pluperfect	Present Subjunctive (Perfect Subjunctive)
je dors	dormirai	dormirais	dormais	ai dormi	avais dormi	dorme
tu dors	dormiras	dormirais	dormais	as dormi	avais ..	dormes
il dort	dormira	dormirait	dormait	a dormi	avait ..	dorme
nous dormons	dormirons	dormirions	dormions	avons dormi	avions ..	dormions
vous dormez	dormirez	dormiriez	dormiez	avez dormi	aviez ..	dormiez
ils dorment	dormiront	dormiraient	dormaient	ont dormi	avaient ..	dorment
(dors, dormons, dormez)				(**dormis**, -is, -it, -îmes, -îtes, -irent)		(aie dormi, aies dormi etc.)

Envoyer *to send* Present participle: **envoyant** Past participle: **envoyé/e/s**

Present (Imperative)	Future	Conditional	Imperfect	Perfect (Past Historic)	Pluperfect	Present Subjunctive (Perfect Subjunctive)
j'envoie	enverrai	enverrais	envoyais	ai envoyé	avais envoyé	envoie
tu envoies	enverras	enverrais	envoyais	as envoyé	avais ..	envoies
il envoie	enverra	enverrait	envoyait	a envoyé	avait ..	envoie
nous envoyons	enverrons	enverrions	envoyions	avons envoyé	avions ..	envoyions
vous envoyez	enverrez	enverriez	envoyiez	avez envoyé	aviez ..	envoyiez
ils envoient	enverront	enverraient	envoyaient	ont envoyé	avaient ..	envoient
(envoie, envoyons, envoyez)				(**envoya**i, -as, -a, -âmes, -âtes, -èrent)		(aie envoyé, aies envoyé etc.)

Faire *to do* Present participle: **faisant** Past participle: **fait/e/s**

Present (Imperative)	Future	Conditional	Imperfect	Perfect (Past Historic)	Pluperfect	Present Subjunctive (Perfect Subjunctive)
je fais	ferai	ferais	faisais	ai fait	avais fait	fasse
tu fais	feras	ferais	faisais	as fait	avais ..	fasses
il fait	fera	ferait	faisait	a fait	avait ..	fasse
nous faisons	ferons	ferions	faisions	avons fait	avions ..	fassions
vous faites	ferez	feriez	faisiez	avez fait	aviez ..	fassiez
ils font	feront	feraient	faisaient	ont fait	avaient ..	fassent
(fais, faisons, faites)				(fis, fis, fit, fîmes, fîtes, firent)		(aie fait, aies fait etc.)

Present (Imperative)	Future	Conditional	Imperfect	Perfect (Past Historic)	Pluperfect	Present Subjunctive (Perfect Subjunctive)

Falloir *to be necessary*   Present participle: **fallant**   Past participle: **fallu/e/s**

Present (Imperative)	Future	Conditional	Imperfect	Perfect (Past Historic)	Pluperfect	Present Subjunctive (Perfect Subjunctive)
il faut	il faudra	il faudrait	il fallait	il a fallu (il fallut)	il avait fallu	il faille (il ait fallu)

Offrir *to offer*   Present participle: **offrant**   Past participle: **offert/e/s**

Present (Imperative)	Future	Conditional	Imperfect	Perfect (Past Historic)	Pluperfect	Present Subjunctive (Perfect Subjunctive)
j'offre	offrirai	offrirais	offrais	ai offert	avais offert	offre
tu offres	offriras	offrirais	offrais	as offert	avais ..	offres
il offre	offrira	offrirait	offrait	a offert	avait ..	offre
nous offrons	offrirons	offririons	offrions	avons offert	avions ..	offrions
vous offrez	offrirez	offririez	offriez	avez offert	aviez ..	offriez
ils offrent	offriront	offriraient	offraient	ont offert	avaient ..	offrent
(offre, offrons, offrez)				(**offr**is, is, -it, -îmes, -îtes, -irent)		(aie offert, aies offert etc.)

Ouvrir *to open*   Present participle: **ouvrant**   Past participle: **ouvert/e/s**

Present (Imperative)	Future	Conditional	Imperfect	Perfect (Past Historic)	Pluperfect	Present Subjunctive (Perfect Subjunctive)
j'ouvre	ouvrirai	ouvrirais	ouvrais	ai ouvert	avais ouvert	ouvre
tu ouvres	ouvriras	ouvrirais	ouvrais	as ouvert	avais ..	ouvres
il ouvre	ouvrira	ouvrirait	ouvrait	a ouvert	avait ..	ouvre
nous ouvrons	ouvrirons	ouvririons	ouvrions	avons ouvert	avions ..	ouvrions
vous ouvrez	ouvrirez	ouvririez	ouvriez	avez ouvert	aviez ..	ouvriez
ils ouvrent	ouvriront	ouvriraient	ouvraient	ont ouvert	avaient ..	ouvrent
(ouvre, ouvrons, ouvrez)				(**ouvr**is, -is, -it, -îmes, -îtes, -irent)		(aie ouvert; aies ouvert etc.)

Partir *to leave* — Present participle: **partant** — Past participle: **parti/e/s**

Present (Imperative)	Future	Conditional	Imperfect	Perfect (Past Historic)	Pluperfect	Present Subjunctive (Perfect Subjunctive)
je pars	partirai	partirais	partais	suis parti(e)	étais parti(e)	parte
tu pars	partiras	partirais	partais	es parti(e)	étais ..	partes
il part	partira	partirait	partait	est parti(e)	était ..	parte
nous partons	partirons	partirions	partions	sommes parti(e)s	étions ..	partions
vous partez	partirez	partiriez	partiez	êtes parti(e)s	étiez ..	partiez
ils partent	partiront	partiraient	partaient	sont parti(e)s	étaient ..	partent
(pars, partons, partez)				(**partis**, -is, -it, -îmes, -îtes, -irent)		(sois parti(e), sois parti(e) etc.)

Pouvoir *to be able to* — Present participle: **pouvant** — Past participle: **pu**

Present (Imperative)	Future	Conditional	Imperfect	Perfect (Past Historic)	Pluperfect	Present Subjunctive (Perfect Subjunctive)
je peux	pourrai	pourrais	pouvais	ai pu	avais pu	puisse
tu peux	pourras	pourrais	pouvais	as pu	avais pu	puisses
il peut	pourra	pourrait	pouvait	a pu	avait pu	puisse
nous pouvons	pourrons	pourrions	pouvions	avons pu	avions pu	puissions
vous pouvez	pourrez	pourriez	pouviez	avez pu	aviez pu	puissiez
ils peuvent	pourront	pourraient	pouvaient	ont pu	avaient pu	puissent
				(pus, pus, put, pûmes, pûtes, purent)		(aie pu, aies pu etc.)

Prendre *to take* — Present participle: **prenant** — Past participle: **pris/e/s**

Present (Imperative)	Future	Conditional	Imperfect	Perfect (Past Historic)	Pluperfect	Present Subjunctive (Perfect Subjunctive)
je prends	prendrai	prendrais	prenais	ai pris	avais pris	prenne
tu prends	prendras	prendrais	prenais	as pris	avais ..	prennes
il prend	prendra	prendrait	prenait	a pris	avait ..	prenne
nous prenons	prendrons	prendrions	prenions	avons pris	avions ..	prenions
vous prenez	prendrez	prendriez	preniez	avez pris	aviez ..	preniez
ils prennent	prendront	prendraient	prenaient	ont pris	avaient ..	prennent
(prends prenons, prenez)				(pris, pris, prit, prîmes, prîtes, prirent)		(aie pris, aies pris etc.)

Recevoir *to receive* Present participle: **recevant** Past participle: **reçu/e/s**

Present (Imperative)	Future	Conditional	Imperfect	Perfect (Past Historic)	Pluperfect	Present Subjunctive (Perfect Subjunctive)
je reçois	recevrai	recevrais	recevais	ai reçu	avais reçu	reçoive
tu reçois	recevras	recevrais	recevais	as reçu	avais ..	reçoives
il reçoit	recevra	recevrait	recevait	a reçu	avait ..	reçoive
nous recevons	recevrons	recevrions	recevions	avons reçu	avions ..	recevions
vous recevez	recevrez	recevriez	receviez	avez reçu	aviez ..	receviez
ils reçoivent	recevront	recevraient	recevaient	ont reçu	avaient ..	reçoivent
(reçois, recevons, recevez)				(**reçus**, -us, -ut, -ûmes, -ûtes, -urent)		(aie reçu, aies reçu etc.)

Savoir *to know* Present participle: **sachant** Past participle: **su/e/s**

Present (Imperative)	Future	Conditional	Imperfect	Perfect (Past Historic)	Pluperfect	Present Subjunctive (Perfect Subjunctive)
je sais	saurai	saurais	savais	ai su	avais su	sache
tu sais	sauras	saurais	savais	as su	avais ..	saches
il sait	saura	saurait	savait	a su	avait ..	sache
nous savons	saurons	saurions	savions	avons su	avions ..	sachions
vous savez	saurez	sauriez	saviez	avez su	aviez ..	sachiez
ils savent	sauront	sauraient	savaient	ont su	avaient ..	sachent
(sache, sachons, sachez)				(sus, sus, sut, sûmes, sûtes, surent)		(aie su, aies su etc.)

Sortir *to go out* Present participle: **sortant** Past participle: **sorti/e/s**

Present (Imperative)	Future	Conditional	Imperfect	Perfect (Past Historic)	Pluperfect	Present Subjunctive (Perfect Subjunctive)
je sors	sortirai	sortirais	sortais	suis sorti(e)	étais sorti(e)	sorte
tu sors	sortiras	sortirais	sortais	es sorti(e)	étais ..	sortes
il sort	sortira	sortirait	sortait	est sorti(e)	était ..	sorte
nous sortons	sortirons	sortirions	sortions	sommes sorti(e)s	étions ..	sortions
vous sortez	sortirez	sortiriez	sortiez	êtes sorti(e)s	étiez ..	sortiez
ils sortent	sortiront	sortiraient	sortaient	sont sorti(e)s	étaient ..	sortent
(sors, sortons, sortez)				(**sortis**, -is, -is, -îmes, -îtes, -irent)		(sois, sorti(e), sois sorti(e) etc.)

Tenir *to hold* Present participle: **tenant** Past participle: **tenu/e/s**

Present (Imperative)	Future	Conditional	Imperfect	Perfect (Past Historic)	Pluperfect	Present Subjunctive (Perfect Subjunctive)
je tiens	tiendrai	tiendrais	tenais	ai tenu	avais tenu	tienne
tu tiens	tiendras	tiendrais	tenais	as tenu	avais ..	tiennes
il tient	tiendra	tiendrait	tenait	a tenu	avait ..	tienne
nous tenons	tiendrons	tiendrions	tenions	avons tenu	avions ..	tenions
vous tenez	tiendrez	tiendriez	teniez	avez tenu	aviez ..	teniez
ils tiennent	tiendront	tiendraient	tenaient	ont tenu	avaient ..	tiennent
(tiens, tenons, tenez)				(tins, tins, tint, tînmes, tîntes, tinrent)		(aie tenu, aies tenu etc.)

Voir *to see* Present participle: **voyant** Past participle: **vu/e/s**

Present (Imperative)	Future	Conditional	Imperfect	Perfect (Past Historic)	Pluperfect	Present Subjunctive (Perfect Subjunctive)
je vois	verrai	verrais	voyais	ai vu	avais vu	voie
tu vois	verras	verrais	voyais	as vu	avais ..	voies
il voit	verra	verrait	voyait	a vu	avait ..	voie
nous voyons	verrons	verrions	voyions	avons vu	avions ..	voyions
vous voyez	verrez	verriez	voyiez	avez vu	aviez ..	voyiez
ils voient	verront	verraient	voyaient	ont vu	avaient ..	voient
(vois, voyons, voyez)				(vis, vis, vit, vîmes, vîtes, virent)		(aie vu, aies vu etc.)

Vouloir *to want* Present participle: **voulant** Past participle: **voulu/e/s**

Present (Imperative)	Future	Conditional	Imperfect	Perfect (Past Historic)	Pluperfect	Present Subjunctive (Perfect Subjunctive)
je veux	voudrai	voudrais	voulais	ai voulu	avais voulu	veuille
tu veux	voudras	voudrais	voulais	as voulu	avais ..	veuilles
il veut	voudra	voudrait	voulait	a voulu	avait ..	veuille
nous voulons	voudrons	voudrions	voulions	avons voulu	avions ..	voulions
vous voulez	voudrez	voudriez	vouliez	avez voulu	aviez ..	vouliez
ils veulent	voudront	voudraient	voulaient	ont voulu	avaient ..	veuillent
(veuille, veuillons, veuillez)				(voulus, -us, -ut, -ûmes, -ûtes, -urent)		(aie voulu, aies voulu etc.)

Other irregular verbs

The forms given here are for the first person singular (**je**) and plural (**nous**).

Verb *meaning* pt. participle past participle	Present	Future/ Conditional	Imperfect
CONDUIRE *to drive* conduisant conduit/e/s	conduis conduisons	**conduir**ai/-ais **conduir**ons/-ions	conduisais conduisions
CONNAÎTRE *to know* connaissant connu/e/s	connais connaissons	**connaîtr**ai/ais **connaîtr**ons/-ions	connaissais connaissions
COURIR *to run* courant couru/e/s	cours courons	**courr**ai/ais **courr**ons/-ions	courais courions
CRAINDRE *to fear* craignant craint/e/s	crains craignons	**craindr**ai/-ais **craindr**ons/-ions	craignais craignions
CUEILLIR *to pick* cueillant cueilli/e/s	cueille cueillons	**cueiller**ai/-ais **cueiller**ons/-ions	cueillais cueillions
ÉCRIRE *to write* écrivant écrit/e/s	écris écrivons	**écrir**ai/-ais **écrir**ons/-ions	écrivais écrivions
LIRE *to read* lisant lu/e/s	lis lisons	**lir**ai/-ais **lir**ons/-ions	lisais lisions
METTRE *to put* mettant mis/e/s	mets mettons	**mettr**ai/-ais **mettr**ons/-ions	mettais mettions

These forms are also the **tu** and **nous** forms of the imperative.
For the **vous** form just add **-ez** to the stem: e.g. **conduis**ez.

Perfect/ Pluperfect	Past Historic	Present Subjunctive	Perfect Subjunctive
ai/avais conduit	conduisis	conduise	aie conduit
avons/avions conduit	conduisîmes	conduisions	ayons conduit
ai/avais connu	connus	connaisse	aie connu
avons/avions connu	connûmes	connaissions	ayons connu
ai/avais couru	courus	coure	aie couru
avons/avions couru	courûmes	courions	ayons couru
ai/avais craint	craignis	craigne	aie craint
avons/avions craint	craignîmes	craignions	ayons craint
ai/avais cueilli	cueillis	cueille	aie cueilli
avons/avions cueilli	cueillîmes	cueillions	ayons cueilli
ai/avais écrit	écrivis	écrive	aie écrit
avons/avions écrit	écrivîmes	écrivions	ayons écrit
ai/avais lu	lus	lise	aie lu
avons/avions lu	lûmes	lisions	ayons lu
ai/avais mis	mis	mette	aie mis
avons/avions mis	mîmes	mettions	ayons mis

MOURIR *to die* mourant mort/e/s	meurs mourons	**mourr**ai/-ais **mourr**ons/-ions	mourais mourions
PARTIR *to leave* partant parti/e/s/	pars partons	**partir**ai/-ais **partir**ons/-ions	partais partions
PLAIRE *to please* plaisant plu/e/s	plais plaisons	**plair**ai/-ais **plair**ons/-ions	plaisais plaisions
PLEUVOIR *to rain* pleuvant plu/e/s	il pleut	il pleuvra/il pleuvrait	il pleuvait
RIRE *to laugh* riant ri	ris rions	**rir**ai/-ais **rir**ons/-ions	riais riions
SOUFFRIR *to suffer* souffrant souffert/e/s	souffre souffrons	**souffrir**ai/-ais **souffrir**ons/-ions	souffrais souffrions
SUIVRE *to follow* suivant suivi/e/s	suis suivons	**suivr**ai/-ais **suivr**ons/-ions	suivais suivions
VALOIR *to be worth* valant valu/e/s	il vaut	il vaudra il vaudrait	il valait
VENIR *to know* venant venu/e/s	viens venons	**viendr**ai/-ais **viendr**ons/-ions	venais venions
VIVRE *to live* vivant vécu/e/s	vis vivons	**vivr**ai/-ais **vivr**ons/-ions	vivais vivions

suis/étais mort(e)	mourus	meure	sois mort(e)
sommes/étions mort(e)s	mourûmes	mourions	soyons mort(e)s
suis/étais parti(e)	partis	parte	sois parti(e)
sommes/étions parti(e)s	partîmes	partions	soyons parti(e)s
ai/avais plu	plus	plaise	aie plu
avons/avions plu	plûmes	plaisions	ayons plu
il a plu/avait plu	il plut	il pleuve	il ait plu
ai/avais ri	ris	rie	aie ri
avons/avions ri	rîmes	riions	ayons ri
ai/avais souffert	souffris	souffre	aie souffert
avons/avions souffert	souffrîmes	souffrions	ayons souffert
ai/avais suivi	suivis	suive	aie suivi
avons/avions suivi	suivîmes	suivions	ayons suivi
il a/avait valu	il valut	il vaille	il ait valu
suis/étais venu(e)	vins	vienne	sois venu(e)
sommes/étions venu(e)s	vînmes	venions	soyons venu(e)s
ai/avais vécu	vécus	vive	aie vécu
avons/avions vécu	vécûmes	vivions	ayons vécu

Some -**er** verbs which have spelling changes in the present and future tenses:

Present tense

acheter   *to buy*   j'achète, tu achètes, il achète, nous achetons, vous achetez, ils achètent

appeler   *to call*   j'appelle, tu appelles, il appelle, nous appelons, vous appelez, ils appellent

commencer   *to begin*   je commence, tu commences, il commence, nous commençons, vous commencez, ils commencent

enlever   *to take off/out*   j'enlève, tu enlèves, il enlève, nous enlevons, vous enlevez, ils enlèvent

envoyer   *to send*   j'envoie, tu envoies, il envoie, nous envoyons, vous envoyez, ils envoient

jeter   *to throw*   je jette, tu jettes, il jette, nous jetons, vous jetez, ils jettent

placer   *to place*   je place, tu places, il place, nous plaçons, vous placez, ils placent

préférer   *to prefer*   je préfère, tu préfères, nous préférons, vous préférez, ils/elles préfèrent

promener   *to take for a walk*   je promène, tu promènes, il promène, nous promenons, vous promenez, ils/elles promènent

Future tense

acheter   j'achèterai, tu achèteras, il achètera, nous achèterons, vous achèterez, ils achèteront

appeler   j'appellerai, tu appelleras, il appellera, nous appellerons, vous appellerez, ils appelleront
Verbs following the same pattern: **épeler**, **rappeler**.

enlever   j'enlèverai, tu enlèveras, il enlèvera, nous enlèverons, vous enlèverez, ils enlèveront
Verb following the same pattern: **relever**.

jeter   je jetterai, tu jetteras, il jettera, nous jetterons, vous jetterez, ils jetteront

promener   je promènerai, tu promèneras, il promènera, nous promènerons, vous promènerez, ils promèneront

INDEX

à 21
  followed by stressed pronouns 96
  ownership, possession 92, 95
achats, les 60
activities 32
adjectives 33
  and adverbs 46
  agreement 30, 34, 35, 36, 38
  demonstrative 22, 27, 61
  interrogative 49, 54
  position 33, 37, 44, 45, 46
  possessive 22, 28, 92, 94, 98
  to ask *questions* 49, 54
adverbs 46, 75, 82, 90
  position 83, 165
  time 75, 84
  for time sequences 125, 128
advice 116
age – in your twenties etc. 41
ago 168
agreement
  adjectives 30, 34, 35, 36, 38, 92
  lequel 54
  past participle 133, 159, 165, 168
  possessives 99
aller 7, 75, 77, 122, 136, 160
anxieties 198
anxiétés, les 198
appartenir 62, 100
argent, l' 147
articles 17, 19, 21, 57
  after a negative 27, 53, 58
  partitive 21, 49, 52
avant de + infinitive 186
avenir, l' 198
auxiliary verb 163
availability 50
avoir
  expressions with 13, 59, 103, 109, 110, 145
  imperative 151
  to form the perfect tense 159, 163

present tense 5
banking 147
banque, la 147
before or after 180
belonging 93, 95, 100
better 68, 73
biens, les 91
by – passive 181
can 103
cause and effect – conjunctions 125, 126, 129
ce que 193
ce qui 193
c'est or **il/elle est** 72
choix, les 60
choses, les 29
commands 149
comparing 61, 62, 68, 73
comparison – better 68, 73
complex sentences 182, 189
computing 178
conditional tense 106, 212, 214, 216, 218, 219
conditional perfect tense 219
conjunctions
  cause and effect 125, 126, 129
  followed by the subjunctive 201
  time 179, 182
connaître 112
courses, les 48
dates 19, 24
days 19, 24
de 21
  ownership, possession 92, 95
  followed by relative pronoun 145, 197
demonstratives
  adjectives 22, 27, 61
  pronouns 65 66
depuis 186
describing – people, places, things 31, 32
désirs, les 198
devoir 106, 112, 114, 117, 216

direct object 61, 67
directions 113, 114, 115, 117, 118
direct speech 177
directions, les 113
dont 145
doubt 200
doubtful information 220
emploi, l' 135
en 67, 123
endroits, les 29
enfance, souvenirs d' 169
engagement 211
-er verbs 5
  irregular 7, 13, 140
  present tense 5, 6
  regular 5, 6
être 133
être – expressions with 13
être
  imperative 151
  to form the perfect tense 159, 164
  present tense 5
events
  future 137
  past 161, 180, 181
  series of 125, 126, 161
explanations 127, 129
expressions
  with **avoir** 13, 59, 103, 109, 110
  with être 13
  impersonal 72, 102, 107, 132
  quantity, size 49, 53, 58, 59
  of time 75, 127, 131, 136, 140, 145,
    161, 166, 173, 176, 208
faire 23, 28
falloir 102, 107, 114, 117, 132, 216
faut, il 102, 107, 114, 117, 132
fears 192, 201
fiançailles, les 211
formality – formal requests 149, 157
formality – instructions 152
frequency 170
future 136, 137
  immediate 77
  plans 137
  tense 138, 139
  time expressions 75, 140, 145
  expressed by the subjunctive 197
  perfect tense 145
gender 10, 15, 58
gens, les 29
getting someone to do something 149, 157
greetings 3
habits 171, 172

have to 101, 112
hobbies 18, 19
holidays 124
hopes 137, 201
how long 186
how you would react 213
il/elle est or **c'est** 72
il faut 102, 107, 114, 117, 132
il y a 168
imagining 213
immediate future 77
imperative 114, 118, 122, 150
  impersonal expressions 157
  irregular verbs 151
  negative 153
  with two object pronouns 154
imperfect tense 170, 172
  direct & indirect speech 177
imperfect subjunctive 209
imperfect and/or perfect 170, 174, 176
impersonal expressions 72, 102, 107,
    132, 188
  imperative 157
  subjunctive 193
impersonally, speaking 132
indicative 150, 190
indicative with two object pronouns 148,
    153
indicative or subjunctive 203
indirect object 115, 119
indirect speech 177, 219
infinitive 136
  after **avant de** 186
  for giving commands, orders 152
  after **il faut** 114, 117
  perfect 186
  or subjunctive 204
  after **venir de** 160
  after a verb 102, 104
information, doubtful 220
informatique, l' 178
instructions 104, 152
interrogative adjectives 49, 54
interrogative pronouns 54
introductions 1, 2
inversion – in *questions* 15, 164
irregular verbs
  -er 140
  imperative 151
  past participle 163
-ir verbs
  irregular 75, 79
  reflexive 87
  regular 61, 63

jobs 135
jouer 28
journeys 74, 158, 178
just – to have just done something 160
knowing – **savoir** or **connaître** 112
lequel 49, 54, 197
likes and dislikes 18, 19, 49
links 142, 180
locating people, places, things 77
logement, le 91
loisirs, les 16
longer sentences 142, 182, 189
mariage, le 211
marriage 211
modal verbs 117
money 147
months 24
mood
  imperative 150, 190
  indicative 150, 190
  subjunctive 188, 190
most, the 76, 84
negative 9, 49, 55, 59
negatives
  articles after 27, 53, 58
  future 140
  of imperative verbs 153
  with partitive articles 27, 53
  perfect tense 164
Nouns
  plural 20
  plural – irregular 27
Numbers 39
  first, second etc. 24
  from 100 41
  in your twenties etc. 41
  ordinal 24, 40
  to 100 2
object
  direct pronouns 61
  direct/indirect? 148
  direct and indirect – two objects 148, 153, 154
  indirect pronouns 115, 119, 123
often 172
-oir verbs 103, 108
order – of *events* 137, 161, 162, 166
orders 104, 149, 157
other people 2, 4, 31
ownership 22, 28, 92, 93
participle
  past 133, 159, 162, 163
  present 46, 83
partitive articles 21, 49, 52

after expressions of quantity 53
after a negative 27, 53
passive voice 132, 133, 185
  present 133
  perfect 179, 183
past historic 208
past
  events 161
  habits 171
  il y a / *ago* 168
  period of time 162, 171
  prepositions 160, 176, 180, 186
  recent 162, 166
  recent – **venir de** 160, 166
  sequencing – time expressions 161, 166
  series of *events* 161, 180, 181
  situations 171
  time expressions 166, 168, 173, 174, 176
past participle 133, 159, 162
  agreement 133, 165, 168
  irregular verbs 163
people 29, 31, 62, 76, 146
perfect conditional 219
perfect and/or imperfect 170, 174, 176
perfect infinitive 186
perfect passive 179, 183
perfect subjunctive 205
perfect tense 159, 162, 163, 164
  with **avoir** 159, 163
  with **être** 159, 164
  reflexive verbs 165
period of time 162
permission 103
personal pronouns 66
places 19, 29, 62, 77
plans 113, 124, 135, 137, 198
pluperfect tense 179, 181
plural 20
plurals – irregular 27
politeness – polite requests 106, 149, 157, 216
position of adjectives 33, 37
position of adverbs 83
possession 91
  à 92, 95
  adjectives 22, 28, 92, 94, 98
  appartenir 92, 100
  de 92, 95
  pronouns 92, 94, 98
  verbs 95, 100
possibility 188, 189
pourquoi 127, 129
pouvoir 104, 218

preferences 62
prendre 71, 75
prepositions 75
  past time 160
  place 80
  relative pronouns after 146
  time 81, 125, 129, 140
  after verbs 87, 143
présentations, les 1, 2
present passive 133, 179
present participles 46, 83
present subjunctive 188, 190, 205
present tense 5, 7
  avoir 5
  for commands 152
  -er verbs 5, 13
  être 5
  for instructions 152
  reflexive verbs 7, 38
prices 50
probability 188, 195
procedures 125, 126
projets, les 113, 124, 135, 137, 198
pronouns
  demonstrative 65, 66
  direct object 61, 67
  en 67, 123
  interrogative 54
  object – direct 61, 97
  object – direct/indirect? 148
  object – indirect 115, 119
  object – two object pronouns 148, 153, 154
  personal 66
  possessive 92, 94, 98
  to ask *questions* 54
  reflexive 123
  relative 142, 188, 197
  stressed 9, 92
  stressed – after **à** 96
  subject 4, 8
  y 121, 123
quand 75, 84, 166, 173, 180, 182
quantities 51, 53
quantity – expressions of 49, 53, 58, 59
que 142, 191
question words 23, 24
questions 4, 8, 15, 77
  formal 164
  future 140
  inversion 15
  with reflexive verbs 39
  in shops 50, 54, 62
  time 126

qui 142
reason – *Why something happened* 81, 127, 129
re- before verbs 71
recent past 162
reflexive pronouns 123
reflexive verbs
  -er – present tense 7, 30, 38
  -ir 87
  -re 87
  passive 185
  perfect tense 165
  questions 39
relating events to one another 142, 180
relative pronouns 142, 188
  ce que 193
  ce qui 193
  dont 145
  lequel 197
  after prepositions 146, 197
  que 142
  qui 142
requests – polite, formal 106, 149, 157, 216
-re verbs
  regular 61, 64
  irregular 71, 75, 78
  reflexive 87
savoir 105, 112
sentences – longer, complex 182, 189
sequencing – the past 161, 162, 166
series of events 125, 126, 161
shopping 48, 60
si 215
signals – subjunctive 188, 192, 196, 202
situations in the past 171
sizes 51, 53
someone else 2, 4, 31
souvenirs, les 169
speaking impersonally 132
speech – direct, indirect 177, 219
stressed pronouns 9, 92, 96
subject pronouns 4, 8
subjunctive
  after conjunctions 201
  to express future 197
  imperfect 209
  or indicative 203
  or infinitive 204
  mood 188, 190
  present 188, 190, 205
  signals 188, 192, 196, 202
  after superlatives 207
suggestions 218
superlatives 76, 84

superlative – followed by the subjunctive 207
telling people to do something 114, 122, 148, 150, 157
tense
  conditional 106, 212, 214, 216, 218, 219
  conditional perfect 138, 139, 219
  future 138, 139
  future perfect 145
  imperfect 170, 172
  imperfect and/or perfect 170, 174, 176
  imperfect subjunctive 209
  past historic 208
  perfect 159, 162, 163, 164
  pluperfect 179, 181
  present 5
  present subjunctive 188, 190, 205
time, telling the 32, 39
time
  adverbs 75, 84
  conjunctions 179, 182
  expressions 75, 127, 128, 131
  expressions – future 136, 140, 145
  expressions – imperfect 173, 176
  expressions – past 166, 168, 173, 174, 176
  expressions for sequencing the past 161, 166
  expressions – subjunctive 208
  a period of, in the past 162, 170
  prepositions 81, 129, 160
tourisme, le 187
travel 74, 158, 178, 187
tu / vous 8, 150
vacances, les 124
venir de 160, 166
verbs
  aller 7, 75, 77, 122, 136
  auxiliary 163
  for giving commands, orders 114, 117, 122, 148, 150, 153, 157
  conditional tense 106, 212, 214, 216, 218, 219
  future – immediate 77
  future tense 138, 139
  future perfect tense 145
  connaître 112
  devoir 106, 112, 114, 117
  -er 5, 140
  expressions with **être** and **avoir** 13, 59, 103, 109, 110, 145
  faire 23, 28
  imperative 114, 118, 122, 150

imperfect tense 170, 172
  followed by an infinitive 102, 104
-ir 61, 63
irregular 103
irregular – **-er** 7, 13, 140
irregular – **-ir** 75, 79
irregular – **-re** 71, 75, 78
-oir 103, 108
ownership, possession 95
modal 117
passive – present 133
past historic tense 208
past participle 133, 159, 162, 163, 165, 168
perfect tense 159, 162, 163, 164, 165
pluperfect tense 179, 181
with prefix **re-** 71
followed by a preposition 87, 143
present participles 46, 83
present tense 5, 7, 13
present tense – **avoir** 5
present tense – **être** 5
-re 61, 64
reflexive – **-er** 7, 30, 38
reflexive – **ir** 87
reflexive – **-re** 87
savoir 105, 112
followed by the subjunctive 192, 193, 196, 202
voice – passive 132, 133
vouloir 105, 149, 157, 212
vouloir – polite requests 106, 149, 157
voyage, le 74, 158, 178
wanting 51, 101, 189, 192
what can you do? 101, 103, 200
what could happen? 213
what would have to happen? 213
what you are going to do 76
what you have to do 101, 112
what you intend to do 137, 139
what you prefer 62
what you thought would happen 214
what you want/wish for 49, 50
what you would like 50, 61
what you would have to 50, 61
when 75, 84, 166, 173, 180, 182
where you are 76, 80
who owns what 22, 28, 92, 93
why? 81, 127, 129
wishing 189, 192, 198
work 135
worries 198
yourself 4
y 121, 123